John D. C Hanna

Centennial Services of Asbury Methodist Episcopal Church,

Wilmington, Delaware

October 13-20, 1889

John D. C Hanna

Centennial Services of Asbury Methodist Episcopal Church, Wilmington, Delaware
October 13-20, 1889

ISBN/EAN: 9783337262990

Printed in Europe, USA, Canada, Australia, Japan

Cover: Foto ©Lupo / pixelio.de

More available books at **www.hansebooks.com**

Asbury Methodist Episcopal Church, Oct. 16, 1889.

THE
CENTENNIAL SERVICES

of

Asbury Methodist Episcopal Church,

WILMINGTON, DELAWARE.

October 13-20, 1889.

Rev. JOHN D. C. HANNA, Editor.

WILMINGTON, DEL.
DELAWARE PRINTING COMPANY
1889.

Pastor,
Rev. John D. C. Hanna.

Local Preachers,
Rev. Chas. Moore, Rev. John Simmons, Rev. J. H. Simms, M. D.

Exhorters,
John Wise, Matthew McGarvey, Charles A. Foster,
Andrew J. Dalbow, Robert G. Humphreys, A. Sergeant.

Stewards,
C. M. Leitch, Recording, Wm. T. Groves, District,
Chas. Moore, J. C. Johnson, John Wise,
Charles Wood, J. T. Mortimer, Wm. F. Maclin,
H. A. Roop, H. H. Ferguson, Chas. H. Heald.
Wm. F. Johnson, Geo. S. Hagany.

Trustees,
David R. Truitt, Pres., John Grey, Benj. J. Downing,
A. Dennis, C. F. Welch, Jas. H. Floyd,
Wm. B. Wharton, David Witsel, T. A. D. Hutson.

Class Leaders,
Rev. John D. C. Hanna, Geo. M. Heisler, Jacob Ellwanger,
Chas. F. Bordner, Chas. A. Foster, B. F. Leonard,
Chas. Moore, Wm. T. Houpt, Jas. E. McKay,
A. Sergeant, Louis M. Maxwell, John Banthrum,
T. B. Ridgway, John Wise, Andrew J. Dalbow,
Noah C. Cunningham, Robt. G. Humphreys, Wm. Pennell,
Wm. B. Genn, Mrs Sallie Moore.

Sunday School Superintendent,
Jas. E. McKay.

Centennial Committee,
Rev. John D. C. Hanna, Chairman, Wm. B. Genn, Secretary,
C. M. Leitch, Geo. S Hagany, John Wise,
John Gray, Mrs. M. A Taggart, Mrs. Sallie Moore,
Mrs. M. R. Lincoln, Miss Sallie Shaw, Lewis M. Maxwell,
C. C. Riley, Jas. E. McKay, Chas. F. Bordner,
Chas. F. Welch, Benjamin J. Downing.

INDEX.

Centennial Quarterly Conference, ... 2
Centennial Ode—Rev. J. T. Van Burkalow, . . 3
Introduction, ... 5
Journal of Centennial Services, ... 8

SERMONS AND LETTERS.

Decisive Tests of Christian Religion. Acts v : 32— Bishop Cyrus
    D. Foss, D. D., L.L. D., ... 17
The Joy of the Lord. Neh. viii : 10—Rev. John A. Roche, D. D., 32
The Power of Christ's Resurrection. Phil. iii : 10—Rev. Chas. Hill, 44
Religious Meditation. Psalm civ : 34—Rev. Wm. C. Robinson, 55
The Fathers and the Secret of their Victories. Psalm xliv : 1,
    Rev. Enoch Stubbs, ... 62
The Scriptural Conclusion and Expedient. Gal. iii : 22—Rev.
    John A. B. Wilson, D. D., ... 72
Past Triumphs and Future Victories. 1 Cor. xv : 57—Rev. W.
    L. S. Murray, Ph. D., ... 86
The Transitory and the Permanent. Heb. xii : 26-27—Rev. Jacob
    Todd, D. D., ... 95
The Heroic Element in Christ's Sympathy.—Luke xix : 7—Rev.
    W. Swindells, D. D., ... 105
Letter from the Rev. Joseph C. Mason, ... 116
Letter from the Rev. G. Oram, ... 118

HISTORICAL PAPERS.

"Then—Now."—Rev. W. L. S. Murray, Ph. D., Presiding Elder, 121

Asbury Methodist Episcopal Church—Rev. John D. C. Hanna, Pastor, ... 135

Asbury Methodist Episcopal Sunday School—Chas. F. Bordner, Esq., 165

"Our Local Preachers"—Rev. Charles Moore, ... 169

Ezion Methodist Episcopal Church—Rev. Jos. R. Waters, Pastor, 172

St. Paul's Methodist Episcopal Church—Joseph Pyle, Esq., . . . 178

Union Methodist Episcopal Church—Rev. Adam Stengle, Pastor, 182

Mt. Salem Methodist Episcopal Church—Rev. Walter E. Avery, Pastor, ... 191

Scott Methodist Episcopal Church—Rev. Vaughn S. Collins, Pastor, 197

Brandywine Methodist Episcopal Church—Rev. C. A. Grise, Ph. D., Pastor, ... 211

Epworth Methodist Episcopal Church—Rev. D. H. Corkran, Pastor, 219

Grace Methodist Episcopal Church—Wm. H. Billany, Esq., . . . 225

Madeley Methodist Episcopal Church—Rev. H. W. Ewing, Pastor, 234

Haven Methodist Episcopal Chapel—Rev. Jas. H. Scott, Pastor, 239

Kingswood Methodist Episcopal Church—Rev. R. Irving Watkins, Pastor, ... 243

Whittington Methodist Episcopal Chapel—Rev. J. A. Richardson, Pastor, ... 249

Swedish Methodist Episcopal Mission—Rev. W. L. S. Murray, Ph. D., ... 257

Silverbrook Methodist Episcopal Church—Rev. Chas. K. Morris, Pastor, ... 260

Wesley Methodist Episcopal Church—Rev. W. G. Koons, Pastor, 268

Cookman Methodist Episcopal Church—Rev. Alfred T. Scott, Pastor, ... 274

Newport Methodist Episcopal Church—Rev. Vincent G. Flinn, . 280

New Castle Methodist Episcopal Church—Rev. E. L. Hubbard, Ph. D., Pastor, ... 287

Edgemoor Methodist Episcopal Church—Rev. J. T. Van Burkalow, Pastor, ... 292

A Centennial Ode.

BY THE REV. J. T. VAN BURKALOW.

Hail, Asbury! first-born of Methodist life
  In Wilmington, now with its progeny rife.
Fair mother of churches and mother of saints,
We gather, in gladness, thro' Love's sweet constraints,
In sermons and songs and reminiscences, now
With Centennial honors to deck thy broad brow.
Thy eight goodly daughters, in love, pure, Divine,
  Swart Ezion, Scott, Union, St. Paul's, Brandywine,
Swall Silverbrook, Wesley and Cookman, all join
With granddaughters, Kingswood, Edgemoor and fair Grace,
Young Haven and Whittington of Africa's race,
And great-granddaughters, Epworth and Madely, to place
On thee, in glad service, through eight hallowed days,
"The Crown of Rejoicing" and "Garment of Praise."

Weird memory and the historical Muse,
The redolence rich of thy passed works diffuse,
Wake echoes of many an eloquent tongue,
Whose accents of truth from thy pulpit have rung.
Among them, the Bishop, for whom thou wast named,
And Harry, his servant, for eloquence famed,
F. Garretson, Sorin, Daily, Atwood and White,
George Quigley, John Inskip, Mast, Kenny, McCombs,
And Gerry, with others—all gone to their tombs.
Besides those deceased, yet alive, there are nine,
Who've preached, as thy pastors, with pathos Divine.
The first and the foremost is golden-mouthed Roche,
Whose power, in the pulpit, but few can approach.
Then Mason, kind-hearted, and Oram, demure ;
Stubbs, Robinson, Murray, all genial and pure ;
Emotional Bryan and Scripturist Hill,
And Wilson, an engine of fire, force and will.
All nine, men of mark, firm, reliable, leal—
As true and as trusty as Bessemer steel.
May still all the graces in these brightly bloom,
Where e'er they may go, to shed heav'nly perfume.

The first mentioned, Roche, still warm-hearted, is here,
Oft taking some part, with deep interest and cheer.
Thy people will long fondly cherish his name;
And long may he live, and the Gospel proclaim.
To Hanna, now, leading thy hosts in the fight,
May unction Divine be imparted to light,
Endue and assist him to win triumphs more
Than any thy pastors enjoyed before.

Ten thousands of saints, born of thy laboring Love,
Have gone to the Kingdom of Glory above;
And thousands still living, in Christ o'er the earth,
Confess that in thee they received the new birth.

The Prophetess, Hope, from success in the past,
Vaticinates fondly that while time shall last,
In all of thy branches, thou'll be a live vine,
Abounding in fruits of the spirit Divine.
Thy altar-fires, burning through one hundred years,
Are bright yet, and ever Shekinah appears,
In joy-lighted faces of real worshippers.

Thy Spiritual Temple, within and around,
The structure, material and hallowed ground,
Appears with the glory of holiness crowned.
The *foundations*, firm, are Salvation-*sapphires;*
The *borders* are *precious stones*, glowing like fires;
The gates are all made of *Carbuncles* of *Praise;*
The *windows* of *rubies*, to receive heav'ns rays;
The whole of *live stones*, erected by God,
His cause to promote and His Name spread abroad;
Prompt sinners to seek for The Pearl of Great Price,
To change them to saints, and restore paradise.

O! Glory to God, for such factors of Grace!
O! Glory to God, for such work for our race!

REV. JOHN D. C. HANNA,

Centennial Pastor of Asbury Methodist Episcopal Church.

Introduction.

Several months before the opening of the year 1889, the pastor and official members of Asbury Methodist Episcopal Church had decided that the centenary of the church should be observed with appropriate services. As they looked back over the century, they had every reason for the profoundest gratitude to Almighty God. Most wondrously had the mother church in Wilmington Methodism been led. The little structure of 1789 had developed by 1889 into a building adapted in every way for the varied work of the church, and sixteen other Methodist Episcopal Churches had arisen in the city to demonstrate the expansive power of our Methodism. Though company after company had departed with the mother's blessing upon them to found church homes of their own, yet the forty-three members of a hundred years ago, despite these frequent depletions, had become nine hundred as the century closed.

The early struggles and heroic sacrifices which characterized our fathers in the founding of the church, the hope alternating with discouragement and culminating in victory which marked her progress, the scenes of triumphant joy about her altars in which thousands were born into the heavenly kingdom, the names of grand men and women both in the ministry and the laity the mere mention of which stirs the heart of the church; these, and many other considerations, concentrated thought upon the worthy purpose of properly commemorating Asbury's hundreth anniversary. It was known, also, that many interesting facts and incidents, stored away in the memory of men still living, relating to the history of the various churches of the city, could not, if we waited a few years more, be gathered at all. Even in the history of the youngest churches, it was believed that there was much of thrilling interest that would be invaluable in another century, or even in a decade or two. The papers read at these services, and contained in this book, will demonstrate the correctness of these views.

When, therefore, in March, 1889, the editor of this volume was appointed pastor of Asbury, he began at once to confer with his brethren in regard to the centenary celebration of the church. There was but one opinion—that we must have a service worthy of so important an occasion. Accordingly, at the Leaders and Stewards' meeting, held in the lecture-room, on Saturday evening, April 27th, a committee was appointed to consider plans for the proper observance of this eventful epoch in the church's history, with instructions to report at the First Quarterly Conference. The following persons composed this committee : The pastor, Rev. John D. C. Hanna, chairman; Rev. Chas. Moore, Geo. S. Hagany, C. M. Leitch, John Wise, Wm. Pennell. They met at the parsonage and drafted a general outline of the exercises, which was submitted to the Quarterly Conference held in the church parlor, June 15, 1889, the Presiding Elder, Rev. W. L. S. Murray, Ph. D., in the chair. This report was adopted and the Quarterly Conference appointed a "Centennial Committee" to take full control of the Centennial proceedings. The committee composed of three members from each of the boards and societies of the church with the pastor as chairman, was as follows : Rev. John D. C. Hanna, chairman; C. M. Leitch, Geo. S. Hagany and John Wise, stewards; W. B. Genn, Lewis M. Maxwell and Chas. F. Bordner, leaders; Chas. F. Welch, Benjamin J. Downing and John Gray, trustees; Jas. E. McKay, C. C. Riley and Miss Sallie Shaw, from the Sunday School Board; and Mrs. M. A. Taggart, Mrs. Sallie Moore and Mrs. M. R. Lincoln, from the Ladies' Aid Society. The committee met at the parsonage on successive Monday evenings, and discussed with great care the arranging of a programme.

It was decided by the "Centennial Committee" that the services should extend from October 13th to 20th, inclusive. Services in the afternoon and evening were to be held each week-day, except Wednesday, which being "Asbury's Centennial Day," was to be observed with appropriate exercises morning, afternoon and night. The ex-pastors were invited to preach on the Sabbaths and on the evenings during the week, with distinguished ministers of the church to take the place of any ex-pastors who might be unable to attend. Historical meetings were to be held each afternoon from Monday to Saturday, at which all Methodist Episcopal Churches related to Asbury should be represented by their pastors with historical papers. The Young Peoples' Christian Endeavor Society was given the Sabbath afternoon of October 13th, and the Sabbath School the afternoon of October 20th, with directions to furnish their own order of exercises. W. T. Groves and W. B. Genn were appointed Directors of Music, and Mrs. Maria Floyd, John T. Askew and Isaac F. Rainear served as Decorating Committee. The Christian Endeavor Society appointed T. A. D.

Hutson, chairman; Jennie Fox, Anna Scott, Sallie Johnson, Harry L. Gray and Alfred Willing, a committee into whose hands was intrusted the management of its service, and the Sabbath School Board appointed a similar committee as follows: H. H. Ferguson, chairman; Miss Ella Marvell, Miss Ella Nowell, Alfred Willing and Anderson A. Fielding. The whole programme will be indicated in the Centennial Journal.

The Centennial Service was a magnificent success. The tasteful and pleasing decorations were in perfect accord with the historic occasion. A beautiful arch spanned the platform, on the keystone of which was inscribed, "1789-Asbury-1889," while the names of the daughters, granddaughters and great-granddaughters of this venerable church were appropriately arranged on each side. Near the base of the arch on one hand were the words, "Thus far have we come, 1789," and on the other, "Hitherto hath the Lord helped us, 1889." Tiers of plants, begonias, palms, ferns, carnations, chrysanthemums and geraniums, rose from the chancel floor to the platform on the right and left of the pulpit, while a scroll of evergreens on which were the words, "1789, First the blade, then the ear, then the full corn in the ear, 1889," adorned the center. The rest of the church was festooned with the country's flag and colors, while at various nooks and corners vases of verdant palms and blooming flowers added beauty to the scene. The well-chosen music was delightfully rendered and full of inspiration; the preaching was most impressive; the historical papers thrilling in interest, and the atmosphere of the Love Feasts more of heaven than of earth. The church was crowded with attentive listeners, and in the evenings hundreds were turned away because standing room could not be obtained.

We are glad to have had a part in this glorious service, and doubt not that while thousands of the seen participated in this spiritual feast unperceived by human eye, a countless host of the redeemed who once worshipped at these altars, cherished shepherds of other days and venerated saints of the flock, joyously mingled with us in our Jubilee.

Upon the pastor, both by the general gathering and by the Centennial Committee, was imposed the duty of editing this volume. In the midst of a busy pastorate he has put forth his best effort to make the book a worthy souvenir of the occasion. And now it is sent forth in the hope that its words may be inspiring to Methodists everywhere, and that it may incite many other churches to gather in some permanent form, facts of their own local history that otherwise will soon be lost forever.   JOHN D. C. HANNA.

Centennial Journal.

SABBATH SERVICES, Oct. 13.

The Centennial Services of Asbury Methodist Episcopal Church commenced at 9 A. M., with a Love Feast in charge of the Revs. T. Snowden Thomas and John D. C. Hanna. As early as seven o'clock the people began flocking toward the time-honored sanctuary, and by nine o'clock the church was filled in every part. For an hour and a half, testimony, song and prayer continued, the interest growing more and more intense to the close. Among others who participated in the experience meeting were Chas. Moore, Ann G. Perkins, Geo. S. Hagany, Cap*t*. Wm. Noble, John Wise, Lewis M. Maxwell, Elisha Cole, Dr. J. H. Simms, Rev. H. Sanderson, and Dr. John A. Roche.

At 10.30 the preaching services of the morning were held. Bishop John F. Hurst, D. D., LL. D., had been secured for this occasion, but not being present, Rev. John A. Roche, D. D., of Brooklyn, pastor of Asbury in 1851-52, kindly consented to occupy the pulpit. Hymns 624 and 726 were sung, Isaiah xii. and II. Cor. viii, were read as lessons, the Rev. H. Sanderson offered prayer, and Dr. Roche preached most eloquently from Nehemiah viii: 10. The service was concluded by singing Hymn 224, prayer by the Rev. J. L. Houston, and the Benediction by the Rev. Chas. K. Morris.

In the afternoon at three o'clock the Christian Endeavor Society was in charge. T. B. Ridgway, Esq., President of the Society, presided. After appropriate music under the auspices of the young people and prayer by the Rev. D. H. Corkran, the Rev. Wm. Swindells, D. D., of the Philadelphia Conference, presented Christ to the audience in a most pleasing and touching manner, from the text, Luke xix: 7.

In the evening at 7.30 Dr. Roche preached again to a delighted audience from Zach. iv: 6, 7. The Rev. J. R. Dill made the opening prayer, and the choir furnished appropriate music. At the close of the sermon, the preacher invited penitents to the altar, and several persons responded. Andrew J. Dolbow, Esq., conducted an overflow meeting in the lecture-room at the same hour.

MONDAY, Oct. 14.

The first historical meeting of the Centennial celebration was held at 2.30 P. M., Joseph Pyle, Esq., of St. Paul's M. E. Church, in the chair, Rev. W. G. Koons, Secretary. After appropriate devotional exercises, the chairman stated that Rev. L. E. Barrett, pastor of St. Paul's Church, was too ill to be present, and so could not take his place on the programme. Mr. Pyle himself, however, after extemporaneous remarks on early Methodist history, read a paper of great interest on "The History of St. Paul's M. E. Church." The paper was discussed by Mrs. Ann G. Perkins, Dr. Roche and Abner P. Bailey, Esq.

A valuable "History of Kingswood" was read by the pastor, the Rev. R. Irving Watkins.

The Rev. E. L. Hubbard read "The History of New Castle M. E. Church," and remarks were made by Dr. Roche and the Rev. N. M. Browne.

"The History of Haven M. E. Chapel" was then presented by its pastor, the Rev. J. H. Scott. Revs. W. L. S. Murray, Ph. D., Presiding Elder of the Wilmington District, and J. T. Van Burkalow expressed their admiration of the paper.

At 7.30 P. M. the Rev. Chas. Hill, of Elkton, who for three terms was pastor of Asbury, preached. After introductory exercises in which Dr. Murray took part, the preacher announced as his text Phil. iii: 10. The sermon was clear, scriptural and impressive, and seekers of this knowledge came in answer to the invitation to the altar. The evening was very inclement, the audience small, but those present felt, "It is good to be here."

TUESDAY, Oct. 15.

At 2.30 P. M. the chairman, John G. Baker, Esq., of Grace Church, called the meeting to order. Jas. C. Pickles, Esq., was elected Secretary and acted in this position through the remainder of the week. After singing and prayer, the chairman announced that the Rev. Jacob Tood, D. D., who had been requested to prepare a "History of Grace Church," had appointed Wm. H. Billany, Esq., to perform that task. Mr. Billany then read an interesting account of the work of Grace Church, which elicited remarks from Drs. Roche and Murray.

A "History of Madeley," a great-granddaughter of Asbury, was then read by the pastor, the Rev. H. W. Ewing, and discussed by the chairman and also by Abner P. Bailey, Esq., Dr. Murray and Mrs. Ann G. Perkins.

Another great-granddaughter's history, the "History of Epworth M. E. Church," was presented to the meeting by the Rev. D. H. Corkran, the pastor. Remarks thereon were made by Wm. H. Billany, Esq., Abner P. Bailey, Esq., Dr. Jacob Todd, Dr. Murray, and the Rev. John White.

The "History of Newport M. E. Church," in the absence of the pastor, Rev. Jas. E. Bryan, was read by the Rev. Vincent G. Flinn, who had prepared the paper with great care. It was claimed by the historian that Newport came to the Centennial not as a daughter, but to offer congratulations to her older sister upon the return of her hundredth birthday. Discussion followed in which the Rev. Daniel Green, of Newport, Solomon Hersey, Esq., Dr. Roche, the Rev. Henry Sanderson, and Dr. Murray took part.

In the evening at 7.30, the Rev. R. Irving Watkins conducted the introductory services, and the Rev. Jacob Todd, D. D., preached with great freedom to a large congregation from Heb. xii: 26-27.

Asbury's Centennial Day.

WEDNESDAY, Oct. 16.

This was a great day in the history of Asbury Church. To commemorate together the Centennial Day, many of the members laid aside all business cares, and spent within their church home the closing hours of the first century and the first hours of the second.

At 10 A. M. Geo. W. Todd, Esq., of Grace M. E. Church, took the chair, and conducted the devotional exercises. Capt. Alexander Kelley, a member of Asbury years ago, was to have presided, but sickness preventing, Mr. Todd kindly consented to take his place. The Rev. W. L. S. Murray, Ph. D., Presiding Elder of Wilmington District, read an essay entitled, "Then—Now." At the conclusion of the paper the pastor, Rev. John D. C. Hanna, introduced the following resolutions, which were adopted unanimously by a rising vote:

We have heard with much interest the paper read by our Presiding Elder, the Rev. W. L. S. Murray, Ph. D. Its descriptions of the trials of the early Methodists, of their triumphs through Christ, and of the peace and victory of the present, have stirred our souls. To-day we thank God for the history of the century past. But above all have

ABNER P. BAILEY, ESQ.,

One of Asbury's Veterans, a true and tried friend of Methodism.

we been interested in the practical suggestions relating to church extension in Wilmington. We are convinced that broader coöperation and greater concentration of effort would produce much more important results; therefore,

Resolved, I. That we have heard our Presiding Elder's suggestions with the conviction that some immediate steps should be taken for the furtherance of Methodism in Wilmington,

Resolved, II. That Dr. Murray be requested to call a convention of the Methodists of Wilmington at the earliest date convenient, to consider plans for the advancement of our church in this city; and that the pastors of the city and two laymen for every hundred members and probationers of each church, shall be delegates to this convention.

General reminiscences were then in order, and for an hour in which sacred song blended with stirring testimony, the delighted audience enjoyed the laymen's reunion. Memory and gratitude were awakened by the remarks of George A. Hartman, Esq., Rev. Chas. Moore, Rev. J. T. Van Burkalow, Dr. Roche, H. H. Ferguson, Esq., Andrew J. Dalbow, Esq., Mrs. Ann G. Perkins, Jas. E. McKay, Esq., and Jas. C. Pickels, Esq.

At 2.30 P. M. the "History of Asbury" was the theme. Geo. S. Hagany, Esq., of Asbury, presided, and after conducting the devotions, introduced the pastor, Rev. John D. C. Hanna, who read the general history, and Chas. F. Bordner, Esq., who presented a "History of the Sunday School." The chairman read an essay entitled, "Our Local Preachers," and the Rev. Chas. Moore spoke on the same subject. General discussion was participated in by Dr. Roche and others, and a "Centennial Ode" was read by Solomon Hersey, Esq.

In the evening every inch of space was occupied and many could not secure an entrance to the building. After C. M. Leitch, Esq., had sung a stirring "Centennial Hymn" composed by Ashley Simpson, Esq., the Rev. Wm. C. Robinson, pastor of Asbury in 1863 and '64, now of Philadelphia, preached an appropriate sermon from Psalms civ: 34. An invitation was given to penitents and several came forward to the altar for prayer.

Thursday, Oct. 17.

The historical meeting of Thursday afternoon opened at 2.30 o'clock. G. W. Joseph, Esq., of Union M. E. Church, presiding. Devotions were led by the chairman, who, after a few general remarks, introduced the Rev. J. R. Waters, of Ezion Church. Mr. Waters read an able paper giving the history of his church. An interesting discussion followed in which the Rev. Chas. Moore, Abner P. Bailey, Esq., Dr. Roche, Dr. Murray and Mrs. M. A. Taggart participated.

The Rev. Adam Stengle traced the "History of Union M. E. Church," and a spirited debate followed participated in by Dr. Roche, Mrs. Ann G. Perkins and Mr. Stengle.

"The History of Wesley M. E. Church," read by the Rev. W. G. Koons, showed that deeds of heroism in our church were not all of the remote past. Remarks were made by Mrs. Ann G. Perkins and Dr. Murray.

Father Samuel Hance, 93 years of age, and a local preacher of much power, being called upon by the pastor, spoke with feeling of his remembrance of the early days, and dismissed the congregation with the benediction.

At 7.30 P. M. the Rev. John A. B. Wilson, D. D., Presiding Elder of the Dover District, and pastor of Asbury in 1878 and '79, preached an earnest sermon. The Rev. J. R. Waters, of Ezion, and the Rev. Alfred Smith, pastor of the Cambridge, Md., M. E. Church, conducted the preliminary exercises. The choir of Ezion Church furnished the music which was highly appreciated by the great audience present. When Dr. Wilson arose to announce his text, every part of the church was packed with attentive listeners. The text was Gal. iii: 22. The sermon was followed by altar work, and the cries of distressed penitents mingled with the songs of the saints, until prayers changed to praise, and tears of sorrow into smiles of delight.

FRIDAY, OCT. 18.

The historical session was called to order at 2.30 P. M. by Lewis T. Grubb, Esq., chairman, who conducted the opening religious services. After an appropriate introductory address by the President, the "History of Brandywine M. E. Church" was read by the Rev. C. A. Grise, Ph. D., and the Revs. Chas. Moore and Eli Mendenhall followed in pertinent addresses.

The "History of Scott M. E. Church" by the pastor, the Rev. Vaughn S. Collins, gave great pleasure to the audience, which was increased by the timely remarks of Dr. John A. Roche.

The Rev. Alfred T. Scott read a history of Asbury's youngest child, "Cookman," showing the struggles and development of this infant society.

On account of the lateness of the hour, the "History of Silverbrook" was posponed until Saturday afternoon, and the audience was dismissed.

At 7.30 P. M. Bishop Cyrus D. Foss, D. D., LL. D., preached a sermon accompanied with great unction and power from Acts v: 32. The simple Gospel was preached by a master, and the great congregation was melted to tears under the Bishop's holy eloquence. At the close of the sermon penitents came to the altar anxiously inquiring the way of life, some of whom were happily converted.

SATURDAY, Oct. 19.

The last historical meeting in which the remainder of the churches related to Asbury were represented, was held at 2 30 P. M. John Haley, Esq., of Mt. Salem M. E. Church, the appointed chairman, was unable on account of sickness to be present, and the Rev. Albert Thatcher, a local preacher of St. Paul's Church, for many years a member of Asbury, was called to the chair and conducted the devotions.

As it had been decided to publish the proceedings of the Centennial services in book form, upon motion of Dr. Murray, the Rev. John D C. Hanna, pastor of Asbury Church, was appointed editor of the volume. This action was afterward confirmed by the "Centennial Committee."

The Rev. Chas. K. Morris then read the "History of Silverbrook M. E. Church," which proved to be very entertaining and instructive. Remarks on this history were made by Dr. Murray and John C. Harkness, Esq.

The "History of Mt. Salem Church," read by the Rev. Walter E. Avery, next demanded the attention of the audience, who listened with delight to a carefully prepared paper. It was discussed by the Rev. A. T. Scott.

"Whittington," a granddaughter of Asbury, was represented by her pastor, the Rev. J. A. Richardson, who read a witty and edifying history of the church, which evoked remarks from the Rev. Albert Thatcher.

The "Swedish Mission of Wilmington," having no pastor in the city, was not represented; but Dr. Murray stated that he would have a history of this work ready for publication in the Centennial Book.

As the daily papers of Wilmington had given wide-spread publication to the proceedings, filling from one to seven columns a day with the historical papers and sermons, resolutions of thanks to them and the gentlemanly reporters attending our sessions which were introduced by the pastor, Mr. Hanna, were adopted unanimously.

A fitting response was made by John C. Harkness, Esq., of the "Daily Republican."

The Rev. J. T. Van Buckalow read the "History of Edgemoor M. E. Church." The pastor, Rev. John D. C. Hanna, thanked all who had participated in these services for the work rendered, and the historical meetings closed with the benediction by Father Hance.

Sunday, October 20.

The first Sunday in the second century of the history of Asbury was a day of wondrous power. All through the Centennial week the interest has been growing, until on this day the fires on the old altars glowed with unusual brilliancy and force. At all the services the church was filled to its utmost capacity with earnest and enthusiastic worshipers, who turned their faces toward the new century thrilled with bright hope founded on unswerving faith in God.

At 9 A. M. the pastor, Rev. John D. C. Hanna, took charge of a Love Feast of such power that all felt God to be present. The experiences related by tried and trusty saints ; the songs of rejoicing that swelled up from the great congregation; the outburst of praise from some souls unable to repress the shout of joy; the tears of happiness on the faces of hundreds, all told that the power of Pentecost and of early Methodism had not passed away. Mother Powell, 98 years of age, and over 70 in the Methodist Church, told with strong voice and dewy eyes that God had never forsaken her. Mrs. Drein was "resting in Jesus." Mr. Abner P. Bailey had been led as a child to old Asbury, Mr. John G. Baker came to this altar, sought Christ three months, and found him to his soul's satisfaction. Bros. Wm. Pennell and John Banthrum sang their experience. Bro. Frank Baker, in the gallery, had come here 25 years ago an ignorant Catholic boy, but sought and found Christ. Bro. Wm. H. Billany claimed a birthright here. Bro. Elisha Cole sang as his experience, "We're Marching to Zion," and the Rev. Enoch Stubbs said that was the way he was marching too. The interest became intense, the rejoicing universal, as Father Hance gave his testimony for his Master. With vigor surprising for so old a man, and with a force and tenderness that caused every sentence to stir the hearts of the audience, he said : " I've been waiting to speak, but I couldn't get a chance. I couldn't get up quick enough. I'm glad the fire has not burned out. This is like the first Love Feast I attended over 70 years ago. I believed then the Lord, the righteous Judge, had a crown for me, and I mean to fight for it until I die; I am still fighting for it this morning, and have the same purpose of heart. I can say to-day, O God, my heart is fixed, but I'm not out of the way of temptation yet. You know I was raised among Quakers. I didn't like the noise Methodists made, and so I thought I would keep the religion to myself. I began to pray in whispers, but finally cried out to God for mercy. I was converted in a storm, and have been going in a storm ever since. I want to be more quiet, but I suppose I have never got established yet. I am in a large place this morning, O hallelujah!" How this old patriarch stirred God's saints! The pastor invited all to sing, "I'll Be There," and shake hands while they sang with everybody in their reach. With this grand song rolling out upon the morning air, the people on their feet grasping by the hand in fraternal sympathy and love those near them, some walking about to rejoice with friends not near enough to be reached by the hand, little groups of shouters all over the church, it was a scene to delight angels and men. But the climax was reached when the pastor cried, "Let all who will promise to meet me there wave back their handkerchiefs as we sing." And immediately while in song they promised, " I'll be there," a thousand snowy white banners of promise from the floor and gallery, and remotest corners of the church waved back the promise, and mighty shouts of anticipation and triumph were heard in every part of the building. It was a thrilling spectacle, and he was fortunate who had a part in that delightful Love Feast.

The Rev. Enoch Stubbs, of Philadelphia, pastor of Asbury from 1872 to 1875, proceeded immediately with the preaching of the morning. The text was Psalms xliv : 1, and the sermon was a most appropriate tribute to the fathers of Methodism. The Rev. Vaugh Smith dismissed the congregation with the benediction.

The Sunday School Celebration was held at 2.30 P. M., the Rev. Enoch Stubbs presiding in a felicitous manner. This was one of the most delightful services of the Centennial week. The music was suited to the occasion and well rendered. Among other appropriate select was a " Centennial Hymn" composed by Miss Eliza Johnson and sung as a solo by C. M. Leitch, Esq., and chorus by the school. The children, trained by Miss Georgie Carver, all of whom acquitted themselves with great credit in their declamations, were Paul Blore, Sallie Sullivan, Anna McClure, Edith Shaw and Bessie B. Johnson. Addresses were made by N. B. Waters, Superintendent of Ezion Sabbath School, Joseph Pyle, Esq., of St. Paul's, A. V. Hysore, Esq., of Union, A.W. Briley, Esq., of Silverbrook, M. A. Pierce, Esq., of Scott, Rev. A. T. Scott, of Cookman, James E. McKay, Esq., of Asbury, and the Rev. A. J. Bohlin, of Sweden.

In the evening in the auditorium, the Rev. W. L. S. Murray, Ph D., Presiding Elder of the Wilmington District, pastor of Asbury from 1883 to 1886, preached an able sermon from 1 Cor. xv : 57. At the same time in the lecture-room, the Rev. Enoch Stubbs addressed the Christian Endeavor Society and invited sinners to Christ. Penitents were at both altars and some were made happy in conscious pardon.

Thus ended the Centennial services of Asbury Methodist Episcopal Church—services that will be remembered by every participant through time and eternity. We have rejoiced in the knowledge that we are a part of the great Methodist Church whose altar fires have never been extinguished, and whose spiritual services are so well adapted to man's needs. Our love has been intensified by the knowledge of the sacrifices made by our fathers, and the price paid for the heritage enjoyed by us. But no unsanctified pride possesses our souls either in the retrospect of past achievements or the prospect of grander conquests to come. Rather would we bow low in humility before God as we study our heroic history, and wait until the Leader of Churches shall endue us with power to make our second century more glorious than the first.

REV. CYRUS D. FOSS, D. D., LL. D.,
Bishop of the Methodist Episcopal Church.

Decisive Tests of Christian Religion.

SERMON BY BISHOP CYRUS D. FOSS, D. D., LL. D.

REPORTED BY THE REV. VAUGHN S. COLLINS.

TEXT: "We are his witnesses in these things; and so is also the Holy Ghost, whom God hath given to them that obey him." These are the words of the Apostle Peter, as found in the fifth chapter of the Acts of the Apostles, and thirty-second verse.

What these things were will best appear by reading a few verses preceding. Then Peter and the other Apostles answered and said, "we ought to obey God rather than men. The God of our fathers raised up Jesus, whom ye slew and hanged on a tree. Him hath God exalted with His right hand to be a Prince and a Savior, for to give repentance to Israel, and forgiveness of sins, and we are His witnesses of these things; and so is also the Holy Ghost, whom God hath given to them that obey Him."

There are two ways of getting at truth. I. Argument; II. Experiment. The one class of searchers take Plato as their head; the other Bacon. One class are continually asking, "What *must* be?" the other class ask directly, "What is?" The two systems might be illustrated by a farmer, who ploughing in his field turns up with his share a piece of glittering mineral, he stoops, picks it up, and says to himself, "Is not this gold? it is a metal; it is yellow; it is shining bright; it is very heavy; gold shows all these characteristics; this must be gold." If, however, he wants to know surely, he will take the mineral to a chemist and let him apply the tests; and then he KNOWS it is gold, which is the better plan.

Four hundred years ago there was no such thing as science; men were busy proving what *must* be, what we now call chemistry was then but the guess work of alchemy; the science of medicine was but quackery; astronomy was but astrolgoy. Bacon arose and said we must inquire by experiment if we would *know*; and acting on his suggestion, by using experiment, oft repeated, the ignorant guesswork of the old system has given way to our present systems of scientific knowledge.

To-night I desire to present to you just a single line of thought: DOES THE CHRISTIAN RELIGION, OR DOES IT NOT, SUBMIT ITSELF TO DECISIVE TESTS, LEADING TO KNOWLEDGE? or in other words, MAY WE PROVE BY ACTUAL EXPERIMENT THAT RELIGION IS A FACT?

The so-called scientist and the careless Christian will perhaps unite in giving a negative answer to this proposition. The scientist will most probably tell you that "religion is mere credulity, not knowledge but speculation;" while the careless Christian may say, "the best any man can say is, *religion is a hope.*"

In answer to the question asked I want to say,

1. That we shall probably find that the religion of the Lord Jesus Christ does submit itself to decisive experiment, leading to knowledge; and

II. That it most certainly does so submit itself.

I. IT DOES PROBABLY SUBMIT ITSELF TO DECISIVE EXPERIMENT. For this proposition I offer three reasons:

(a) Only thus can it be the religion of the world at large.

If it is to be the religion of all nations, all races, all classes, it must be such a religion as all these can prove for themselves. Now the Christian Religion is clearly intended for the entire world. When at His birth the Star of Bethlehem shone, the angels sang "on EARTH peace, good-will to MEN." The Jews tried hard and long to shut up even this promise to Judea; but it could not be so shut up. When the Manger Babe came to manhood, and lived and taught just what He meant, just before leaving the earth, with one foot already in the Angelic Chariot that was waiting to bear Him back to His Celestial Home, in order that there might be no doubt about this, He said to His Disciples, "go ye into ALL the WORLD, and preach the gospel to EVERY CREATURE," so it was clearly meant for the race, the whole race of man.

In this it is sublimely unique. No one had ever before dreamed of such a thing. The wisest of the ancient sages would have laughed such an idea to scorn. "A religion for all nations? For all peoples? Impossible! Like language, each nation must have a religion of its own, to suit the fancies and conditions of its own people. How could it go? The great mass of people are compelled to work many hours a day with their hands; what time would they have to learn a religion, or to spread it? What will be your tests? Must a man learn Hebrew?

Shall those only be saved who have mastered Algebra?" All such talk is vanity. When our God would tell us what it is like, and how we are to test it, He compares it to "water," and to "bread," common food, and common drink, which king and peasant must use. These are the metaphors by which our God informs us how universal this religion of His is to be; an everyday, universal religion, one that is as good for a man on Tuesday as it is on Sunday.

(b) Again, only thus, can it be the religion of ALL MEN, at ALL TIMES. Any religion, or no religion, might do perhaps when everything was bright and prosperous; but if our religion will not stand the test of the adversity, what is it good for? We need something upon which to rely in hours of darkness, in times of trial and affliction, pain and tribulation come with their giant flail and beat us all down What then? Are we to be counseled and comforted as a philosopher? No, but as a sinner saved by grace. When Bengel, the learned author of the "Gnomon of the New Testament," one of the most learned men Germany ever produced, lay a-dying, he turned to a divinity student standing near and said, "Give me some word of scripture to comfort me." The student, abashed in the presence of the great man who knew so much more about the scripture than he, stammered out that he was not able. "What," replied the old philosopher; "a divinity student, and yet not able to speak a word of comfort from the word of God to a dying man?" Urged by this half rebuke the student quoted, "The blood of Jesus Christ His son cleanseth us from all sin." "O, that is it, that is it," exclaimed the dying saint: "His blood cleanseth us from all sin." The poorest peasant in all Germany could have taken that promise to his heart just as well as the learned Bengel.

(c) Again, it is propable that God would have arranged for a religion that could be tested, because we find it is the best way to gain knowledge in other things.

In all other search after truth we have to build on facts. This is the way from the cradle to the grave. Along every line of knowledge and action we have facts as a basis. Suppose religion were different: it would be but building on air instead of on the rock. When everything else about us responded to test and experiment, if religion contained nothing but hypotheses, would we not have bitterly complained, "O that God had given us a few facts."

The old adage is true: " An ounce of fact is worth a ton of argument." Dr. Lardner I believe it was, who many years ago proved most satisfactorily to himself, that no vessel could ever cross the ocean by power of steam alone. His demonstration ran thus: " To propel the vessel so many miles, would require so many revolutions of the wheels;

so many revolutions of the wheels will require so much power; so much power will require so much steam; so much steam will require the combustion of so many tons of coal. And when he had figured it all up as nice as nice could be, according to his calculation it would require so much coal that it would sink at the dock any vessel ever built. A very pretty, ingenious calculation; but the very first steamship that crossed the ocean brought the argument over in her hold. What did the long argument amount to when you had the fact? Since God has so arranged it then, that in all other things, from the cradle to the last breath, that all knowledge is to be built on facts, is it not probable that anything so important as religion would also be based upon fact?

I might go on and make this probable argument much stronger; but I must pass on to notice in the second place.

II. WE MOST CERTAINLY DO FIND THAT GOD HAS GIVEN US A RELIGION THAT SUBMITS ITSELF TO DECISIVE TESTS.

(a) In the scriptures.

Where shall we look for the proof? At the first altar ever reared; and standing beside it we find righteous Abel rejoicing because he *knows* that God is well pleased with his offering; "God testifying of his gifts: and by it he being dead yet speaketh." Coming on a little farther and we find Enoch "was translated that he should not see death; and was not found because God had translated him: for before his translation he had *this testimony, that he pleased God.*"

Coming on a little further we find David rejoicing that he has also tried it and proved it. Hear him singing from his full heart, "He brought me up also out of an horrible pit, out of the miry clay, and set my feet upon a rock, and established my goings. And he hath put a new song in my mouth, even praise unto our God." In every age there have been the same clear demonstrations of this truth; always some man to stand up for God, and say, "We are His witnesses of these things." Not to tell of Paul, or of the other Apostles, let us look at what John says in his first general epistle. Let us see whether John had any experience, whether or not John knew for himself that he was born of God. "O, well," you say, "John is not a fair test. John was always sweet and amiable, even from his birth." Do not make a mistake. When John first came under the influence of Jesus he was a "son of thunder." Aye, he was a son of "lightning" as well, fiery and impetuous. It was this same John, together with his brother James, who besought the Master to let them call down fire from Heaven upon the inhabitants of a certain village because they would not believe, like Elijah of old. Such was John ; but grace made him all over—not *nature*, but GRACE, made John the sweet, loving man that we know. Now let us turn to his epistle. In our ordinary Bibles it covers about three pages; but, short as it is, it is a most wonderful book. Again and again it says, "*we know*," "*we know*." Nineteen times in three pages John distinctly declares "we *know* him;" and one time he gets so much in earnest about it he declares, "*we do* KNOW that we know him." With only a slight change in phraseology, John in this short letter declares fifty-one times that he *knows* what he is talking about. But there is no need of telling Methodists that the Bible says a man may know his acceptance with God. *You* know it; not from the Bible only, but like John you know it for yourselves.

(b) Again, the whole experience of the Christian church of all ages has given its strong AMEN to this proposition.

Now do not understand me as saying that we can dictate experiments to God. We can not. The Pharisees and Sadducees came more than once to the Master and demanded a "sign," some great demonstration of His power. True, He was daily working miracles, healing the sick, casting out devils, cleansing the lepers, and even raising the dead; but that was not enough. They were not satisfied with these proofs of His divinity. They wanted to have a great miracle done just their way; just as they dictated. In every such case the Master flatly refused to gratify their unholy curiosity. Nor do I forget that when He hung on the cross men insultingly demanded, "Come down from the cross, if You are the Christ; You pretended to save others when You were going about. If You can save others You can certainly save Yourself, so let us see You come down now, and we will believe." But He came not down. To have come down would have been to have left us without salvation. O, how His divinity shines forth as He hangs there, suffering, insulted, dying; refusing to do what He could so easily have done, in order that we might never die!

Nor can we say on what conditions we will believe. We are to accept the conditions as we find them. Here is the unfairness of such tests as that prescribed by Prof. Tyndall. "Take two wards in a hospital, of same size, same number of patients; one ward is to be prayed for, and the other not; and see which ward has the most recoveries." Only let it be known to the Christian world that there was one whole ward of sufferers deliberately given up to disease and death without a word of prayer for their alleviation and recovery, and the whole world would pray for the neglected ward. Yet, while we can not dictate terms, and tempt God with these foolish experiments, there are tests, real and true tests, that may be tried, and have been tried; and through all the ages from righteous Abel to the last poor penitent sinner there comes swelling one long, O sweet, sublime chorus, "Not one word faileth of all He hath promised us."

Why can not men learn from science? You take a piece of charcoal to a chemist and he will tell you it is pure carbon. Take him a diamond and he will tell you that also is pure carbon. Then why not cause the charcoal to become diamond? Because no man knows how to do it. One is crystallized, the other uncrystallized; but how to change one into the other is the mystery. But if a man tries to effect this change, as men have done and failed, do men say there is nothing in chemical knowledge? Because you fail to work the transformation, do you refuse to believe that they are both one identical substance in two forms? Not at all. A man may try an experiment nineteen times and make an utter failure to find out anything new; but if the twentieth experiment enables him to find out a hair's breadth more about the subject of his experiment, he is heralded far and near as a great discoverer. If men would only give the Bible and religion an equal chance, what manifold greater results they would get.

A learned, pious Scot, it is said, went through the whole Bible with this one question in his mind, "How many promises are there?" He is said to have found eighteen thousand. Just think of it, eighteen thousand promises! I do not know whether that is just the true number or not; but I do know there are enough—enough for all, and enough forever. Eighteen thousand promises; and every one an invitation from God to try experiments on Him; and he stands pledged to stand by the man that makes the experiment. Hear Him: "Wherein God, willing more abundantly to show unto the heirs of promise the immutability of His counsel, confirmed it by an oath; that by two immutable things, in which it was impossible for God to lie, we might have a strong consolation, who have fled for refuge to lay hold upon the hope set before us."

There are two or three classes of these promises I might mention. How clearly defined, how distinct do they stand out, on this great background of God's everlasting oaths of fidelity; and God will come down from heaven and die, ere He will allow a single one to go unfulfilled.

(a) Willing obedience the solvent of doubts.

While on earth Jesus left this test: "If any man will do His will, he shall know the doctrine, whether it be of God." The revised version makes it clearer, and renders the Greek more accurately: "If any man *wills to do His will*, he shall know." Here is a pledge, a promise, a test. God says he will not leave such a one in the dark.

When I was a young pastor in New York City I had a call from a young art student, the son of a Canadian Methodist minister. It was not long before he brought it around in conversation so as tell me that he did not believe in the Bible. His father a minister of God, his mother a Christian woman, and the son did not believe in the Bible! I was so surprised I asked him over again: "You say you do not believe in the Bible?" "No." "Well how did you come to disbelieve the Bible? If you were trained by a Christian father and mother, you surely must have believed in the Bible when a child ; then how it is you do not believe now? Certainly upon so important a subject you must have spent much time and study before rejecting the Bible? I suppose you have read the Bible through two or three times at least?" "No; I have never have read it through." "Did you ever read the New Testament through?" "No." "How long since you read your last chapter?" "O, about five or six weeks." I must confess I felt like saying to him what Dr. Lyman Beecher said to a man who was ranting about his scepticism: "You are no sceptic, it takes *brains* to be a sceptic." Here was a beardless youth of nineteen, who had never read even the New Testament through in his life, pretending to deny the Bible of his father and mother! But I did not say anything sharp like the master when a certain young man came to him, and when "he looked on him he loved him;" so as I looked on this young man I loved him; and I determined to save him if I could, looking at him I said gently, "Pardon me, but may I ask if your Bible is not now in your trunk?" He answered that it was. "And is it not away down in the bottom of your trunk under all your clothes?" He blushed and said, "Yes, it is at the bottom." "Pardon one more question; when you left home to come to New York, did not your mother put your Bible in your trunk with her own hands, right on top of everything, so that it would be in full view the moment the lid was opened?" I saw his embarrassment, and his evident confusion; and as he did not reply at once I continued, "now no one has told me anything about it ; I never saw you or heard of you in my life until you introduced yourself a few minutes ago ; and all I know about you is what I have gathered during our conversation." He then acknowledged that my surmise had been correct. After chatting a few minutes he arose to go and I said, "Well, my young friend, you have taken an hour of a very busy man ; I have given it to you cheerfully, however, and am willing to do what I can for you; may I make one request of you?" "Why, certainly, I will do anything I can for you; what is it?" "Before you retire to-night will you not take your Bible out of your trunk and read two or three chapters of the gospel according to Luke? and do this every day until I see you?"

At first he hesitated; but at last he promised to do as I requested, and he went home.

Three weeks from the next Sunday I baptized that young man into the Church of God, the happiest of converts.

Young brethren of the ministry, what are you going to do about it? How shall doubters be convinced? Will you refer them to the large volumes of Watson, or Pope, or Butler? Do not do this. Send them to the Bible. The New Testament and prayer is the short road out of scepticism. The way of salvation is by faith; and to get faith we must come to Jesus, for He is both the "Author and Finisher of our faith."

(b) Another class of promises: "He that believeth shall be saved." Does any body know that? [Voices, "Yes!"] "We are witnesses of these things; and so is also the Holy Ghost, whom God giveth to them that obey Him." We must emphasize the teachings of the Holy Ghost.

Some time ago I heard a most able address by Dr. Patton, of Princeton, before the convention of the Y. M. C. A. He was speaking of the evidences of the truth of the Bible and religion. He said it was as a man going on a journey of a thousand miles, but stops a half mile from home. He is not at home. So he argued that all the authority of the scriptures and of tradition, all history and all logic, all learning, does not complete the journey. What about that last half mile? The Holy Ghost takes you the last half mile. "We are his witness of these things, and so is also the Holy Ghost."

Does any body know that? Saint Paul insists that he has no remedy in his whole *Materia Medica* but "Believe and thou shalt be saved." I see him in Troas, alone, meditating. One comes unto him saying, "Come over into Macedonia and help us." He takes it as the voice of God, sets sail across the blue ægean, and finds his way to Philippi. He goes out to the place of prayer and finds there certain faithful women, whom he tells of Jesus. Among these is Lydia, a seller of purple, of the city of Thyatira, whose "heart the Lord opened;" and Lydia believed and was converted, the first convert in all Europe. "O, well she was only a woman; a good, pure, gentle woman. It is easy enough to get her to believe and profess. Let us have another case, Paul. Lydia won't do. We want to see you try it on some bad, sin-polluted, determined man. Take another case, Paul, before you ask us to believe you have a sure cure." All right. Here he is, right in this same city of Philippi, the hard-hearted, iron-handed Roman jailer. Paul and Silas have been thrown into prison. With backs gashed by the scourge and bleeding, with their feet fast in the stocks, these two sing hymns and praise God. It is no low humming; but they sing out so loud "all the prisoners heard them." It is midnight; and as they pray God sends in his "amen" with an earthquake. The foundations of the prison are shaken, the doors are all open, and the shackles fall from every prisoner. The jailer in alarm springs from his bed to find the doors all open; and thinking the prisoners are surely gone he draws his sword and is about to fall on it when Paul calls out, "Do thyself no harm, we are all here." The jailer calls for lights, and comes in; and falling down before Paul and Silas asks, "What must I do to be saved?" Now, Paul, here is your case. Here is a poor, hardened wretch. What will you do with him? And Paul pulls out the same old medicine, saying, "Believe on the Lord Jesus Christ and thou shalt be saved." The remedy works just as well as in the case of Lydia; for he believed, and was converted and baptized, and received into church all between midnight and day.

I know something of this from personal experience. From nine years of age until I was eighteen I was bowing at every Methodist altar I could get to. Never was an invitation given but I accepted it and went forward. All these years I was seeking for light and pardon —praying and groaning for salvation. I wondered how it was that God would convert harlots and drunkards and all that were vile, and leave me, a good, moral, truthful boy, who had never done anything very bad, in the dark. But at eighteen I saw that during all these years I had been a poor, little, miserable Pharisee, thinking I was something when I was nothing. Then I cried, "O Lord, I am poor and vile, and I cannot save myself. Have mercy upon me, poor, miserable sinner." And the Lord heard me, and answered me; and I knew for myself that God does forgive sinners. The same God that converted that little son of a poor Methodist preacher will save all who put their trust in him.

Does anybody else know this?

Years ago I heard Bishop Janes tell of a little Jewess who lived in Baltimore. Her husband was a gay young man, who spent his evenings away from home, and his wife was left to entertain herself as best she could. One evening having nothing else to do, merely for the sake of amusement she went into the basement of a church where they were holding a protracted meeting, and heard for the first time in her life a Gospel sermon. She was highly amused at the singing and prayer, and the preaching seemed perfectly ridiculous to her. Being so much entertained she came the next evening, and was, if possible, even more amused than the first time. But somehow during the hours of the next day she could not help but think, "Well, now suppose what the preacher said is true; suppose this Jesus is the Christ, the promised Messiah." She went to the meeting the third evening, and she became very much exercised. It seemed that the sermon came directly to her. She left the church at the close of the sermon feeling that "this Jesus must be the Christ, the Messiah for which the Jews have been looking; and my people murdered him." She was under deep conviction. She could not go to bed. Her husband came in about midnight and found her bathed in tears. He wanted to know what the matter was, and she told him. He begged her to come to bed, telling her that she was just nervous and excited; but she said no; she could not go to bed. She wanted him to go right out and get her a New Testament. He told her the stores were all closed, and she must wait until morning; and besides what a curse would come on them from their people. "No," said she. "I must have it now. Please go get me one from a neighbor's." When he found he could not dissuade her he set out, and going to the house of a Christian neighbor rang the bell. Roused from his slumber the good man came to the door and inquired what was wanted. The husband replied, "I am sorry to trouble at this hour of the night; but my wife wants a New Testament." "You shall have it," replied the good man; and gave him the desired Testament. As soon as the young husband was gone the good neighbor, one of those lynx-eyed watchmen on the walls of Zion, always looking about to see where the arrows from the pulpit are striking, put on his clothes and went to call up another brother. "What do you want?" asked the brother disturbed. "Put on your clothes and come go with me. I think the Lord has a mission for us to-night. You remember that little Jewess who has been to our meeting for three nights? Well, her husband has just been to my house and got a New Testament, saying his wife wanted it. I think we ought to go see if we can not help her." So these two started to the Jew's house.

Meanwhile, the husband of the Jewess had returned to his home, and handed his wife the much coveted New Testament. She received it with as much reverence as if it had been the Ark of Jehovah itself. She hastened to her own room, and clasping the book in her arms prayed "O God of Abraham, Isaac and Jacob, give me light! give me light! give me light!" With trembling hands and palpitating heart she opened the book. Her eye fell upon the first chapter of Paul's letter to the Romans; and with bated breath she read: "Paul, a servant of Jesus Christ, called to be an Apostle, separated unto the Gospel of God, which he had promised afore by his prophets." "Why that means our Jewish prophets. So then they, our own prophets, prophesied of this Jesus, 'Concerning His son Jesus Christ.' Why here again this Jesus is called the Christ, the Messiah "our Lord." Why this Jesus is here called our Lord. Can it be so? 'Which was made of the seed of David according to the flesh.' Why that was what our prophets all said the true Messiah should be. 'And declared to be the son of God with power,' son of God? Why this must be true. This Jesus must be the true Messiah. Help me, O Lord!" and on she read and prayed, on down to the sixteenth verse where she read, "For I am not ashamed of the Gospel of Christ: for it is the power of God unto salvation to every one that believeth." Every one that believeth; why that must mean me. 'Every one!' 'Unto the Jew first!' Is it so? 'Unto the Jew first?' Why praise the Lord, that means me sure. Unto the Jew first: I see it now! I am saved. This Jesus is the Messiah, and He is my Savior." When the two good brethren rang the door bell she had no need of their help; but filled with joy, she shouted to them, "I have found Jesus, the son of God, the son of Mary; and He is my Savior."

"O, that is all imagination!" Imagination? Then in the name of scientific honesty give us a fact? Do we know anything that we can not see and hear? Do I know that I love my wife and children when I return from my long journeys? And my boy, just budding into manhood, and my darling daughter, and my faithful loving wife meet me with kisses and words and looks of tenderest affection? Do I know that I love them? If so, why do I not know that I love my God, who has done and is still doing so much for me?

Bishop Janes said that to his personal knowledge, for fifteen years from that midnight hour, that woman showed forth by her walk and conversation that she had indeed found Jesus. You want facts? The Roman Empire and the old red sandstone are no more facts than are such experiences in religion.

Have no more doubt about experimental religion. Here is the citadel. Here is the central, pivotal point of the war against sin. Never worry about scepticism, or rationalism, or pantheism, or any other "ism," as long as you are living "witnesses of these things." Twenty or thirty men raised from the death of sin to life in the Lord Jesus Christ is a standing argument that religion is true; and all the argument in the world can not overturn such evidence.

In my world-ranging tours I find everywhere men and women who rise and testify that they *know* that they have proved God—they *know* they have peace, and joy in the Holy Ghost. There are living to-day a host as great as that John saw, "that no man can number," who can truthfully testify that they have tried and proved that God is true, and that He does fulfill His promises to men.

Yet there are those who say they doubt about there being any such thing as experimental religion; that such talk belongs to the old days of superstition (by which they mean theology). "But we have reached a higher plane in learning now—we have got to the solid basis of fact."

Now, my doubting friend, I want to ask you two or three plain questions, to see what you mean by your oft-repeated boast of scientific knowledge. In the first place I will ask you:

(a) Is mystery the proof of absurdity?

You claim that it *is*, in the case of religion; and because of its mysteries you refuse to believe the Bible and its teachings. Then where, prey you, is your boasted science? I have a handful of cambric needles, and I throw them on the Bible here. I take an ordinary horseshoe magnet and move it near them, and find the needles at once follow the magnet. No matter which way I turn the magnet the needles follow. I ask some bright school boy of twelve, "What makes the needles follow the magnet?" at once he replies, "Magnetism." I ask, "And what is magnetism? Can't tell me, eh? Don't know? Very well my lad, don't worry; Professor Tyndale says he don't know either. I raise this hymn book a few inches and let go of it, and down it falls; why? "Gravitation," you reply. Yes; but what is gravitation? No man on earth knows, or ever will know. Here are these simplest of scientific facts that no scientist can explain—mysteries just as great as those we find in the spiritual world. Explain to me, who can, the mystery of magnetism, and I will undertake to unfold to you the mystery of the Trinity. When you can tell me the mystery of gravitation, whether it is in the matter, or outside of matter, or something different and apart from matter, then it will be my time to tell you the mysteries of salvation.

It is strange, yet not strange, to see what men will believe, and what they refuse to believe. A heathen king of an oriental country was being entertained by a philosopher, who had been traveling in Arctic regions, with an account of his travels. The traveler was recounting a series of sights and adventures as marvelous as those of Munchausen or the Arabian Nights; and the king drank in every word as the most sacred truth. Presently the traveler said that he had seen water frozen hard into a substance called ice; and when thus frozen it became so hard that men and horses, and even elephants, could walk on it like it were the solid ground beneath their feet. "O stop, stop," said the now excited king; "now I *know you are lying*." He refused to believe, because in his hot country he had never seen ice.

Walking down the street there comes a lean, lank, parchment-faced philosopher, whose head is packed with what he calls "scientific learning." On her way to school comes tripping past a bright-eyed little girl with her satchel of school books on her arm, singing out from her merry heart,

> "Jesus loves me, this I know,
> For the Bible tells me so ;
> If I love Him, when I die,
> He will take me home on high."

The cold-hearted philosopher looks after the child in pity, and says " What a shame that the Sunday School should teach that bright child such nonsense. What a shame to impose so upon her childish credulity. However, I will not undeceive her." Which of the two is to be pitied ? O, sing on, little maid, sing on. You are not deceived. You are only practicing the song of salvation which you shall one day sing with the redeemed in Glory. Sing on, and do not let the grumbling of the philosopher whose soul is blind hinder you in your happy march to Zion, the bright city of God.

And I would ask my scientific doubter one other question :

(b) Do you not hold that the law of need is universal ? That for every need there is, there must be, a supply ?

Certainly science does hold this as a cardinal truth. Light is for the eye, honey for the honey bee, water for the fish.

Blasting in a mine five hundred feet below the surface a skull is found. At once science says, " this creature moved upon the surface of the earth." It may be a skull like none other ever found. It may seem to be that of neither bird, beast, nor human ; and yet at once the scientist says, " the owner lived on the surface of the earth." Why ? Because in this skull are sockets, and sockets mean eyes for the sockets, and eyes mean light, demand light. So disease demands a cure ; and I have no question that there are hidden in mineral and vegetable a cure of every disease. It is the part of medicine to hunt these out.

But there is something else beside these material demands. I have an intellect that demands truth ; it craves knowledge. Well do I remember how the blood tingled in my very finger tips and in my toes when I mastered the multiplication table. Truth ! my mind demands it ! the whole universe is my teacher : mountain, river, ocean, plain, my text books.

Is that all ? No, I worship. I want a God ; I want salvation ; I want immortality. Saint Paul but voiced the wail of thoughtful men of all ages when he cried, "O, wretched man that I am, who shall deliver me from the body of this death?" These are the seers of the race. Men have gone up and down this earth weeping and wailing, "O, where is my Father? where is my God?" The thunder peals in the Heaven above, and some say "that must be God;" and worship. Some beholding the sun shining in his strength and bringing light and life, say "that must be our God," and worship.

The storm, the wind, the rushing waters, each have spoken; and various races have said, "these must be God;" and have worshiped. I hear a voice. Whence is it, of Heaven, or earth, or from within? False or true, whence is it? It is beside me, it is within me, sweetly saying, "Our Father." Praise His name! I have found Him! my God, and my Father!

Now a word in closing.

There are those who are *practically* infidels. I take my Bible and start through this congregation and ask you one by one, "Do you believe this book?" Every one of you would indignantly reply, "Yes." Let me ask you one more question before leaving you, "Do you *live* as though you believed it?" You hang your heads, and mumble something about "doubting experimental religion." Then why say you believe the Bible, when all the time you are practically living an infidel life? Doubt on, and you can only have, and you must surely have, the same terrible fate as those who refuse God.

Passing along the street I meet a man of fair intelligence, and pointing to the second brightest star that to-night is shining in the heavens, I say, "Does not Jupiter and his four moons look beautiful to-night." He replies, "I don't believe in Jupiter's having four moons. Such talk is all nonsense. I never saw them in my life, and I don't believe any one else ever did." "Well, my friend, you may not be able to see them with the naked eye; only about one man in ten thousand can; but if you will come home with me and look through my telescope I will show them to you." So together we go to my home. As he takes my arm to climb the observatory steps, I notice he leans rather heavily on my arm. Reaching the top I turn my telescope upon the planet Jupiter, fix the focal distance until it is just right, then ask him to come look. He comes stumbling along and puts his eye to the glass, and grumbles out, "I see no Jupiter, nor the four moons." Amazed I look at the man, and see *he is blind!* No wonder he does not see. But shall I let that blind man made me believe that the four moons of Jupiter all imagination merely because *he* can not see them? So in spiritual things. It is not to be expected that the natural man shall see and understand spiritual truth. They are spiritually blind. The Bible distinctly says, "The natural man receiveth not the things of the Spirit of God; for they are foolishness unto him; neither can he know them, because they are spiritually discerned."

But suppose the blind man refuses to put his eye to the glass; is he not still more inexcusable? Blind at best, and now refusing to put his eye where he might have his vision aided; would you not say he was a most presumptuous man to dare stand up and speak against the four moons of Jupiter as being a fable? That is just the position of some here to-night; blind, and yet refusing to come put their eye to the only place on earth whence they may be able to see. The Master when on earth at one time cried out, "Ye *will* not come unto Me that ye may have life." "Ye WILL not." There is the trouble. You refuse to do just what God says you *must* do in order to see. How long will you go on in your blind, stubborn way, refusing the mercy of God?

Suppose, however, I get the blind man to believe that if he will only come and put his eye to the telescope, he will receive his sight, and will be able to see just as well as I. He has never seen in all his life before; so he makes up his mind to try. With trembling step he approaches the telescope, puts his eye close up to the lens, turns his face up toward heaven, and at once the scales fall from his eyes. "Why, I do see something. I see a beautiful bright spot of light, set in a background of richest, deepest blue; is that Jupiter?" "Yes." "And I see circling about that bright spot four brilliant points of light. Are they the four moons?" "Yes." "O, then I see them, I see them too. No doubt about it. Whereas I was once blind now I see." You now have a life witness that Jupiter has four moons.

O, blind man, troubled with doubts, if you would see and know for yourself the power of God to save sinners, come put your eye to the Gospel telescope. Don't doubt, don't scoff; but try it! *try it!!* TRY IT!!!

The Joy of the Lord.

SERMON BY THE REV. JOHN A. ROCHE, D. D.

Neh. 8: 10. *The joy of the Lord is your strength.*

With nations and churches as with individuals, "There is a time to weep and a time to laugh." In ancient times (Dut. 16: 15) the feast was to be kept with rejoicing. The context presents an occasion that justified intensest joy. We witness one of the sublimest spectacles in the world's history. God's chosen people, long in captivity, have returned to Jerusalem. They who "by the rivers of Babylon sat down and wept, when they remembered Zion," are back in the city of Solemnities, male and female—all of understanding assemble, as upon a plazza before the water gate and ask Ezra the scribe to bring the book of the law of Moses. He stood upon a pulpit of wood and read and caused them to understand. He blessed the Lord, the great God, and all the people with uplifted hands and bowed heads, answered amen. Memory awoke, gratitude glowed, hearts melted.

Can we imagine greater joy except with those who return and come to Zion with songs and everlasting joy upon their heads? Nehemiah wished the people to appreciate their condition—"to eat the fat to drink the sweet, and send a portion unto them for whom nothing was prepared." He desired others to sympathize with the occasion and share in its delights. The day was holy unto the Lord and it forbade sorrow, and urged joy *as their strength*. With a like spirit this honored church of a hundred years, asks its friends far and near to rejoice with them and profit by the holy services of its first centennial. They would not eat their morsel alone. They rather say "Eat O friends and drink. Yea, drink abundantly. Magnify the Lord with us and let us exalt his name together."

Appropriating the language of the text to the child of God.

1. We shall endeavor to show that the joy of the Lord is the Christian's strength.

Joy is a delight of the mind to which men of the world are not

REV. JOHN A. ROCHE, D. D.
Pastor of Asbury Methodist Episcopal Church, 1851-53.

strangers. It may arise from riches gained, from learning acquired, from stations reached and from influence at their command. This delight may be largely of the animal spirits, or it may be mere mental buoyancy. It may be the joy of success, or of deliverance from danger; as men enjoy in time of harvest, or as when some great evil has passed. But the text presents "the joy of the Lord." He is its source, its substance and its support. At one time it may be expressed as serenity and satisfaction. At other times it rises to transport. The inhabitants of the rock sing; they shout from the top of the mountain. Christian joy is rooted in faith, grounded in love and increased by exercise. "The Lord Jehovah is their strength and their song."

We sometimes say of a man he is strong in logic, or in eloquent speech. This man's strength is in grasping great principles and that man is strong in the administration of government. The strength of the athlete is in his muscle. The strength of the philosopher is in his mind. The strength of the millionaire is in his coffers. But the joy of the Lord is the strength of the Christian. He may be the scholar, the statesman, the man of wealth and of earthly power. But joy in God distinguishes him as an heir of heaven. He has the best cause for joy and its cultivation is both his duty and his interest. There is a joy of the world that from its origin and excess is followed by lassitude and depression. It re-acts. Not so the joy of the Lord.

Let us consider Divine joy as an element of power in Christian character.

1. As the highest inspiration to noble deeds. Of joy in general we may say it is an *inspiration*. Gloom enervates. A depressed spirit has enough to do to attend to its own sorrows. But the faculties of the mind, the passions of the heart and all the forces of nature respond to joy. It is the sunshine of the soul in which things appear in the best light, and all the fruits of the spirit ripen; even the dearest relations of life fail to exert their due influence when sadness is allowed. The parent, the companion, the child, each of whom should be happy in the relation subsisting, experiences none of the delights that should distinguish the place and condition.

In business life the wheels of commerce stand still when depression paralyzes. The mariner would make no voyage, and except in desperation the soldier would fight no battle. An officer received orders from his superior to take a stronghold. He replied, "It is impossible." He was relieved. To another the commander said, "Take that fortification." The reply was, "I am unable." To a third was given the order. He saw the difficulty but answered, "It shall be done." He marched;

he charged; he fought; it fell. The one was buoyant, the others depressed.

The sculptor had his ideal. Before him lay a rude mass of marble. What was in that block more than in many others in the same quarry? He took his chisel; devoted his skill; labored in faith. The form, the features came out; the links, the chain, the manacles were revealed, and before an admiring world stood "The Greek Slave." The ideal was actualized and the voice of freedom was heard from lips of stone. It immortalized the artist who worked with cheer.

In art, in science, in literature, in government, in all the departments of thought and action, joy is a power to be confessed. It kindles the imagination of the poet; it fires the heart of the patriot and causes the tongue of the statesman to flame with consuming eloquence.

If *such is the influence of earthly joy*, what shall we say of the "joy of the Lord?" It is more exalted in its origin, more intense in its action, more certain in its results. The soul under its power is ready, if not eager for any work. The young man hears God say, "Go into all the world and preach the gospel." One of observation sees he is exercised about his duty, and ventures to say, "Pause, you have talents that will distinguish you in law, in medicine, in commerce; your talents qualify you for the grandest spheres of human action." Talk to a rock! you may as soon move it. Assure him of the estate of an Astor or a Vanderbilt; of the pre-eminence of a Webster or a Gladstone; name to him all the difficulties of a Divine vocation. He is honored by fortune or favor, and the difficulties do not deter him for a day. He says, "The Everlasting God is my portion, and they who turn many to righteousness, shall shine as the stars for ever and ever." Hear Melville B. Cox. Africa, is on his heart! A friend says such a mission is certain death. "Then, replied he, "when I fall come over and write my epitaph." "What shall I write, inquired he? "Write, let a thousand fall before Africa is given up." He went! He fell! He rose! He lives the inspiration of the missionary of the cross.

What is it to-day that makes Bishop Taylor the grand man that he is on the Congo? A wonder of labor in advanced age! A hero in suffering and danger! "The joy of the Lord is his strength." There is a young lady who has been reared and educated in the refinements and luxuries of one of the most distinguished families in New York City. The cause of missions stirs her. She married one of like mind and they go as missionaries to a distant and dangerous field. Her husband dies. With an infant she is left among a people whose only claim to her love is that they have souls. Her father wishes her return to the comforts at home, but she remains and amid the privations of her condition and place that she may do the work that her missions afford. What animates her? What sustains her? It is the joy of doing good! This is a strength worthy the name. Behold the action of this element in the Apostle Paul. He is just converted. He had great and protracted sorrow. Now he has indiscribable gladness. Joy thrills him. Love to Christ consumes him. He cannot be restrained in the exhibition of his zeal. Prudence might suggest, "Go up to Jerusalem to them that were Apostles before him" He would be like an angel flying with the everlasting Gospel to preach to men on earth. When Edward Taylor, the eloquent mariner's preacher of Boston, would describe a converted sailor in his haste to save sinners he said: "It was as if you had put spurs to lightning, that hardly had he kindled the holy fire in one port before he was off to another to set it on blaze." We know how it was with Andrew. "He first findeth his brother and brought him to Jesus." *This joy prompts the adoption of all means available to the Divine purpose.* Time, talent, and treasures are at ready command. Paul shows this in the church (cor. viii: 1) of Macedonia how that in a great trial of affliction, an *abundance* of their joy and their deep poverty abounded unto the riches of their liberality. For to their power, yea and beyond their power, they were willing of themselves. Praying us with much entreaty to receive the gift and minister to the saints. So *now there are laymen* who though they cannot be misionaries and ministers, give much of their time and talent and secular gain to the advancement of the cause of Christ, and who like Zaccheus are ready to give half their goods to feed the poor.

Joy in God makes a ready and cheerful offering. Nothing is difficult to him who acts under its power. Who shall describe this joy in the first realization of the beauties and blessings of vital piety? It sparkles in the eye, speaks in the voice, shines in the countenance and is itself a quiet demonstration of the influence of the good. Joy that is the highest inspiration of genius secures the sublimest manifestation of the saintly devotion, and affords the clearest evidence of its presence in strengthening and sustaining Christian character. Did not David show a just judgment when he said: "Restore unto me the joy of Thy salvation; then will I teach transgressors Thy ways and sinners shall be converted unto Thee."

2. The joy of the Lord is a support of the Christian in the labor and trials to which he is called. As these are efforts that would never be put forth if the joy of the Lord did not impel them, so there are difficulties that we could not overcome if joy did not sustain us. The minister enters his study with the "burden of the Lord." The mis-

sionary goes to his work with a knowledge that he lacks the success he seeks. The Bible reader, the Sabbath School teacher retires from the lesson and the class with the feeling that nothing seems to come from all this effort. The exhorter, the class leader, the laborer in God's vineyard, in whatever department, is tempted to say: "What good?" The tear falls; the heart aches. He enters his closet; "he prays to the Father." The soul struggles; faith reaches up; the hand grasps the arm of Jehovah and Omnipotence yields to importunity. A voice from the throne proclaims, "As a prince Thou hast power with God and hast prevailed." Now comes the sustaining power of holy joy. Behold Elijah when sorrow took him to the juniper tree and then God so feeds him that he goes on the strength of the meal for forty days.

Holy Samuel Rutherford, amid the imprisonment to which his preaching Christ subjected him, writes in his joy: "From Christ's Palace at Aberdeen." This joy in God sustained Francis Asbury on this peninsula in the season of his "dumb Sabbaths," when in the Revolution of 1776, he was pursued by those who did not comprehend his mission and character. This joy kept Freeborn Garretson faithful to the ministry that he had received of the Lord, when in his native state he was beaten by his persecutors and left unconscious on the highway. And who can ever forget the joy of Paul and Silas, that gave them such songs in the night, when an earthquake shook the prison, and the jailer was made an heir of heaven?

In whom can we find a fuller illustration of the sustaining power of Christian joy than in the Apostle to the Gentiles? He declares "God has set forth us the Apostle, as it were appointed to death. We are made a spectacle unto the world, to angels and to men. Even unto the present hour we both hunger and thirst and are naked and have no certain dwelling place, and labor with our own hands. Being reviled we bless; being persecuted we suffer; being deformed we entreat. We are made as the filth and offscouring of all things unto this day."

Think of a man of such origin, education, endowments. Think of him of such capabilities of worldly distinction. Think of him as such an Apostle of Jesus Christ, and yet subjected to such contempt. Think of the extent of his labor, the character of his solicitude, and the fierceness of his persecutions. Take his own account: "In prisons frequent, in deaths oft, of the Jews five times received I forty strips save one! Thrice was I beaten of rods, once was I stoned; thrice I suffered shipwreck; a night and a day have I been in the deep; in all kinds of perils;" in "waters" with "robbers;" with his own "countrymen" and "heathens;" in the "city" and in the "wilderness," and "among false brethren." Beside those that are without that which came upon him daily the care of all the churches. What unaided mortal could bear this with mental serenity?

But amid these diverse and trying experiences, he maintained a courage, revealed a wisdom and achieved results to which God alone could make him equal. With a moral heroism that showed the real grandeur of the man when so sustained, as if disdaining the thought of cowardice, as if utterly superior to all thought of regret at his course, he eloquently declares, "None of these things move me, neither count I my life dear unto myself, that I might *finish* my course with *joy*. What orator, poet, philosopher, or divine, can tell the strength to labor or endure, of him whose "sufficiency is of God?" Only the infinite can gauge the soul that grace fills. The Lord alone can measure the depths and heights and breadths of that love that passeth knowledge.

We know that the Christian has tribulation as well as joy. But we have not forgotten the words of Him who said, "Ye now have sorrow, but I will see you again, and your heart *shall rejoice* and *your joy* no man taketh from you." Thus in the past have the children of God been enabled to perform the most difficult service and withstand all the fiery darts of the devil.

There are those around us to-day who stand as the beaten anvil to the stroke, and the hammer will break, and the arm that wields it fall powerless before the soul shall yield to the strokes, though the heaviest that were ever given.

3. The joy of the Lord is our strength as a means of turning souls to Christ. Is there any thing in the Christian that attracts attention and awakens desire in those not saved like a cheerful and exultant spirit? The desire of happiness is innate; one exclaims: "O, happiness, our being, end and aim." The rich seek it; the poor long for it; the good have it. Dr. Samuel Johnson says: "The habit of looking on the bright side of things is worth a thousand pounds a year." The Scriptures declare a "merry heart doeth good like a medicine." May we not assume that the religion that does not invite by its benignity repels by its austerity? Religion is supposed to make us at once good and happy. And we so present it. If in this it fail, we fail. A man was recommending his medicine for a particular disease. The patient looked and said, "I perceive you have the same trouble; why does not your medicine *cure you*?" *It killed the cure*. Joy is diffusive, and there associates with it a sweetness and suavity that admits no counterfeit. I had almost said there is in the very manners of some Christians a divine urbanity as unlike merely artificial courtesies as the sun's rays are unlike the beams of the

moon. "They saw the face of Stephen as it had been the face of an angel." Paul tells of Nebuchadnezzer's wish to have some of the children of the captivity trained for superior wisdom and service. They should be fed with meat and wine from the king's table. They refused and asked only "pulse and water." After ten days they were examined and were fairer and fatter than those who ate at the king's table, and they were ten times wiser than all the magicians and astrologers. Zach. viii: 23 speaks of ten men of all languages that shall take hold of him that is called a Jew, saying we will go with you, for we have heard that God is with you. It is not the form but the spirit of religion that wins. Who will long prefer a bird of plumage to a bird of song?

Joy was a distinguishing characteristic of early Methodists. The witness of the spirit to adoption into the heavenly family and the earnest it gave of the inheritance that is incorruptible, undefiled and that fadeth not away, justified their highest expressions of delight. Lady Hastings, converted through Mr. Wesley's influence, declared to Lady Huntingdon: "Since I have known and believed in the Lord Jesus Christ for life and salvation I have been as happy as an angel!" Such an experience must win. It did in Asbury church in its earliest history. It does to-day. In your graveyard and in your records may be found the names of some of the leading families of this State and through Delaware and this peninsula, Methodism in her first efforts was instrumental in the convertion of some of the most distingushed layman that have honored her history. The spirit she revealed won not only the poor and uneducated, but the rich and learned.

When Whitfield asked an unbeliever in Christianty what it was in his sermon that convinced him of the truth of religion? he replied "Nothing," but added "As I was passing from the church and old woman was about to fall, I caught her; the look that she gave me and the 'God bless you,' that she pronounced convinced me that she had something that I had not."

The truth is many Christians must either be strong in *joy* or in nothing. They are not strong in learning, in riches, in worldly fame or position. They can only say "What I am I am by the grace of God." What I am not by grace, I am not.

Two Christians I observed in my youth to be impressed by them. I marked the contrast in them: one sighed, the other shouted; one told by his life that grace is not gloom and sanctification is not sadness. It drew me, won me.

On my first circuit there were two members of the charge who commanded me by their joyful spirit. They were a power! When they prayed the heavens bowed. When they spoke in love feast the assembly shook.

Who confesses not the power of sacred song? Who that heard it in the united voices of the congregation that our Fathers addressed will doubt its benefits. It came from the holy joy that lifted the soul of the singer. This joy is the very thing that all want to make life happy, death welcome and heaven a thing of *certitude*.

The late Samuel Halsted, of New York, and a man of precious memory, as one of the most successful laymen in bringing souls to Christ, was in nothing more distinguished than in his ardent zeal, his cheerful spirit and his practical and earnest exhibition of what he called "good religion," that made him happy in every place and service. The sight of him to many persons was a benediction.

He gave a narrative of two men who spoke in love feast. One was in a complaining mood. The preachers, the members, the times received his censure. To a warm meeting it was like a cold douche. The other man was in ecstasy and regretted that he who had just spoken lived in "Grumble street." He confessed that he was once there but he disliked it and left it. It was narrow and not clean and he had bad neighbors. Now he was living in Thanksgiving avenue and was delighted there. It was wide and clean. The air was pure, he had good neighbors and he was happy all the time.

Who that reads Christ's life does not see that though the world's moral woes were on Him, he carried joy wherever he went. He gave joy at the wedding feast; to the woman at the well; to Zaccheus who received him joyfully; to the two Disciples as they walked to Emmaus. And in his presence children by the wayside shouted Hosanna.

Do not facts justify us in saying with Dr. Young, "Retire and read thy Bible to be gay."

There is a moral gaity that grace induces. There is that exhilarates more than wine. Peter defended the disciples of Pentecost against the charge of drunkenness, by quoting from the Prophet Joel, in relation to the pouring out of the spirit in the latter days. These days we see. Will it then be deemed harsh to say "'Tis impious in a good man to be sad."

Would that we could be properly impressed with the fact that the Christian and the church that fail in the joyful prosecution of our work, *denies to the world one of the most influential means of bringing it to God.*

4. The joy of the Lord is our strength in the conquest of our final foe.

Death is before us; it meets us in every avenue of life. It comes under all circumstances and in many forms. To human nature it is an event of perpetual revulsion. The old as well as the young, the poor as well as the rich would shun it. It is the King of Terrors and the terror of kings; but there is no discharge in this war. "We must needs die." But how shall we meet death? With nothing but manly courage; with nothing but human philosophy? Will it be enough to say "The sword devours one as well as another?" Will the death of the many change the death of the individual? Alone I must meet God; alone I must be judged. If David Hume joked as death approached did it prove exemption from fear? His levity not less than another's gravity, was a recognition of that which he would fain disguise. The affectation meant apprehension.

Men brave in battle cower in the sick room. Behold the sinner as he faces death. His anxiety increases the solicitude of his friends. What will they do? Will they enumerate his social, domestic and political virtues? Will they tell the orator of his eloquence in the senate, or the financier of the skill by which he saved the credit of a tottering government; or will they emphasize the unequalled wealth of him that is about to depart?

Would not the dying man say, "Miserable comforters are ye! I am entering a world where these things do not avail?" This is true. The wreaths of earthly immortality wither before the tomb. Fame has no voice in the silence of the sepulchre, and flattery cannot soothe the dull cold ear of death.

Now is wanted what the dying man has not.

If God has made it possible for a departing soul to triumph over death, then that which he has provided is a boon worthy of universal and profoundest gratitude. Grace in the heart, through the death of Christ, and by faith in His blood is the death of death; the funeral of our sorrows. Here where unaided human reason fails, where philosophy hangs down its head, and skepticism carps no more, religion wins her brightest trophies and reveals its sovereign power. In yielding the ghost the Christian is more than conqueror.

Bunyan represents the pilgrims as entering the land of Beulah; the air is sweet and pleasant; the birds sing; the flowers appear, and the voice of the turtles is heard in the land; the sun is shining night and day; they are out of the reach of "Giant Despair," and cannot so much as see "Doubting Castle." They are in sight of the city, but there is a river and there is no bridge over it. All save Enoch and Elijah have had to cross this river. *Doubt* makes Christian sink; *joy* makes Hopeful brave. One is troubled with apparitions, hobgoblins, and evil spirits, but Hopeful says, "I feel the bottom." Christian in his doubting has a fainting fit, but when he *believes* "the enemy is as still as a stone;" they see the shining ones enter heaven and are safe.

So have I seen a saint go up to God; Glory filled the room and she said, "The angels had come;" with them she went and left us. Is there not strength in such joy of the Lord? Hear Paul when martyrdom was before him :

"I am now ready to be offered, and the time of my departure is at hand ; I have fought a good fight ; I have finished my course ; I have kept the faith; henceforth there is laid up for me a crown of righteousness, that the Lord, the righteous judge, will give me in that day, and not to me only, but to all them also who love his appearing." *Joy to the last, and culminating joy in the final conflict.* Yes, yes, "the joy of the Lord is our strength, and the more we have, the stronger we are to *do*, to *suffer*, or to *die*.

Who wonders then that such fact should inspire the genius of even Alexander Pope to write :

> "Vital spark of heavenly flame.
> Quit, O quit this mortal frame.
> Trembling, hoping, lingering, flying ;
> O the pain, the bliss of dying !
> Cease fond nature, cease thy strife,
> And let me languish into life.
> Hark ? they whisper ; Angels say,
> "Sister spirit come away !"
> What is this absorbs me quite
> Steals my senses, shuts my sight,
> Drowns my spirit, draws my breath !
> Tell me, my soul, *Can this be Death ?*
> The World recedes—it disappears ;
> Heaven opens in my eyes, my ears !
> With sounds seraphic ring.
> Lend, lend, *your wings! I mount! I fly!*
> O grave where is thy victory !
> O death where is thy sting ?"

Is this dying? O this is beginning to live with grander capabilities and for a higher realm. Call this transport! beatitude! call it the gate of heaven, with much of heaven in it!

People of Asbury! honored members of the charge of a hundred years! we cordially congratulate you in your history. You have no cause to blush at your origin or to be ashamed of your record. The temple where you worship perpetuates the memory of "The Apostolic Bishop" of earliest Methodism. No church in the denomination can boast of nobler names than those of your first pastors. Yours was the ministry of Ezekiel Cooper, distinguished for logic, illustration and strength; of John Emory, afterwards Bishop, and one of the ablest men that this country has produced; of Lawrence McCoomb, the Boanerges of the Conference; of Solomon Sharp, the colloquial, the expository and the patriarchal; of Lawrence Laurenson, who rose to the heights of impassioned eloquence; of the pathetic and searching Henry White; of the courteous and fascinating John Kennedy; of the majestic Matthew Sorin, and of the seraphic Joseph Lybrand. These are a few of the men of the first half century. All these I personally knew. Of those who have filled your pulpit in the second half century, some of you know as well as the speaker.

Of the thousands of souls—*I mean thousands*—converted at your altars we need not tell you. Their names are in "The Book of Life." In this, where is the church that transcends you? Nor is it the least of the facts of which you may exult that God has made you the mother of so many churches. The light of their knowledge and purity is shining all around you, and yet in the brightness of their beams you are not eclipsed or obscured. He that holds the seven stars in His right hand will cause you to shine on. In all that constellation there is no "Star called wormwood, whose fall makes the waters bitter." Organizations do not, like saints, have crowns in heaven; but Asbury is *crowned on earth*. Shall we say with *eleven stars?*

Oh, to-day as you are about entering upon your second century, resolve that with additional opportunities you will give it a character not less exalted for wisdom, for virtue, and for usefulness. Let it be seen that the ardor of your zeal in the past is equalled by the fires of your love in the present. Oh, honor your origin. Emulate the graces of the fathers, and still exhibit the energy that made you what you are. *Increase if you may, if you may not multiply the successes of the past.*

May the pulpit be as true to the *Truth*. May the altar glow with intenser fires! The living this day celebrate the victories of a hundred years. But the dead! the ascended saints, have they no share in this great interest and assembly? It seems not fancy but fact. It is *vision*. The veil lifts and I behold a cloud of transported witnesses. They look with love; their shining faces tell the "joy of the Lord above;" even greater than we are having below. I recognize many of them. Some seem incapable of perfect rest till they see us crowned. Rest! rest departed ones, we will join you; in the race where you ran, run we; on the field where you fought we are making our arms tell. We have the same great enemies that you encountered; some of them seem even stronger, but by the means of your conquest we shall be victors. Even now our hearts are saying, "Thanks be to God, who always causeth us to triumph in Christ, and maketh manifest the savour of his knowledge by us in every place."

The Power of Christ's Resurrection.

By the Rev. Chas. Hill.

"That I may know Him and the power of His resurrection." Phil. 3: 10.

Experience is the test of truth, a fact which is recognized in the realm of nature and of grace, of science and religion. However skeptical a man may be concerning a discovered fact of nature, if he will submit the truth to the proper tests without prejudice or cavilling, all doubts will disappear from his mind, and compelled by the light of truthful investigation, he will exclaim, "I know." When Fulton announced the theory that boats and ships could be propelled by steam, his statements were doubted, and the people were ready to regard him as a monomaniac and his theory the product of a diseased brain. But when his theory was tested, and the little craft, under the influence of steam, moved forward as a thing of life, their doubts disappeared and they could say, "We know it to be true, vessels can be propelled by steam." So when Professor Morse in 1832 conceived the idea of a magnetic telegraph and sought in 1837 an appropriation from Congress for an experimental line from Baltimore to Washington, he was met with skepticism; the people doubted the truth of his theory. The idea of sending messages on a wire to distant points with the rapidity of the lightning's flash appeared to them as an absurdity. But when they saw the theory tested, when they saw the message sent and the answer received on the trembling wires, skepticism gave way and now men everywhere have such a conviction of the truth of telegraphy that they talk of its wonders without doubt. So when Cyrus Field spoke of laying the Atlantic cable, to establish telegraphic communication between England and America, many doubted the

REV. CHAS. HILL,

Pastor of Asbury Methodist Episcopal Church, 1861-'63, 1869-'72, and 1880-'83.

possibility of such a thing. But when the cable was laid and the experiment made, when they saw the firey message go into the sea and almost the same moment flashing out the words on the other side "Glory to God in the highest, peace on earth and good will to men," all doubt on the subject ceased, and men now believe the truth in this respect as firmly as they believe their own existence.

As these and other truths are tested they gain experience and experience produces knowledge; indeed all experience is knowledge. They can say, having tested the truth we know its reality. The same thing holds true in religion; tell a man there is power in the religion of the cross sufficient to change the heart and to fashion the soul after the image of the Creator; tell a skeptic that there is efficacy in the great atoning scheme, sufficient to raise him from a life of sin to a life of righteousness, as he listens to your statements perhaps he will say in the language of Nicodemus, "How can these things be?" But let him put the truth to the test, let him examine the doctrines and commit his soul by faith to those doctrines, let him bring his heart to the battery of divine truth and have his soul surcharged with fire from heaven's altar; in a word, let him do the will of God and he will know the truth.

This is what Jesus meant when he said, "My doctrine is not mine, but his that sent me. If any man will do his will, he shall know of the doctrine, whether it be of God or whether I speak of myself." St. Paul had made a personal test of the truth and realized its saving power. Hence, he said, "What things were gain to me I counted loss for Christ." He had by actual experience such a clear perception of the divinity of Christ, such an unshaken faith in a risen Redeemer that he regarded no sacrifice too great, no labor too severe and no suffering too intense if he could thereby know Jesus and the power of His resurrection. The text suggests that the Christian, in his experience, witnesses the truth and attests the power of Christ's resurrection. The resurrection of our Lord Jesus Christ from the dead is fundamental to the truth of the Christian system. It is the foundation doctrine; with it the whole scheme of human redemption stands or falls. Upon this single doctrine the apostle stakes everything when he says, "If there be no resurrection from the dead, then is Christ not risen, and if Christ be not risen, then is our preaching vain and your faith also vain; yea, and we are found false witnesses of God because we have testified of God that he raised up Christ, whom he raised not up if so be that the dead rise not. For if the dead rise not, then is not Christ raised, and if Christ be not raised, your faith is vain, ye are yet in your sins. Then they also which are fallen asleep in Christ are perished." This is as if he had said, If Christ has not risen from the dead, there is no proof that he has not justly been put to death. If he were a malefactor and justly put to death, he has made no atonement and ye are yet in your sins, under the power, guilt and condemnation of them. If Christ be not risen our preaching is vain and your faith is vain; if Christ be not risen, we are found false witnesses of God. If Christ be not risen then they which are fallen asleep in Christ are perished. In a word, if Christ be not risen, then the whole system of Christianity built upon it is false. But the Apostle adds, "Now is Christ risen from the dead and become the first fruits of them that slept." This is as if he had said, "His resurrection has been demonstrated by eye-witnesses and by many infallable signs. He has become the first fruits of them that slept and our resurrection necessarily follows; as sure as the first fruits are the proof that there is a harvest, so surely is the resurrection of Christ a proof of ours. He was delivered for our offenses and raised again for our justification." The question arises, How does a Christian, in his experience, witness the truth and attest the power of Christ's resurrection? I answer in the first place, by the operation of the Divine Spirit upon his heart. Jesus said to his disciples while he was yet with them, "It is expedient for you that I go away; for if I go not away the comforter will not come unto you; but if I depart, I will send him unto you." We have the fulfillment of this promise recorded in the second chapter of Acts. "When the day of Pentecost was fully come, they were all with one accord in one place. And suddenly there came a sound from Heaven as of a rushing, mighty wind, and it filled all the house where they were sitting. And there appeared unto them cloven tongues like as of fire, and it sat upon each of them. And they were all filled with the Holy Ghost and began to speak with other tongues as the Spirit gave them utterance." When this was noised abroad, the multitude were amazed and were in doubt saying one to another, "What meaneth this." Others, mocking, said, "These men are filled with new wine." Peter, standing up with the eleven, said, "These are not drunken as ye suppose, seeing it is but the third hour of the day. But this is that which was spoken by the prophet Joel. And it shall come to pass in the last days, saith God, I will pour out my spirit upon all flesh, and your sons and your daughters shall prophesy, and your young men shall see visions and your old men shall dream dreams. And on my servants and on my handmaidens I will pour out of my spirit."

After vindicating the conduct of the disciples and pressing upon the people the fearful sin of crucifying the Lord of life and glory, he said, "This Jesus hath God raised up, whereof we all are witnesses. Therefore being by the right hand of God exalted, and having received of the Father the promise of the Holy Ghost, he hath shed forth this which ye now see and hear."

The Holy Spirit was poured out as the result of Christ's death, resurrection and ascension into heaven." He said, "If I depart I will send him unto you." Therefore we may conclude that the coming of the Spirit is the proof that Jesus has triumphed over death and has ascended up on high, leading captivity captive and receiving gifts for men. The question comes, what is the office of the Spirit in the work of man's salvation? I answer, He reproves of sin, of righteousness and of judgment. He enlightens the mind, he takes the things of Christ and shows them to us, he regenerates our nature and attests our acceptance with God. Hence believers are spoken of as being born of the Spirit, renewed by the Spirit, comforted by the Spirit, sanctified by the Spirit, and sealed by the Spirit, unto the day of redemption. Now in as much as the out-pouring of the Spirit or the coming of the Comforter is the proof of the resurrection of Christ, and in as much as the believer knows that the Spirit has been poured out by the operations of the spirit upon his heart, enlightening his mind, regenerating his nature, attesting his acceptance with God, then we maintain that every Christian in his experience witnesses the truth and attests the power of Christ's resurrection, and can say with Job, "I know that my Redeemer liveth."

Again, the Christian witnesses the truth and attests the power of Christ's resurrection in his conversion. Conversion signifies in its common use a change; and when applied to moral nature, it is a change wrought in the governing purposes of the soul, in the great aim and object of life. A change of the will, of the heart and of the affections. It is a change from the rejection of Christ to a cordial reception of Christ. It is a change from death unto life. It is a change from hatred to God to love for God, and therefore it is a change of moral nature. This is what Paul meant when he said, "If any man be in Christ he is a new creature, old things are passed away and behold all things have become new." His thoughs are new, his dispositions are new, his objects and aims are new, regulated by new principles and controlled by new laws and consecrated to new ends. It is important to a proper understanding of our subject to remark that this change is in the will, the affections and the governing purposes of the man. It does not affect immediately his intellect, his mental capacity or his distinguishing characteristics. In conversion the same elements of character and the same mental peculiarities remain as before. It is the new direction which the powers take that constitute the change. In conversion the individuality of the man is preserved and his mental characteristics are retained, but the constitutional powers are intensified and turned in a new direction. The things he once hated, he now loves and the things he once loved he now hates.

Love and hate exists after conversion even as before but they are turned upon different objects. Old things have passed away and all things have become new. To be converted is to be renewed in the spirit of our minds, created anew in Christ Jesus and therefore the subject of this change knows God, loves God, has peace with God and rejoices in God his Saviour by whom he has received the atonement. The question comes, How does a Christian in his conversion, witness the truth and attest the power of Christ's resurrection? I answer because, faith in a living Redeemer is the condition of conversion. St. Paul in writing to the Romans said, "The righteousness which is of faith, speaketh on this wise; say not in thine heart, who shall ascend into heaven, that is to bring Christ down from above, or who shall descend into the deep, that is to bring Christ again from the dead, but what saith it, the word is nigh thee, even in thy mouth and in thy heart; that is the word of faith which we preach, that if thou shalt confess with thy mouth the Lord Jesus, and shalt believe in thine heart that God hath raised him from the dead, thou shalt be saved. For with the heart man believeth unto righteousness and with the mouth confession is made unto salvation." The apostle evidently teaches that faith in a living Redeemer is the condition of salvation. If thou wilt believe that he was delivered for thy offences, has been raised again for thy justification thou shalt be saved. The faith then which bringeth salvation is faith in a living Redeemer; not simply in the fact that Christ was crucified, although faith takes hold of this also; but it rests implicitly for justification upon the glorious truth of his resurrection. He was delivered for our offences and raised again for our justification. St. Peter teaches the same truth when he said, "Blessed be the God and Father of our Lord Jesus Christ, who according to his abundant mercy hath begotten us again unto a lively hope by the resurrection of Jesus Christ from the dead, to an inheritance incorruptible, undefiled and that fadeth not away reserved in heaven for you, who are kept by the power of God, through faith unto salvation ready to be revealed in the last time." Faith in a living Redeemer is the condition of conversion, and just as soon as the penitent shall grasp by faith the great truth that Jesus was delivered for his offences and raised again for his justification, as soon as his faith appropriates the merits of a living Redeemer, who ever lives to make intercession for him; as soon as he believes in his heart that God hath raised him from the dead, just as soon will he know Christ and the power of his resurrection. Nothing but the power which raised Jesus from the dead can possibly raise a soul from the death of sin to a life of righteousness, and this saving power becomes available only on condition of faith in a living Redeemer. When the Philippian jailer cried out, "What must I do to be saved," he received the ready answer. "Believe on the Lord Jesus Christ and thou shalt be saved." When Paul was earnestly inquiring what he should do, Ananias, under the direction of the Spirit, went to him and said. "Brother Saul, the Lord even Jesus who appeared to thee in the way as thou camest hither, hath sent me that thou mightest receive thy sight and be filled with the Holy Ghost." Paul, in his conversion, exercised faith in a living Redeemer, and in his experience witnessed the truth and attested the power of Christ's resurrection. So every convert knows Jesus and the power of His resurrection. They know Him as their living Redeemer; they know Him as their personal and all-sufficient Saviour; they feel the resurrection power in their hearts; they realize the efficacy of the great atoning scheme, and as they realize the power of His resurrection they sing,

"I know that my Redeemer lives,
What joy the blest assurance gives,
He lives, He lives who once was dead,
He lives, my everlasting head.
He lives, and grants me daily breath,
He lives, and I shall conquer death,
He lives, my mansion to prepare,
He lives, to bring me safely there.
He lives, all glory to His name,
He lives, my Saviour still the same,
What joy the blest assurance gives,
I know that my Redeemer lives."

Do you ask, what this faith is which brings the knowledge of a living Redeemer into the soul? I answer, it is taking God at His word; it is believing the testimony which God has given of His son; it is taking hold with a firm grasp of such truths as these. "He was delivered for our offences and raised again for our justification, and ever lives to make intercession for transgressors." Again—a Christian in conversion, witnesses the truth and attests the power of Christ's resurrection, because conversion is the gift of a living Redeemer. We have seen that conversion is the work of God in the soul, changing the moral nature to such a degree that the individual now lives to glorify God. We have also seen that the atonement as completed by the sufferings, death, resurrection and ascension of our Lord Jesus Christ, constitute the ground of God's ability to save the soul from sin and renew it in righteousness and true holiness. If this be true, then it follows that conversion is the gift of a living Redeemer. "The God of our fathers," saith the apostle, "hath raised up Jesus and hath highly exalted him with his right hand to be a Prince and a Saviour to give repentance unto Israel and the forgiveness of sins." He is exalted for the express purpose of giving repentance and remission. He says, "I am He that blotteth out thy transgression for my own sake, and will not remember thy sins." Again, he says, "Come unto me all ye that labor and are heavy laden and I will give you rest." Therefore when a penitent comes to a throne of grace, he comes to a living Redeemer; or in the language of St. Peter, he comes to a living stone, rejected of men but chosen of God and precious. He has not entered into the holy place made with hands, which is the figure of the true, but into heaven itself, there to appear in the presence of God for us, and now he bestows repentance, forgiveness or conversion, upon all who come to the throne of grace with boldness. If there are persons present who are seeking the great blessing of pardon and peace, let me say to them—look to Jesus the living Redeemer and expect to receive these blessings as a gift. You can do nothing to merit salvation; you can do nothing to purchase salvation. No pilgrimage, no penance or bodily mortification can bring peace to the soul.

> "Could my tears forever flow,
> Could my zeal no languor know,
> These for sin could not atone,
> Thou must save and thou alone !
> In my hands no price I bring:
> Simply to the cross I cling."

By grace are ye saved through faith and that not of yourselves, it is the gift of God. It is not of works lest any man should boast. Now in as much as conversion is the gift of a living Redeemer, and as faith in a living Redeemer is the condition of conversion, then we insist that a Christian in conversion witnesses the truth and attests the power of Christ's resurrection, and possessing this knowledge, he can say with Paul, "We know that if our earthly house of this tabernacle were dissolved, we have a building of God, an house not made with hands eternal in the heavens." Again a Christian witnesses the truth and attests the power of Christ's resurrection in his every day life. Jesus said, "Abide in me, and I in you. As the branch can not bear fruit of itself, except it abide in the vine, no more can ye, except ye abide in me. I am the vine, ye are the branches. He that abideth in me, and I in him, the same bringeth forth much fruit; for without me ye can do nothing." It is just as impossible for a man to do anything acceptable to God while separated from Christ, the true vine, as it is for the branch to live and thrive and bring forth fruit while separated from the vine.

A living branch attests a living vine. If you pass along the street and see a branch full of verdure and fruit; you know, although you do not see it, that there is a living vine with which that living branch possesses a vital connection. So a living Christian, adorned with the fruit of righteousness, attests a living Redeemer. When a Christian gains the victory over the world, when he resists and overcomes his spiritual foes, when he triumphs in the midst of the afflictions of life, in every such triumph he attests the power of a living Redeemer, for without Him we can do nothing. The Christian has many enemies to contend with who excel him in strength ; he has many trials to endure which are too great for his unaided strength, he has many temptations to encounter which he is not able to resist successfully without Divine assistance ; hence he needs Divine strength, he must be Divinely aided; he must be strengthened everywhere and everywhere Divinely fortified by the energies of the Holy Spirit or he will be overcome. Therefore when you see a Christian conquering his enemies, resisting temptation and rising superior to the trials of life, when you see him living in the discharge of duties, standing with the world beneath his feet, we conclude that he is Divinely helped, and that there is a redeeming power among men, made available by faith in a living Redeemer. In all this he witnesses the truth and attests the power of Christ's resurrection.

This great truth is illustrated always and everywhere in the experience of God's people. Take Paul as an example: when the great duties of life presented themselves for his consideration, he said, "I can do all things through Christ which strengtheneth me." When a messenger from Satan was given to buffet him, he took it to the living Redeemer in prayer and received this glorious promise, "My grace is sufficient for thee, my strength is made perfect in weakness." When persecution assailed him and when martyrdom looked him full in the face, he said, "None of these things move me neither count I my life dear to myself so that I may finish my course with joy and the ministry which I have received of the Lord Jesus to testify the gospel of the grace of God." We need not go back to the days of the Apostles. We read of a gracious woman, in the time of persecution, who was called before bloody Bonner, then Bishop of London, and placed upon trial for her faith in Christ. He threatened to take her husband from her, but she said "Christ is my husband;" he threatened to take away her child, she replied "Christ is better to me than ten sons." He threatened to take away all her outward comforts, she answered "Christ is my comfort and you can not strip me of him." The knowledge of a living Redeemer and the assurance that Christ was hers, sustained her heart and quieted her spirit under all her trials. "You may take away my life," said Basil, but you can not take away my comfort, you may take my head but you can not take my crown; if I had a thousand lives I would lay them all down for my Saviour's sake who has done so much for me." John Ardly, when about to be burned for his religion, said to Bonner. "If I had as many lives as I have hairs on my head, I would loose them all in the fire before I would forsake my Saviour." What gave such triumph in the midst of such trial? I answer the knowledge of a living Redeemer. But we need not go so far back. Have there not been times in your own experience when you have been sorely pressed? difficulties have been upon the right hand and upon the left; the Red Sea rolled at your feet while Egypt's war chariots thundered at your back. Destruction seemed imminent, but at the command of God you went forward. As you advanced the sea of difficulties divided and you passed over without harm. Again, a Christian witnesses the truth and attests the power of Christ's resurrection, in his death. Death is something from which there is a general shrinking on the part of our nature and yet the dying Christian realizes the truth of Christ's resurrection. As he descends to the tomb he hears it said by Him who conquered death. "I am the resurrection and the life," and as he hears he exclaims, " Oh death, where is thy sting." Paul realized this truth as he cried out in full view of the executioner's block, "I have fought a good fight; henceforth there is laid up for me a crown." Thousands since the days of Paul have experienced the same in the hour of their dissolution. It was my privilege to visit, during his death sickness, Elijah Reynolds of Port Deposit. His tongue was paralyzed, he could not speak and when I asked him of his religious state, he made signs for the Bible to be handed him, opened to the fifth chapter of Romans and placed his finger on the first verse.—"Being justified by faith we have peace with God;" then turned to CIII Psalm and first verse.—"Bless the Lord, oh my soul and all that is within me bless his holy name." He then turned to CXXI Psalm and pointed to the second verse, "My help cometh from the Lord which made heaven and earth." Mrs. Hewitt who died in Elkton, said, as we were leaving at the close of a visit made her in company with several others, "Brother Perkins, I want you to be one of my bearers. When you lower my body in the grave, sing.

> "And let this feeble body fail,
> And let it faint and die
> My soul shall quit this mournful vale
> And soar to worlds on high."

then cover me up and sing, 'Praise God from whom all blessings flow,' then go to your homes and leave me until the morning of the resurrection." The Christian in his dying hour realizes the presence of Jesus with him and therefore witnesses the truth and attests the power of Christ's resurrection and he will witness the same glorious truth in his resurrection. If you believe that Jesus died and rose again, even so also them that sleep in Jesus will God bring with him at His coming. Then—

> "Break off your tears ye saints and tell
> How high your great Deliverer reigns.
> Sing how He spoiled the hosts of hell
> And led the monster death in chains."

I shall close with an inference or two; first, if the Christian witnesses the truth and attests the power of Christ's resurrection, we infer that Christianity carries with it its own attestation. Everyone who embraces it knows the truth for himself; he becomes conscious that the gospel is the power of God unto salvation, and under the enlightening, renewing and attesting influences of the Holy Spirit he can say, "I know that my redeemer liveth." No man need travel in search of evidence to sustain the truth of the Christian religion; no man need devour books to find proof of its sustaining power; only let him come and test its truths by actual experience and he will have evidence sufficient to prove that the religion of Jesus can accomplish what it proposes to do. A camp-meeting was held, as I have been informed, in one of the townships of Penn, in a grove owned by a man who was skeptical in his religious views. That gentleman, although a skeptic, attended the meetings and was present at nearly all of the services. During the meeting prayer was offered for his conversion. The preachers knowing his condition so constructed their sermons that he might see his error and forsake it; but nothing seemed to move him, and the friends of Jesus began to fear that the meeting would close without producing any good results on his mind. Towards the close of the camp, an experience meeting was held, and during the progress of the meeting, two men in the congregation were seen to rise and lift up a chair upon which sat a poor little crippled boy. The child proceeded to tell how the spirit of God strove with his heart and how he had been brought to a saving knowledge of the truth; and then he said, "Although I am crippled and deprived of the sports of other children, I am happy in God, my Saviour." As he reached this point, the skeptic rose to his feet, and with tears in his eyes, started towards the cripple exclaiming as he went, "There must be something in it, there must be something in it." Yes, there is something in it; all that we ask is that you shall come and try it, then you will know for yourself and not another. Come, touch but the hem of His garment and you will feel healing and cleansing virtue to flow into your soul and as you feel it you will exclaim with us,

Jesus' blood hath healed my wounds,
O the wondrous story!
I was lost but now I'm found
Glory, glory, glory.

Again, I infer that there is no saving religion without the knowledge of a living Redeemer. There is no other name given under heaven among men, whereby a man can be saved. Paul was willing to count all things but loss, if he might thereby know Jesus and the power of his resurrection. Men may talk of their morality and church membership; they may talk of confirmation and baptism; they may speak of orthodoxy and consistency; they may be possessed of everything else besides, but if they have not the knowledge of a living Redeemer, it is of no avail. Other foundations can no man lay save that which is laid. A knowledge of Christ in the remission of sins is indispensible to salvation. Christ is to the sinner what the life-boat is to the drowning mariner. He is the only passage from the power of darkness into the kingdom of grace, for he hath said, "I am the way, the life and the truth, no man cometh unto the Father but by me." Therefore without the knowledge of a living Redeemer we can not be saved. This being true, let me ask, Have you felt the resurrection power raising you from the death of sin to a life of righteousness? Can you say with Job, "I know that my Redeemer liveth?" If so, hold on to this knowledge, hold everything in subordination to it, maintain it at all hazzards. If you will, it will sustain you in the midst of life's trials, it will disarm death of its sting and will be the condition on which you will be received into everlasting habitations, where you will dwell in the immediate presence of Him who sits upon the throne and be forever with the Lord. But if you have not this knowledge of a living Redeemer, if you do not know Him in the power of His resurrection, whatever hope you may indulge in is as worthless as the baseless fabric of a vision. God can only save you through the son of his love. Time is short with you, life is uncertain, the thunders of God's violated laws are against you, the horrors of an endless hell are moving to meet you at your coming, death is pursuing you, the decisions of a general judgment are just before you, there is no safety for you, not a shadow of hope anywhere but in the knowledge of a living Redeemer. Then come to Jesus just as you are. Come, confessing your sins; come and accept Him as your Saviour, and as you accept Him, He will receive you. He says, "Behold I stand at the door and knock, if any man," no matter who he is, no matter if he is almost damned, "if any man hear my voice, and open the door, I will come in unto him and will sup with him and he with me." May the Lord help you to come!

REV. WM. C. ROBINSON,

Pastor of Asbury Methodist Episcopal Church, 1863–'65.

Religious Meditation.

By the Rev. Wm. C. Robinson.

"My meditation of Him shall be sweet, I will be glad in the Lord." Psalms civ : 34.

There is, in all probability, no religious exercise that sustains a more important relation to our spirituality than religious meditation ; and there is no duty more uniformly neglected. How few among us of set purpose and at fixed times engage in close consecutive religious thought. As remarked by one "It is easier, after listening to a sermon, to walk six miles than to meditate upon it for fifteen minutes ;" and I may add that there is no fact in our experience which reveals more potently, though secretly and silently, the alienation of our nature from God than this indisposition to engage in religious thought. How cheering is the assurance brought to us in the Gospel that one of the sublime achievements it accomplishes in the life and upon the heart of the believer, is that of "Casting down imaginations and every high thing that exalteth itself against the knowledge of God, bringing into captivity every thought to the obedience of Christ." (II Cor. x : 5.) Accordingly says the Psalmist in the words of my text, "My meditation of Him shall be sweet."

MEDITATION.

By meditation is to be understood the exercise of the power of continued thought. This power is God-given. "There is a spirit in man, and it is the inspiration of the Almighty that giveth him understanding." It may be employed in Divine contemplation or in the consideration of the leading truths of the Gospel and of practical piety. This power distinguishes our species from the lower order of animals; a power possessed by all men in a greater or less degree except of insanity or idiocy, or as may be in the case of very little child ren. A power by which we are enabled to analyze, to compare, to judge and to act wisely; in the rightful exercise of which we are so happy; in which is constituted to so large an extent our personal responsibility before God, and for the abuse of which the eternal displeasure of God will be visited upon us. "The wicked shall be turned into hell with all the nations that forget God." (Isa. ix : 17.)

THIS POWER INFLUENCED.

Our knowledge will be found to be the substance of our meditation and at the same time will prove its limit. The man of capacious intellect well stored with knowledge will enjoy the advantage arising from meditation to a much larger extent than the man of feeble intellect, however great may have been the latter's opportunities for the acquisition of knowledge. A Newton, a Locke, a Bacon, a Wesley, a Watson, and a Clarke enjoyed the advantages of continued reflection in a fuller measure than most of their contemporaries. Likewise, in our times, those who improve their opportunities for enlarging the bounds of their knowledge enjoy an intellectual life which is far above and beyond that enjoyed by those who neglect to add to their intellectual stores.

Our five senses are not only the avenues through which we form an acquaintance with the material world but they are stimuli to thought. What the eye sees or the ear hears awakens a corresponding perception in the mind. All our sensations have the power of suggesting ideas.

The tempers we cherish will assert a mastery over our thoughts. The avaricious man, the great object of whose life is to get gain, will find it much more difficult to withdraw his thoughts from these objects than he who considers himself the steward of a Divine Master. So, likewise, is it with those who have cherished the passions of vanity or pride; who are fascinated by a beautiful face, an elegant form or a large estate and expensive equipage; who are happiest when they can excite the envy of others. The staple of their thought will be on the line of the passion they have indulged. A miser who had hidden his treasure in the ground was robbed and found a stone put in the place of his hoarded wealth, was lamenting his loss to a friend, when his friend remarked, "You are really none the worse off, for you would never use the money." "True," replied the miser, "but I am mad—it almost kills me to think that some one else is so much richer." The same is true of the licentious who live to the gratification of the "lusts of the flesh, the lust of the eyes, and the pride of life;" they will find that, notwithstanding the impulses of a nobler nature, their thoughts will be controlled by the momentum of their passion.

The habits formed by us will exert a most potent influence over our thought. It has been remarked, "Habits are chronic diseases of the mind," and we are accustomed to say, "I am so habituated to the thing that I did it without thought." Some are constitutionally indolent and stupid; others, through excessive eating or drinking, have their perceptions blunted or inflamed according to temperament; and, if circumstances prohibit the gratification of their desires, they become violent.

Our associations will be found to be commanding in their influence. We are social beings physically, intellectually and morally, and formed for one another's society. How readily we imbibe one another's spirit. We mutually impart our spirit and partake of the spirit of the society we enter. It is impossible to accept voluntarily the society of the profane, the licentious and the proud without contamination. "Can two walk together except they be agreed?" (Amos iii: 3.) The influence of these associations will extend beyond the moment of contact, intruding upon the privacy of the closet, arresting and polluting our thoughts, and we would give worlds, if we had them, to be released from their power. Herein lies the hidden virus of novel-reading in which one associates with the characters figuring prominently in the plot. The Rev. Robert Hall, of England, who was induced to read the novels of a distinguished authoress of his day, declared the effect to be the destruction of all spiritual enjoyment and this condition of mind continued for weeks.

There is another agency influencing our meditation which should not be overlooked in this discussion—I allude to the power of the Evil One. Through any of the means mentioned or independent of them all he can inject a thousand thoughts. This will not be doubted by any who believe in the divine inspiration of the scriptures and the immateriality of the human soul, or by those who have simply noted the operations of their own minds. A single example will suffice: When the devil tempted Jesus, "Command these stones that they be made bread," and upon the pinnacle of the temple, "Cast Thyself down from thence, for it is written I have given my angels charge over Thee," and upon an exceeding high mountain where he showed Him all the kingdoms of this world and the glory of them saying, "All these will I give unto Thee if Thou wilt fall down and worship me." I will not discuss the questions as to whether the devil appeared to Jesus in a bodily shape or spoke in an audible voice. The only use I desire to make of this allusion is that the devil did have the power to insinuate thoughts of evil into the mind of Jesus. If this were possible with the immaculate Jesus he certainly possesses the same power over the human mind.

> "Angels our march oppose
> Who still in strength excel,
> Our secret, sworn, eternal foes
> Countless, invisible.
> From thrones of glory driven
> By flaming vengeance hurled,
> They throng the air, they darken heaven
> And rule this lower world."

THE VARIED EFFECTS OF THESE AGENCIES IN THE DEVELOPMENT OF CHARACTER.

With the unconverted these agencies, i. e. knowledge, the senses, tempers, habits and associations are like so many demons let loose from the bottomless pit goading the wicked onward to the gratification of every depraved appetite, propensity, and disposition, until, insane with passion, he plunges into the abyss of endless woe. These are the suicides, the assassins and the vile of every age. Here we have a development of that doctrine—Total Depravity—so largely taught in the Word of God, confirmed to our experience and observation. Total, not in the sense that men cannot become worse but as involving every faculty, function and power. It is only upon this theory that the appalling character of crime can be explained. Otherwise, how could the drunkard with his eyes open to the ruin that is impending to health, to reputation, to estates, to family and to his immortal soul, press the fatal cup to his lips? Otherwise, how could a man consent to such villiany as to rob his benefactor of his hard earned and honestly gotten gains, merely to enrich himself or to expend it on his lusts? Otherwise, how could the assassin place the knife at the throat of his fellow and with one stroke put out that light that no power at his command can relume? It is only explicable upon the theory that the human heart, unrestrained by Divine grace, is a perfect hell of passion. "For the imagination of a man's heart is evil from his youth." (Gen. viii: 21.) It is true that there are divinely appointed restraints upon the thoughts and passions of men secured through the atonement of Jesus; namely: the power of truth, the influence of the Holy Spirit, the society of the godly and the Church of God. To these and kindred agencies is to be attributed the civilization we enjoy, the good order we witness in society and the respect of ungodly men for what is right. Until the renewing and sanctifying grace of Christ asserts its power upon the hearts of men, society has nothing to expect but that men will continue to become vile in every form. Education will not correct the evil, it will only make a man refined and accomplished in his wickedness.

OUR NATURE FITTED FOR RIGHT THOUGHT.

It is the work of our holy Christianity to sanctify knowledge, to to make a man to see with new eyes, to hear with new ears, and to taste, smell and feel with new emotion. It awakens heavenly tempers, leads to the formation of new habits and introduces into new associations. The converted man is begotten again to new hopes, new longings, new joys, a new life, and, in an important sense, a new world. The den of vipers, the cage of unclean birds, the sephulchre of dead men's bones, the strong man armed, the legion of devils have all been cast out and substituted by tempers of a heavenly origin. The image of the devil has been effaced and the image of God has been restored. Old things have passed away and behold all things have become new. The things once loved are hated and the things once hated are loved, and thus the circumstances of life which hurry the unconverted onward to perdition, give impulse to the good in the way to heaven!

The religion of Jesus alone fits the mind for devout meditation, for it alone can bring man's nature into harmony with God. Previous to conversion the understanding was darkened. "The natural man receiveth not the things of the Spirit of God for they are foolishness unto him, neither can he know them for they are spiritually discerned." (I Cor. ii: 14.) His thoughts are now in harmony with the Infinite Mind; the will, once opposed to the law of God and His Providence, is now brought into subjection to the Will of God. The new convert can say, "It is the Lord; let Him do unto me as seemeth to Him good." (I Sam. iii: 18.) "Let me not fall into the hands of man but into the hands of God." (I Chron. xxi: 13.) "Not my will but Thine be done." (Luke xxii: 42.) This is one of the most difficult lessons to learn, and the Christian character has no more positive test of its genuineness than this. A Christian lady whom I knew told me that in the course of six short weeks she was bereaved of her husband and three children, and lost an estate worth $35,000, and through it all she was enabled to say, "The will of the Lord be done." The affections are now in harmony with God. We love Him perfectly, whereas we were His enemies, and can say with Peter, "Lord, Thou knowest all things, Thou knowest that I love Thee" (John xxi: 17), and with the Psalmist, "Whom have I in heaven but Thee, and there is none upon earth I desire beside Thee." (Psalms lxxiii: 25.) In fact the whole nature is brought back into harmony with God. We are one with God as the foundation is one with the superstructure built upon it, as the branch is with the vine, as the head, the hands and the feet are one with the body. So are we as Christian members of His body and His flesh and His bones; "For this cause," says Paul, "shall a man leave father and mother and cleave to his wife and they twain shall be one flesh. This is a great mystery but I speak of Christ and His Church." (Matt. xix: 5.) Our life is hid with Christ in God. We are lost and swallowed up in Him. As Christ prayed "That they all may be one, as Thou Father art in Me and I in Thee, that they may be one in us that the world may believe that Thou hast sent Me." (John xvii: 21.) These are not mere figures of speech but the statement of a great fact which has taken place in the life of the believer. It is by this change that we are brought into sympathy with the Triune God, as well as the author of my text.

FITTING THEMES FOR MEDITATION.

1. The being and perfections of God. It is true we may never fully comprehend the Nature of God. "Canst thou by searching find out God? Canst thou find out the Almighty to perfection? It is as high as heaven, what canst thou do? It is as deep as hell, what canst thou know? And the measure thereof is wider than the earth and broader than the sea." (Job xi: 18.) A certain Armenian philosopher when asked, "What is God?" after prolonged study replied, "The more I think of God the more incomprehensible He seems." Nevertheless to the extent He has been pleased to reveal Himself, He is an inexhaustible source of thought. In His works, in the natural world, above us, beneath us, around us and within us, and through every season of the year. There are but few studies in which the littleness of man's knowledge is more apparent than in astronomy. "The heavens declare the glory of God, and the firmament showeth His handiwork." (Psa. xix: 1.) "The invisible things of God are clearly seen being understood by the things He has made, even His eternal power and Godhead." (Rom. i: 20.)

2. In providence He covers the heavens with clouds and causes the grass to grow upon the mountains, filling His hands with bounties and satisfying the wants of every living creature. He causeth the sun to shine upon the evil and the good and sendeth the rain upon the just and the unjust. He controls amid the circumstances of life and all things work together for good to them that love Him. "Oh, the depth of the riches both of the wisdom and the knowledge of God, how unsearchable are His judgments and His ways past finding out." (Rom. xi: 23.)

3. In the great work of human redemption the love of God is the moving cause, the sacrifice of Christ is the procuring cause and the Spirit and the word are the instrumental causes. "God commendeth

His love to us in that while we were yet sinners Christ died for us." Rom. v: 8.

> "Here the whole Deity is known
> Nor dares a creature guess
> Which of the glories brightest shone
> The justice or the grace."

4. We may meditate upon Him in His word, in the privacy of the closet, in the sick room and by night upon our bed. What admonition! What comfort! "Oh how I love Thy law." (Psalms cxix: 97.) "More to be desired are they than gold, yea, than much fine gold." (Psalms xix: 10.)

[HAPPY THOUGHTS TO-DAY.

This day, as we participate in these centennial services, our attention is arrested by the events of a hundred years. We are delighted to be reminded of the labors of such Christian heroes as Captain Webb, who was said to equal Whitefield as a declaimer; Francis Asbury, the self-forgetful apostle; Richard Whatcoat, who resolved never to be angry under any provocation; Thomas Coke, the ardent missionary, and others whose memory we cherish with equal warmth, going as far back as 1769. What Gospel sermons have been preached in this place and on this spot. How great has been the power of God displayed on these occasion in all these years. "Old Asbury." What a host of souls have been saved through the instrumentality of these services. How vast the number that have passed triumphantly through the changes of death into the realities and circumstances of another life. These all are interested in the scenes which now engage us. There is an unusual sensation to-day among those who have gone up from "Old Asbury" redeemed and glorified.

> "Shall we in heaven ne'er review
> The scenes from which we sever?
> Or will our recollections leap.
> O'er death's dark gulf at times.
> To keep with earth's acquaintance ever?
> In life we love the blessed past,
> It clings upon us ever.
> The songs of childhood and of home.
> Like music when the minstrel's gone,
> Live in the heart forever."

I congratulate the pastor and members of this goodly old church. as well as the Methodism of Wilmington and throughout the State of Delaware, and in all the peninsula, because of this centennial and the important relation this church organization has sustained to the success of Christ's cause throughout the whole land, in all of which our God has been so wondrously glorified.

The Fathers and the Secret of Their Victories.

By the Rev. Enoch Stubbs.

Text, Ps. xliv: 1.—"We have heard with our ears, O God, our fathers have told us what work Thou didst in their days, in the time of old."

The wonderful works of God are accomplished mostly by human instrumentality, even if all that man can do is to stretch forth a rod for God, or to blow a ram's horn We look back to-day to times of wonderful accomplishment; what victories were achieved through the labors of our fathers of a hundred years ago upon the spot where we now stand.

OUR THEME

is "*The Fathers, and the Secret of their Victories.*"

We are ever fascinated with the past. We stand amazed before the accomplishments of the ages gone by. Stone Henge, Karnac and Solomon's Temple astonish us. We read Homer's Iliad and study Plato's Philosophy, feeling "there were giants in those days." The past is too precious to be forgotten, hence we carve it in stone and write it in history. But there is no department so full of wonderful achievements as that of religion. Its activities are on a higher plane and in a wider sphere than any other, and its victories are more mighty, far-reaching and enduring. The battle may look ridiculous to a world that cannot comprehend spirtual issues, but the result concerns every member of the human race. When John Wesley, struggling through the slough of religious uncertainty, reached a place where "his heart was strangely warmed," it was a victory, not for himself alone but for the millions who have pressed after him into the same assurance of Divine acceptance. Hence the veneration in which he is held. So those who opened to us the gates of conscious

REV. ENOCH STUBBS,

Pastor of Asbury Methodist Episcopal Church, 1872-'75.

salvation on this side the ocean, by presenting to our fathers the Gospel in its simplicity, must be held in precious commemoration. Let preacher and poet, history and "centennial" keep alive the memory of these heroes, whose spiritual triumphs have done more for us than all the Waterloos the world has ever seen.

True, the faces of John and Charles Wesley smile down from the walls of Westminster Abbey, and we might be moved to rear similar memorials to Coke and Asbury on this continent. But they need no other monument than the living verities of to-day—the souls saved, the churches ringing with salvation and bristling with innumerable agencies for the extirpation of sin—verities which are the outcome of their heroism and faith.

WHAT MONUMENTS

they have in the multitudes who bear the Methodist name! It is said, there are more Methodists in the world to-day than there were English speaking people at the time of Wesley's conversion. What a monument is found in the experience of these millions; their eyes opened to see God and eternal things; their ears to hear the trump of Sinai and the coming judgment day, softened by the sweet notes from Bethlehem and Calvary. "Peace on earth." "Father forgive them." This nation is a monument, for it has been lifted to a table land of higher possibilities than could have been occupied had the voice of our Methodist Fathers never been heard. Families, by thousands, are in sunlit parlors, and in a joyous salvation, who would have been in cellars of moral and social neglect and wretchedness, if the itinerant preacher had not found them.

As it would be almost an impertinence to add to the brief record upon Benj. Franklin's tombstone, since every telegraph pole is a monument to his memory, and ten thousand telegraphic machines are clicking eloquently his praise, while the very lightnings, in brilliant penmanship write his name on the sky; so there needs no other memorial to those who brought spiritual lightnings from the heavens, illuminating hearts and homes, and warming the world with the rich glow of a moral and spiritual incandescence, than the souls and lives of the millions of men and women, who in the past hundred years have been brought from darkness to light, and are to day shining on earth, or resplendent in heaven. We had better

BE SURE THEY ARE DEAD

before we bury and monument the Fathers of American Methodism. They live in more than thirty thousand ministers, forty-five thousand local preachers, and five million Methodists on the soil of North

America. This pyramid of souls is the standing memorial of their work for God; nor these alone, but the countless host whose names are on the registers of church and class meeting, but who have passed their Gethsemane and Calvary, mounted the Olivet of ascension and are entered into the "many mansions" that Jesus promised to prepare for them. To the toilers of the century, in the pulpit and out of it, on this hallowed spot, there is a record on high, in the many whom they found within an inch of hell, but are now casting their crowns at the Saviour's feet.

The times when our fathers were laying the foundations of this present Methodism were not specially favorable to easy triumph. What religious ignorance and unbelief, and what worldly and indifferent churches there were one hundred years ago! Some souls were open to conviction and hungry for the living bread, but others were clad in the armor of unbelief. From the work shops of Hobbes, Voltaire and Tom Paine there were malignant opposition and persecution, and the attack must be made with skill and courage. There must be wise generalship and apostolic faith; guns of large calibre, sword of fine steel, and temper and skill to use them. Our fathers were not mere

"THEOLOGICAL IRONSIDES."

Though an invincible battalion of the great army, it was not by intellectual "might or power" their victories were won. They were clad in the panoply of Emmanuel, and shone in the burnished armor of love, truth and faith, by which many a fortress deemed impregnable was taken with a bound and a shout.

It is always refreshing to recall the days of the early itinerant preacher—the spiritual cavalry of the Great Captain's forces. With souls and saddle bags filled with ammunition, they wrote salvation songs as they went, composed sermons at a jog trot, and discharged them with a power that has made the echo audible, and the vibration still powerful after the lapse of a hundred years. Such men could afford to lie down, without pomp, when their work was done. "Their works do follow them." But what a resurrection must await them. Perhaps there will be no special displays over the humble mounds under which they "rest in hope;" but when they see on every hand the "fruit of their labor" and the "travail of their souls," they will begin the resurrection life with louder doxologies than ended this.

THEIR HALLELUJAHS RANG

many times in this ancient sanctuary. Their feet have walked these aisles; around these altars they have wrestled for victory, and it seems to me on this occasion, they must be here, an invisible but a much greater company than the visible hovering o'er us, "unperceived amid the throng."

It would be impossible to measure their influence upon the Wilmington of to-day. Many are sitting by rivers of prosperity, that overflow with blessings like the Nile. If they will seek for the sources of this stream, they will find them *here;* fifty, seventy-five, and one hundred years ago. Here your fathers tasted of salvation waters. Sermons preached here enlightened the mind and aroused the conscience. From these altars they went with souls renewed, and with lives made holy. As sin went out, not only peace, but prosperity came in. Truth, sobriety and diligence, characterized them as they came and went between these pews and their ever brightening homes. Religion was found to have the "promise of the life that now is." Yes; it was here the seed was sown that has ripened in your days into a harvest of material as well as spiritual plenty. Thus, in temporal things, the living of to-day are indebted to the spiritual heroes of the century gone. They touched you, though yet unborn, in the homes you occupy; the business conducted in your name; the amount to your credit in the city bank ; the comforts that surround you ; the luxuries upon your tables and the education privileged to your children. Uninfluenced by their ministrations, though so long ago, all had been different ; instead of avenues and stone fronts, a sea-side cottage for vacation, and a tree in the corner at Christmas, it might have been hovel and lane ; no Christmas tree, but that seen from the icy street through some other man's window, and some well clad hearer, this morning, in jail, or perdition, instead of here, rejoicing in God.

LET US KNOW,

however, that these blessings are held only on probation. Where are we scattering what we have reaped ? Are we sowing in Vanity Fair ? Is the fruit trodden under foot in the theatres and ball rooms ? Sow it in the benevolent fields of the church to which, under God, it is due, that it may spring up all over the earth to the salvation of lost millions. As our Fathers sowed that we might reap, let us scatter for the gathering of others, in distant ages and places. This is God's order, it is the soul of Methodism. If we prove unworthy to occupy this high palace of privilege, we shall receive orders to vacate, that others more loyal to the divine plan may enter and take possession. There is in operation a stern law for the "survival of the fittest," and the " fittest " are those who accept the Gospel, and employ the blessings it confers for the good of others. If we fail, others will occupy our position by and by, while we settle back to the place where good

Bishop Asbury and his noble helpers found our parents a hundred years ago. Advantages are continually changing hands upon this principle. Who can say where he would have been, if these "fishers of men," baiting their hooks of gospel steel with many a sweet story and apt illustration, had not caught and lifted that thoughtless sire or maternal ancestor from the stream down which they were drifting to darkness and death. It is evident that in saving their souls, they also

MADE THEIR FORTUNES

and those of their children.

We have wondered, oft, whether the prophets of ancient Israel caught glimpses of the glory that should result from their faithfulness and sacrifice, and whether their souls would not have been intoxicated by such a revelation. So we wonder now whether these prophets of early Methodism could have seen, without dangerous self-complacency, the outcome of their faithful toils in Wilmington and elsewhere. Let us emulate their example and work for posterity as did they.

If I could bring before you now in succession the men and women of God who have labored here for the past century, some in the office of pastor, others as local preachers, and others as exhorters, class leaders and prominent laborers at these altars, what recollections and emotions would be stirred? Here is the one who found you in the brickyard of spiritual slavery, and here you would have lived and died; but, as a Moses, he brought down upon your Egypt such plagues that you were aroused and departed. Here is he who when the rocks enclosed your path and the sea rolled across it, bid you "stand still and see the salvation of God," and with his rod stretched forth and pointing to the promise, the way of duty was made plain and a path opened through the deep. Here, too, is one that held up his hands in prayer for you until your Amalek was driven back. Here the Miriam that lifted your soul to holy enthusiasm with her song and timbrel of joy. This one seemed to stand between you and God. Through him the Infinite spoke to your very soul. He stood upon this pulpit like the law-giver on Sinai handing down to you the truth written as by God's own finger. Here comes another, pre-eminently a preacher and expositor. His text might look like a rock, hard and dry. But as he smote "firstly, secondly and thirdly," it was rent at every blow, the waters of life gushed out as fountains, and the streams therefrom have never ceased to flow. And still another of these fathers was of all things a pastor. How he fed his flock! What rich pastures he found. Though the world was a desert to you, under his tender leadership you gathered manna fresh every day. What "coriander seed" dropped from his loving lips, still lie in the corners of memory! And thus one was your Joshua leading you into the promised land, another, your David felling Goliath from your path, another your Solomon rearing silently in your soul the beautiful temple of a holy character. This one the tearful Jeremiah weeping over your spiritual retrogressions; that a Josiah demolishing your idols and with royal skill reforming your life. Here is a Daniel following you into your spiritual Babylon; there a very Paul shaking your jail as with earthquake power, and here one that turned your Patmos into Paradise and put your spiritual sky aflame with visions of mercy and judgment and the city of jasper and gold. Truly in the services of such a ministry and a succession of such apostolic men, Wilmington has been "lifted to heaven with privileges."

WHENCE THIS SUCCESS?

is a question of the first importance; for it devolves upon the present generation to carry forward what the fathers began.

One secret of their success was the *fundamental character of their work*. They were not superficial. They dug down to the native rock, and laid their solid blocks of truth upon it. There has been no settling of foundations. If the walls have cracked anywhere it has been the fault of careless building thereon. We need no modification of foundations—no change of doctrine, or aim, for our fathers built on the Word of God.

They were *men of simple faith*. This was another secret of their success. They believed the powers that protected ancient Israel were around them. That they were doing work for God, co-working with the Infinite King for the betterment of the race. How could they fail? Would not God protect and prosper His own cause? This made heroes of them all. There was nothing they would not attempt at the bidding of His Providence. Odds against them were nothing, for with God on their side they were ever in the majority. They re-enacted the scenes of Jericho, taking many a city with the "ram's horn" of attack and the shout of victory; but their sublime faith was the invisible inspiration of both.

Their faith was *truly divine and philosophic*. They were not trusting in their own efforts, but in invisible forces, which to them were tremendously and gloriously real.

INVISIBLE FORCES!

All power is invisible; gravitation is invisible, but it brings down the sturdy oak, and the mighty avalanche; cohesion is invisible; but it holds the universe in a grip so powerful that no world, however ponderous, can tear itself from its hold.

The invisible is the foundation of the visible. The human body is built upon the invisible spirit. When that slips away the body is but a handful of dust. The universe floats in the invisible, all pervading presence of Deity. Invisible powers supports the whole. So society at its best, a society of love and goodness, can only exist upon a foundation of invisible truth. Our fathers built the church on this invisible but Divine basis; they harnessed the chariot of Methodism to these unseen, but irresistible forces. They could not fail while such a faith united them with the power of God.

Men are apt to cling to what is visible for protection; they will trust a fetich; depend on a horse shoe; follow a fanatic—something they can see, but they are slow to trust the invisible power that upholds all things. Israel distrusted God, the unseen but omnipotent, but could worship a golden calf, and would doubtless have worshipped the bones of Moses could they have found his place of burial. But our fathers of the century past, well knew that power was with the invisible Jehovah, and they looked "not at the things which are seen but at the things which are unseen;" hence their victories.

A GLORIOUS MACHINE,

however, was the organized Methodism which our fathers left us. If the power that saves is invisible, they well knew that its operator must be *through a visible and tangible organism*. Steam is invisible, but its force must be exerted through piston, crank, and wheel. Invisible wind must have a sail against which to press its sturdy shoulders if it must push our commerce from shore to shore. Mind, as invisible as either, must be furnished with body of visible form and tangible material if its plans and volitions are to effect changes in the world. What steam would be without engine, wind without sails, and mind without brain and hand, God's truth and spirit would be in this world without an organized church. None knew this better than the Methodist fathers, and they organized the redeemed souls about them, using each as his talents would permit, until Methodism with its itinerant ministry, local preachers, class meetings, camp meeting, love feasts and protracted meetings, was a steam engine for God, through which his power divine could be applied to the saving of the world. Well might beholders say they were "all at it" and

"ALWAYS AT IT."

Another secret of their success was the presentation of *practical, saving truth*. Theoretical and metaphysical questions touching Divine and eternal things are intensely interesting, but with a perishing world around them our fathers had no time for them. They set forth with solemn earnestness, the doctrine that make wise unto salvation: the Trinity of the Godhead, Father, Son and Holy Ghost; man's fall; sin and condemnation; mercy, free, full and universal. With unconditional election and reprobation they had no sympathy. It has never recovered from the blows they dealt it, and to-day efforts are being made to modify those dogmas by the people who have taught them.

When Rowland Hill was reproved for not preaching to the elect only, he requested his reprover to mark the elect with a bit of chalk, that he might address them in the future. Our fathers saw every soul marked not with chalk, but with the tear drops and the bleeding finger tips of Him who "gave His life for the world;" and they proclaimed His Gospel to all men. They preached repentance, faith and holiness, attainable in this life, and a final judgment day with an eternal heaven and an everlasting hell beyond it.

One great source of their influence was the *well defined and orthodox meaning of the terms they used*. Sin, to them, was not a trifling disease of the soul, incidental to its normal development and likely to be outgrown. It was a leprosy, deeply seated in the very centre of man's being, which only a Jordan of redeeming blood could wash away.

Human depravity did not mean a slight derangement of man's moral constitution.

A SCREW LOOSE SOMEWHERE.

so that a turn here and there would put man all right again. It was such a complete disorganization as required the taking to pieces of the whole machinery, that it might be put together new and aright by the original maker of the soul. "Ye must be born again," was a frequent text in the early Methodist pulpit.

God's law was put forth in no doubtful tone. To them the Ten Commandments were not the production of Moses as an Egyptian scholar; excellent advice but without binding authority. They were the words in which the Eternal God had formulated the principles of His moral government of the world, given for the enlightenment of the human conscience. God was not a myth or an impersonal force, but a Personal and Eternal Deity—making sun, moon and stars with His "fingers"—but holding the saints "in the hollow of His hand." He was a father, loving man even in his wanderings, sending His son to bring the prodigal home again; preparing a celestial feast where he shall be presented in the robes, ring and shoes of his original sonship, and inviting all to be present when the universe shall dance its joy at his restoration.

To our fathers Christ was not a celestial personage bringing us an example, but leaving unsolved the soul's greatest and most awful problem. "What must I do to be saved" from my past record and future consequence of sin? He was the Second Person of the Godhead, with an incomprehensible love, exchanging a throne for a cross that He might, by His vicarious death, make salvation possible and just. Nor was the

BIBLE A STRING OF BALLADS AND TRADITIONS,

with the string cut so that each might take out the leaves he wished. No; it was a solid book. The covenant of God with man, for the salvation of the race; inspired by His Spirit; written with His fingers ; protected by His Providence ; a complete rule of faith and practice; opening with the only reliable account of creation ; bound together by the "scarlet thread" of Redemption, and closing with an apocalypse of glory for all who "obey this Gospel," and an eternal anathema against them that shall "take away from the words of the book of this prophecy."

With our fathers hell was not a mere probationary annex to the present life, where the belated scholar might learn the lessons he had neglected here, and take his place in the Kingdom of God after all—a doctrine that must encourage indifference to the opportunities offered here, besides having no foundation in the word of God. To them it was the place burning with the fire and brimstone of Divine indignation and human remorse "for ever and ever." Deliverence therefrom was by faith in the atonement of Jesus Christ, a faith attested by a life of practical obedience to God. In the *earnest and faithful presentation* of such unequivocal Law and Gospel we find another of the great secrets of our fathers' victories. They fought the Lord's battles with the Lord's weapons. But no small part of the solution is in what they *were by the saving grace of God*. They were earnest men because they had found themselves sinners. They had been to the brink of the awful abyss, had seen its fiery depth, had well nigh slipped over, but being graciously saved and called of God to proclaim the deliverance to others they went forth equipped, like Gideon Ousley, with the knowledge of

THE DISEASE AND THE REMEDY,

and determined to make it known wherever the sun shone, or a sinner could be found.

And was their not a power in their manner of its proclamation. They did not eulogize the gospel; they preached it. They made no apologies for the gospel; they simply gave it utterance. To the assemblies gathered to worship God and receive the bread of life, they did not defend the Omnipotent against some blasphemer, a frail man of dust, breath and sin, until then unknown to the people, and after the hour thus spent send the hungry home with a stone, and the young with doubts instead of faith, or bits of infidelity to gnaw upon. They sought to convict of personal sin and save the soul. They sought "the lost."

To us is committed the perpetuity of this great work, you begin here

A SECOND CENTURY.

If you would have it close one hundred years hence with results worthy the sons of such sires, maintain in all essential respects the doctrines and principles which make this such a

GLORIOUS CENTENNIAL.

The Scriptural Conclusion and Expedient.

By the Rev. John A. B. Wilson, D. D.

Gal. iii : 22. "But the scripture hath concluded all under sin, that the promise by faith of Jesus Christ might be given to them that believe."

The Bible contains the statement "Surely the wrath of man shall praise thee," Psalm lxxvi : 10; and it furnishes its own demonstration of its correctness, one of the strongest of which is the epistle now before us.

To Paul, the doctrinal and practical errors of the Galatian churches were an unmixed cup of bitterness. Yet, in the providence of God, even these heresies were made the occasion of an inspired defence of the very cardinal principles of Christianity. A defence which has come down the ages ever an armory and a bulwark to the church when assailed. A defence, that amid the darkness of Arianism, the storms of Romanism, the murk of Antinomianism, the fog of Rationalism, like the Eddystone out in the midst of the troubled waters it rears its head unshaken by the fury of the blast; throwing out to the tempest-tossed a light which indicates at once the rocks of danger and the course of safety, until the storm has spent its rage and the darkness is past. And it still stands to encourage and assure those whom it saved in the hour of danger.

No question can be more practical or more important to man than that which enlightens him as to the attitude of his Creator toward himself, and how that attitude may be made most favorable. And for this purpose comes the conclusion and expedient of the text for "the scripture hath concluded (shut up, delivered over) all under sin that the promise by faith of Jesus Christ might be given to them that believe."

REV. JOHN A. B. WILSON, D. D.,
Pastor of Asbury Methodist Episcopal Church, 1878–'80.

The text presents two propositions for consideration:

I.—THE SCRIPTURAL CONCLUSION WITH REFERENCE TO THE MORAL CONDITION OF MAN.

"The scripture hath concluded all under sin."

II.—THE SCRIPTURAL EXPEDIENT IN VIEW OF THAT CONCLUSION.

"That the promise by faith of Jesus Christ might be given to them that believe."

I.—THE SCRIPTURAL CONCLUSION.

We must remember that a conclusion is not a wish, opinion, or argument, but a fact. Not a process of deduction or of induction but a result; the correctness of which depends upon the character of the premises, the knowledge, wisdom and integrity of the reasoner. Here it is said that the scripture hath concluded: meaning that this is the end reached by its author and herein recorded. Now, if it is true that "all scripture" is given by inspiration of God then is He the author, hence the reasoner, hence the conclusion is His; and upon His knowledge, wisdom and truth depends correctness of the deduction. But who shall doubt this when "The Lord is righteous in all His ways and Holy in all His works."—Ps. cxlv: 17. "He is wise in heart and mighty in strength, who hath hardened himself against Him and hath prospered." Job. ix: 4. "With Him is wisdom and strength. He hath counsel and understanding."—Job. xii: 13. So that we may "Ascribe greatness unto our God, He is the Rock, His work is perfect, for all His ways are judgment, a God of truth and without iniquity, just and right is He."—Deut. xxxii: 3, 4.

The conclusion of scripture is sustained by reference

1.—To the condition of the world.

"The scripture hath concluded (or shut up) all under sin." And this conclusion, with the moral condition pre-supposed, appears in every age; and in the institutions and records of every dispensation. It is manifested in the religious observances of the heathen and in their ceaseless efforts after propitiation.

2.—It is confirmed also by the Patriarchal allotment.

It is seen in the discipline of labor, the bloody sacrifice of Abel, the destruction of the Old World, the calling of Abraham and the promise to him of an universal blessing through his seed, implying an universal need; which universal need is the legitimate offspring of universal sin. And sin in its relation to the Divine authority and person is the traitor's act which aims at the overthrow and death of his sovereign. It is that which, could the Divine Governor cease to be, would be sufficient to bring it about. Sin is treason against His government and warfare against His person.

3. It is also illustrated by the Mosaic ritual.

Under the law I find frequent atonement; sacrifices for the sins of the whole people. And why for the whole people if the whole people are not under sin. "Now we know that what things soever the law saith it saith to them that are under the law, that every mouth may be stopped and all the world become guilty before God."—Rom. iii: 10.

4.—It is further shown by the expiation of Jesus.

In the sacrificial death of Christ for the sins of the whole world we have a demonstration that the whole world is under sin. "Wherefore as by one man, sin entered into the world and death by sin; and so death passed upon all men for that all have sinned."—Rom. v: 12.

5.—This conclusion is corroborated by human reason, experience and observation.

Dr. Luther T. Townsend says: "Though we meet with much that is amiable, refined and apparently lovely in humanity, we must remember that merit or demerit consists not in mere possession; and it makes a world of difference whether a man has made for himself a heavenly disposition, or whether he received it [as a natural endowment] from his Creator. A beautiful face may excite our admiration, but whether the beauty has come from the personal development of a lovely disposition, or from a smiling Providence, decides whether she is to be commended or God thanked. These indwelling good qualities, so far as they are not the product of personal conquest and development are the gifts of God, and no thanks to man for his endowments. As well might we say the blessings of wealth shows a man to be free from the dominion of sin as to say that a kindly disposition indicates the same. And the good possessions of human nature do not preclude their opposites."

The state of the world and the experience of men in all ages makes evident the reasonableness of the conclusion. Pascal understood humanity when he said, "What a chimera is man; what a singular phenomenon; what a chaos; what a scene of contrariety. A judge of all things, yet a feeble worm; the shrine of truth, yet a mass of doubt and uncertainty; at once the glory and the scorn of the universe. If he boasts I lower him; if he lowers himself I raise him; either way I contradict him until he learns that he is a monstrous, incomprehensible mystery. Oh, the grandeur and the littleness, the excellency and the corruption of life."

One has said, "We have known men of such correct life that we have thought evil entirely foreign to them, yet how little we know of the conflicts that wage in their breasts. The best of men living tell us that they are sometimes startled almost out of their wits by the horrid suggestions that spring up within them. And these fiery darts of the devil, as they touch and enter the soul seem to come in contact with things frightfully inflammable."

Boyce says, "No man can know the fiftieth part of the good that is in him, nor the hundreth part of the evil. Good men have confessed that without the slightest reason and from no recognized agency they have felt of a sudden an impulse to commit the most horrid crimes ever perpetrated. They would tempt and ruin some victim, strike some fatal blow, or leap from a precipice upon the rocks or into the sea."

Said the noble Ralph Erskine when he saw a robber led to execution: "But for restraining grace I had been brought to this same condition."

Said John Bradford, the English martyr, when he saw a man going to Tyburn to be hanged for crime: "There, but for the grace of God, goes John Bradford." The devout Samuel Marsden, the New Zealand missionary had been basely slandered by some bigoted enemies; he replied to a friend who had reported to him the slander: "Sir, these men do not know the worst; if I should walk through the streets with my heart laid bare, the very boys would pelt me." "I have never heard of any crime," says Goethe, "which I might not have committed."

Says Thomas Shepard: "There is never a wicked man almost in the world, as fair a face as he carries, but hath at sometime or other committed some such secret villiany that he would be ready to hang himself for shame if others did know of it."

The outward world of evil finds such full and ready response from within, that even devout men are at times well nigh terrified at themselves. President Edwards, speaking of himself, says: "My wickedness as I am in myself has long appeared to me perfectly ineffable and swallowing up all thought and imagination, like an infinite deluge or mountains on my head. I know not how to express better what my sins appear to me to be than by heaping infinite upon infinite and multiplying infinite by infinite. * * * When I look into my heart and take a view of my wickedness it appears an abyss infinitely deeper than hell."

Who is free from this terrible experience of sinfulness in some degree? He who resists it with most determination is most aware of its presence and has the lowest conception of his own goodness. He who best understands the nature of God and the character of Jesus is most humiliated by the awful contrast between Him and himself. "For I know that in me (that is in my flesh) dwelleth no good thing, for to will is present with me, but how to perform that which is good I find not. For the good that I would I do not, but the evil which I would not that I do. Now if I do that I would not it is no more I that do it but sin that dwelleth in me."—Rom. vii : 18-20.

All have felt the presence of sin and writhed beneath its power. It is a fell blood poison breaking out in the most loathsome of diseases. The sweet children that play about knees to-day may in after years with murderous hand pluck the life blood from your bosom. You do not think so, and yet such is your knowledge of human nature that you dare not say impossible.

Perhaps you are familiar with the oft-repeated story of an artist who, desiring to make a picture of innocence, found his ideal in the face of a little child upon the bosom of its mother. Years after, wishing to place upon canvas a terrible conception of wickedness, found his subject in the person of a criminal behind the grates of a prison, but learned afterward that the child in his conception of innocence and the felon in the painting of depravity were one and the same person.

Fletcher says: "Bad roots which vigorously shoot in the Spring will naturally produce their dangerous fruit in the Summer." Where is he who has reached the age of thirty whose depravity has not broken out into the greatest variety of wanton acts? Among the persons of this age who were never esteemed worse than their neighbors shall we find a forehead that never betrayed daring insolence? A cheek that never indicated concealed guilt by an involuntary blush or unnatural paleness? A neck that was never stretched out in pride and vain confidence? An eye that never cast a disdainful, malignant or wanton look? An ear that an evil curiosity never opened to frothy, loose or defaming discourse? A tongue that was never tainted with unedifying, false, indecent or uncharitable language? A palate that never became the seat of luxurious indulgence? A throat that was never the channel of excess? A stomach that never felt the oppressive load of abused mercies? Hands that never touched or plucked the forbidden fruit of pleasing sin? Feet that never once moved in the broad downward road of iniquity? A bosom that never heaved under the dreadful workings of some exorbitant passion? Where is there a face ever so disagreeable that never was an object of self-worship in a glass? And where a body, however deformed, that was never set up as a favorite idol by the fallen spirit which inhabits it?"

Alas, the scriptural conclusion that all are under sin is more than confirmed by the condition of the world, the patriarchal allotment, the tutelage of the Mosaic ritual and the expiation of Jesus. What is thus confirmed is further corroborated by human reason, experience and observation as found in the testimony of the wisest and best of the race. And if it be so with these, what must be the sad experience of the rest of the world. What wonder that Paul cried out, "I see another law in my members warring against the law of my mind, and bringing me into captivity to the law of sin which is in my members. O wretched man that I am, who shall deliver me from the body of this death?—Rom. vii : 23, 24.

Iniquity works by all the powers and has broken out in its terrible disease through all parts of the being. What if I knew and were about to relate the hidden sins of your life, the thoughts of evil and deeds of darkness; what imploring would there be, what shrieks of anguish, what emptying of coffers to purchase silence. O, man, may God save thee from the fiend of thine own life, and the hell of thine own bosom.

Wisely, justly hath the scripture concluded all under sin. "For all have sinned and come short of the glory of God."—Rom. iii : 23. "For we have before proved both Jews and Gentiles that they are all under sin ; as it is written. There is none righteous, no, not one; there is none that understandeth, there is none that seeketh after God. They are all gone out of the way, they are together become unprofitable; there is none that doeth good, no, not one. Their throat is an open sepulchre; with their tongues they have used deceit; the poison of asps is under their lips; whose mouth is full of cursing and bitterness; their feet are swift to shed blood; and destruction and misery are in their ways, and the way of peace have they not known; there is no fear of God before their eyes."—Rom. iii : 9-18.

This conclusion is the verdict of a Divine jury, the opinion of the Judge of all the earth. It has not been reached upon the testimony of fallible witnesses, but from the actual observation of the Lord of all. "And God saw that the wickedness of man was great in the earth, and that every imagination of the thought of his heart was only evil continually. The earth also was corrupt before God, and the earth filled with violence. And God looked upon the earth and behold it was corrupt, for all flesh had corrupted his way upon the earth."—Gen. vi : 5, 11, 12.

"For the Lord looked down from heaven upon the children of men, to see if there were any that did understand and seek God.

They are all gone aside, they are altogether become filthy; there is none that doeth good, no, not one."—Psa. xiv : 2, 3.

All are under the dominion, power and delusion of sin, and if all are under sin, then the doom of sin is the doom of all.

In courts of justice the jury hear the evidence; and though some of it is contradictory and much of it circumstantial, yet from its general bearing they unanimously conclude the prisoner guilty and convict him. The judge, from the verdict of the jury and the law in the case, concludes to condemn and pronounces sentence. The governor, from the finding of the jury and the sentence of the court concludes to sign the death warrant. The sheriff in obedience to his instructions and with the death warrant in his hand, concludes to execute the sentence of the law upon the wretched prisoner; and upon the day appointed he dies. But, when God through the scripture concluded all under sin, it was—"That the promise, by faith of Jesus Christ might be given to them that believe."

II—THE SCRIPTURAL EXPEDIENT IN VIEW OF THE CONCLUSION.

The blessed Jesus took the testimony of the witnesses, the verdict of the jury, the sentence of the judge, the warrant of the governor, the instructions of the executioner; and nailing them to His cross baptized them with the blood which flowed from His wounds in rivers of mercy for the healing of the nations.

"The scripture hath concluded all under sin, that the promise by faith of Jesus Christ might be given to them that believe."

1.—*The promise to which the text refers*

is that of universal blessing through His seed made to Abraham; which seed is Christ and which blessing is the salvation by Him procured. "The scripture [hath not only concluded all under sin, but] foreseeing that God would justify the heathen through faith preached before the gospel unto Abraham saying, in thee shall all nations be blessed."—Gal. iii : 8. "Brethren, I speak after the manner of men; though it be but a man's covenant, yet if it be confirmed, no man disannulleth or addeth thereto. Now to Abraham and his seed were the promises made. He saith not, And to seeds, as of many; but as of one, And to thy seed which is Christ. And this I say that the covenant that was confirmed before of God in Christ, the law, which was four hundred and thirty years after, cannot disannul, that it should make the promise of none effect. For if the inheritance be of the law, it is no more of promise; but God gave it to Abraham by promise. Wherefore then serveth the law? It was added because of transgressions, till the seed should come to whom the promise was made; and it was ordained by angels in the hands of a mediator. Now a mediator is not a mediator of one, but God is one. Is the law then against the promises of God? God forbid: for if there had been a law given which could have given life, verily righteousness should have been by the law. But the scripture hath concluded all under sin, that the promise by faith of Jesus Christ might be given to them that believe."—Gal. iii: 15-22. The promise is not annulled by the law nor opposed by it, the one is the complement of the other. The promise is for salvation, the law for conviction, for "by the law is the knowledge of sin." It shuts the sinner up when he cannot but realize his danger and the futility of depending on the law, his captor, or on his own efforts for escape from the thraldom of guilt and sin.

There is not only harmony between the two, but the "scripture hath concluded all under sin" for this very purpose, "that the promise might be given." Hence we see the absolute necessity of the law to the success of the gospel. The conclusion is essential to a realization of the promise.

Men reject the proffer of unnecessitated grace. I say to a man, "Sir, I have a pardon from the governor for you." "For me? What do you mean, I don't need a pardon?" "But have you never violated the law?" "That is neither here nor there. I have never been charged with, indicted for, or convicted of violation, so your pardon is a dead letter so far as I am concerned. You will therefore please give yourself no further concern about me." Try it on that poor convict who watches you through the grates of his cell and raises manacled hands to accept your proffer. Ah! grace must be necessary to be acceptable. And, as I understand them, here is where Calvinism and so-called Liberal Christianity fail. The one is all law: dark, malignant and forbidding, from which men disparingly turn and regard its author with horror. The other being all grace is equally disregarded, men recognizing no necessity in the absence of law.

A man must sense the fact, not only that it is a good thing, but that he is in a strait where he must perish without it.

Doubtless to the angels the atonement is the sublimest spectacle, the most beautiful bow that spans the world. But to us, lost by the fall and cursed by the law, it is salvation, life, all! Hope is seen only under its arch, peace approaches beneath its canopy alone, and heaven is accessible but by its bridge.

Without the law and the concluding under sin the Gospel would be but a beautiful picture, the masterpiece of a great artist; and the

Golgotha scene but a gladiatorial for the entertainment of creation. But shut up under sin by the law which we have violated, with agony of longing I turn my eyes to Calvary and cry,

> "Jesus, the sinner's friend, to Thee,
> Lost and undone, for aid I flee,
> Weary of earth, myself, and sin,
> Open Thine arms and take me in.
>
> "Pity and heal my sin-sick soul,
> 'Tis Thou alone canst make me whole ;
> Dark, till in me Thine image shine,
> And lost I am till Thou art mine.
>
> "At last I own it cannot be
> That I should fit myself for Thee ;
> Here, then, to Thee I all resign ;
> Thine is the work, and only Thine.
>
> "What shall I say Thy Grace to move?
> Lord, I am sin—but Thou art love ;
> I give up every plea beside—
> Lord I am lost—but Thou hast died."

Concluding all under sin makes Cavalry practical and Jesus Lord and Saviour instead of the benevolent prince of tragedians. And in place of the greeting of complaisant plaudits and floral tributes of admiration, we humbly confess Him with Thomas, "My Lord and my God," and cry with Blind Bartimeas, "Jesus, Thou Son of David, have mercy on me," and forget the inherent virtues of humanity and the moral dignity of man while we offer Him "the sacrifice of a broken spirit," and sing :

> "Just as I am, without one plea,
> But that Thy blood was shed for me,
> And that Thou bidst me come to Thee,
>   O Lamb of God ! I come, I come !
>
> "Just as I am, and waiting not
> To rid my soul of one dark blot,
> To Thee whose blood can cleanse each spot ;
>   O Lamb of God ! I come, I come !
>
> "Just as I am though tossed about
> With many a conflict, many a doubt,
> Fightings and fears, within and without,
>   O Lamb of God ! I come, I come !
>
> "Just as I am, poor, wretched, blind,
> Sight, riches, healing of the mind,
> Yea, all I need, in Thee to find,
>   O Lamb of God ! I come, I come.

"Just as I am, Thou wilt receive.
Will welcome, pardon, cleanse, relieve;
Because Thy promise I believe,
    O Lamb of God! I come, I come."

"Just as I am, Thy love unknown,
Hath broken every barrier down;
Now to be Thine, yea, Thine alone,
    O Lamb of God! I come, I come!"

Until by faith in His atoning merit we accept Him as our present, sufficient and abiding Saviour, and He touches our hearts with a new life and our lips with a new song and we break forth in rapturous praises with.

"O happy day that fixed my choice
    On Thee my Saviour and my God.
Well may this glowing heart rejoice
    And tell its rapture all abroad."

"'Tis done, the great transaction's done
    I am my Lord's and He is mine;
He drew me and I followed on
    Charmed to confess the voice divine."

"Now rest, my long divided heart,
    Fixed on this blissful centre rest;
Nor ever from thy Lord depart
    With Him of every good possessed."

"High heaven that heard the solemn vow
    That vow renewed shall daily hear;
Till in life's latest hour I bow
    And bless in death a bond so dear."

"What shall we then say to these things? If God be for us, who can be against us?

He that spared not his own Son, but delivered him up for us all, how shall he not with him also freely give us all things?

Who shall lay anything to the charge of God's elect? It is God that justifieth.

Who is he that condemneth? It is Christ that died, yea rather, that is risen again, who is even at the right hand of God, who also maketh intercession for us.

Who shall separate us from the love of Christ? shall tribulation, or distress, or persecution, or famine, or nakedness or peril, or sword?

As it is written, For thy sake we are killed all the day long; we are accounted as sheep for the slaughter.

Nay, in all these things we are more than conquerors through him that loved us.

"For I am persuaded, that neither death, nor life, nor angels nor principalities, nor powers, nor things present, nor things to come,

Nor height, nor depth, nor any other creature, shall be able to separate us from the love of God, which is in Christ Jesus our Lord."
—Rom. viii: 31-39.

2.—*The condition of the promise.*

"The scriptures hath concluded all under sin, that the promise by faith of Jesus Christ might be given to them that believe."

The blessing is conditioned upon faith in Jesus.

It is man and not God that puts salvation at the end of a long series of improving processes. God puts it at the beginning, with faith as a condition, upon Jesus as the object; and improvement and moral development as the essential resultant of it. It is not deliverance from the consequences, but from guilt and sin. So that, "if any man be in Christ, he is a new creature, old things have passed away, and behold, all things are become new." II Cor. v: 17.

But to all this faith is the divinely and naturally imposed condition. Hence it is not secured as a result of moral character, social standing or intellectual status, but on the exercise of an universal faculty. It is not he that is, he that knows, or he that does, but he that believes in Jesus.

Did you ever discover the depths of philosophy and benevolence in this condition? Did you ever think that however low the organism, or sensual the mind, or groveling the character, or deplorable the ignorance; yet the capacity of faith inheres in every man. Aye, even the brute is possessed of it. "The ox knoweth his owner" (believes he will feed him); "The ass his master's crib" (believes there is corn there). And on this commonest of all and universal faculty salvation impinges, conditioned only upon its exercise, an exercise precisely analogous to its every day activities. And to whomsoever, by whomsoever, it is exercised and Christ accepted comes, who shall describe it? What tongue portray the transformation? "There is joy in heaven over one sinner that repenteth." Ring all the bells of the glory world; let the minute guns boom the triumph from celestial parapets; let the blood washed redeemed parade the city, displaying the battle flags of the cross; let the angel orchestra make the eternal arches reverberate with the symphonies of the skies. An adoption is made, a prince is inaugurated; a sinner saved takes his place on the earth, "a king and priest unto God." "The scripture hath concluded all under sin that the promise by faith of Jesus Christ might be given to them that believe."

For Christ is the end of the law for righteousness to every one that believeth.

For Moses describeth the righteousness which is of the law, That the man which doeth those things shall live by them.

But the righteousness which is of faith speaketh on this wise, Say not in thine heart, Who shall ascend into heaven? (that is, to bring Christ down from above.)

Or, Who shall descend into the deep? (that is, to bring up Christ again from the dead.)

But what saith it? The word is nigh thee, even in thy mouth, and in thy heart: that is, the word of faith, which we preach;

That if thou shalt confess with thy mouth the Lord Jesus, and shalt believe in thine heart that God hath raised him from the dead, thou shalt be saved.

For with the heart man believeth unto righteousness; and with the mouth confession is made unto salvation.

For the Scripture saith, Whosoever believeth on him shall not be ashamed.

For there is no difference between the Jew and the Greek: for the same Lord over all is rich unto all that call upon him.

For whosoever shall call upon the name of the Lord shall be saved. —Rom. x: 4–13.

5. — *The terms of the promise.*

The Divine blessings are free. In nature there is no bargaining for sunshine, air or water. He gives enough of each for all. So the promised salvation cannot be secured by barter. It is not exchanged for so much of feeling, of penance, or penitence, or prayers. He gives it to them that believe.

Sinner, it is not at this stage a question of doing on your part, but of acceptance. "But to him that worketh not but believeth on him that justifieth the ungodly, his faith is counted to him for righteousness."—Rom. iv: 5.

I dare to say that, so far from your salvation being difficult, apart from yourself, the Father hath made it so plain and brought it so near that it is impossible for you to be lost but by the most persistent rejection of His Son. "The word is nigh thee, even in thy mouth and in thine heart the word of faith which we preach."—Rom. x: 8.

Whatever has been or may be your course toward Him, God seeks thee to-day. Out on the mountains of sin and waste of folly, He seeks for His lost one, and long has He toiled in the search. "He never gives up a soul so long as in the economy of His grace there is one resource left, or in His infinite ingenuity one untried suggestion. God give up a soul! The thought would darken His great white throne with suspicion. God give up a soul! It is not the loss of the soul that gives the climax to such a suggestion, but the fact that it takes the godliness out of God."

Though He is discarded of thee, thou art not rejected of Him. To-day He invites thine acceptance of His Son as thy Saviour; to-day he proffers thee His grace; to-day He tenders thee a free and full pardon of all thine offences; to-day He offers thee Sonship with Himself and brotherhood with the Saviour.

But though so free, it is offered only on this condition. Jesus says: "I am the way, the truth and the life; no man cometh unto the Father but by me."—John xiv : 6.

"I am the door; by me if any man enter in, he shall be saved, and shall go in and out, and find pasture."—John viii: 9

"Neither is there salvation in any other, for there is none other name under heaven given among men whereby we must be saved." "He that believeth on Him is not condemned."—Acts iv : 12.

"The scripture hath concluded all under sin." You are included. Shall the object of this conclusion in your case be secured? "that the promise by faith in Jesus Christ might be given to them that believe." He, He alone hath made the atonement for the sins of the world, complete and sufficient to all eternity, and God is satisfied with the propitiation of His Son. So that you have not to bring additional worth to be accepted. And this is true of every sinner, however great his guilt.

"Naught of merit or of price
 Remains to justice due ;
Jesus died and paid it all,
 Yes, all the debt I owe."

"When He from His lofty throne
 Stooped down to do and die,
Everything was fully done,
 'Tis finished was His cry."

"Weary, working, toiling one,
 O, wherefore toil you so ;
Cease your doing, all was done,
 Done ages long ago."

"Till to Jesus' work you cling
 Alone by simple faith,
Doing is a deadly thing,
 Yes, doing ends in death."

"Cast your deadly doing down,
Down, all at Jesus' feet;
Find in Him your all in all,
All glorious and complete."

Oh man! woman! child! I dare not tell you anything to-night in the doing of which you might be lost. Should I tell you to meditate upon these things you might obey, go out and perish; should I say pray about it you could do it, go forth and be lost. I urge upon you now the immediate, right now acceptance of Jesus Christ as your only Saviour. "For as many as received Him to them gave He power to become the children of God even to as many as believed on His name."—John i: 12. You cannot be lost in doing this. Receive Him and be saved. Believe it when I tell you that God accepts every sinner as saved who accepts His Son as Saviour. Will you do it? Will you do it now?

"O, believe the record true,
God for you His Son hath given;
You may now be happy to
Find in Christ the way to Heaven;
Live the life of Heaven above,
All the life of glorious love."

"This the universal bliss,
Bliss for every soul designed,
God's original promise this,
God's great gift to all mankind;
Blessed in Christ this moment be,
Blessed to all eternity."

"For the scriptures hath concluded all under sin that the promise by faith of Jesus Christ might be given to them that believe."—Gal. iii: 22.

Past Triumphs and Future Victories.

By the Rev. W. L. S. Murray, Ph. D.

"Thanks be to God who giveth us the victory through our Lord Jesus Christ."—I Cor. xv: 57.

The proposition laid down by the apostle in this sublime argument is that the religion of Christ is either false or true. If it be false then it follows that "our preaching is vain and your faith is also vain; yea, and we are found false witnesses of God. Ye are yet in your sins. They also which are fallen asleep in Christ are perished. If in this life only we have hope in Christ we are of all men most miserable."

But if the religion of Christ be true then none of these things follow. Whether it be false or true depends upon the resurrection of Christ from the dead. If He rose not then His religion is false and Christ is a deceiver and ought to have died on the cross, His ministers are false prophets, His believers false witnesses and the whole system a *falsehood*.

"But now is Christ risen from the dead and become the first fruits of them that slept." "He rose again the third day according to the scriptures, He was seen by Cephas then of the twelve. After that He was seen of above five hundred brethren at once, then by James, and last of all He was seen of me as of one born out of due time."

Of the resurrection of Christ we have, besides others, three proofs. First, The annual celebration at Easter, and a striking illustration in the recurring springtime, when nature rises from the icy tomb of Winter to the beautiful life of Spring.

Second, The weekly proof in the recurring Sabbath. It is one of the best authenticated historical facts that the Sabbath has been changed from the seventh day of the week to the first day, and called the Lord's day because of the resurrection of Christ on the first day.

Third. The daily or, better still, the momentary proof of Christ's resurrection. This is found in the life and testimony of Christians, for says the Apostle, "We are begotten again to a lively hope through the resurrection of Christ from the dead, which hope is as an anchor to the soul, sure and steadfast." For these and many other reasons, it follows for us as well as for the Corinthians that our preaching and your faith are not in vain. Those who have testified that Christ rose from the dead are not found false witnesses, and those who have fallen asleep in Christ have not perished, and instead of our being of all men the most miserable we are, through our hope in Christ, of all men the most happy.

Paul rejoiced in the Christian's victory over four things, viz : The law that condemned, sin that defiled, death that destroyed, and the grave that consumed. His glowing logic breaks into flaming rhetoric. His prose into poetry. His reasoning into fervid exclamation when he shouts. 'O death, where is thy sting? O grave, where is thy victory? The sting of death is sin and the strength of sin is the law.' But thanks be to God, which giveth us the victory through our Lord Jesus Christ."

In these Centennial services now closing, which have continued for a whole week, which have been so full of interest, so replete with hallowed association, so fruitful of sacred reminiscences, with so many able historical papers, with such preaching of the word of God in demonstration of the spirit, and with power by leading and eminent divines, with such a revival spirit inducing sinners to seek pardon, and members of the church power we give thanks unto God that we now have the victory.

1.—*Over ignorance.*

By this we do not mean to say that all Methodists are classical or have been trained in the academies, colleges or universities, but we do mean to say that a great many have and that the facilities have been wondrously multiplied.

Rev. J. A. Roche, D. D., who served this church a full term beginning 1851, said during these services. "Sixty years ago we did not believe there were three Doctors of Divinity or a half dozen graduates in our ministry, but to-day there are many. While Methodism in this country had its birth in a sail-loft, in England it was born in a university. Ignorance is weakness, and knowledge is power. We rejoice in what our church has done in the last century in supplanting the former and in planting the latter. In the annual report of the Board of Education of the Methodist Episcopal Church, issued January, 1889, we find the following summary:

Class of Institutions.	No. of Schools.	Value of Buildings and Grounds.	Endowments.	Debts.	No. of Teachers.	Students last year.	Students from the beginning.
Theological Institutions	12	$631,500	$1,250,000		67	883	4,233
Colleges and Universities	56	6,326,774	9,398,982	$432,300	863	16,185	111,404
Classical Seminaries	54	1,951,325		386,700 171,500	576	10,167	172,979
Female Colleges and Seminaries	9	801,000	25,000	60,000	118	1,150	22,774
Foreign Mission Schools	66	373,126	5,000	29,300	171	3,941	8,163
Total	197	$10,083,725	$11,079,682	$684,100	1,595	32,276	319,553

INCREASE IN FOUR YEARS.

	In 1885.	In 1889.	Increase.
Theological Institutions	10	12	2
Colleges and Universities	45	56	11
Class Seminaries and Mission Schools	86	120	34
Whole number of Institutions	142	197	55
Total number of Teachers	1,405	1,595	190
Total number of Students	28,591	32,276	3,685
Value of Buildings and Endowments	$14,023,342	$20,479,307*	$6,455,965
Students from the beginning		319,553	

*Less debts.

The editor of the Christian Advocate, Oct. 17, 1889, in sending out an educational supplement of one of the most able of all Christian papers claims that no such paper as the supplement has ever been sent forth in the history of Methodism.

2.—*Victory over pinching poverty.*

We have been astounded while listening to the historical papers of this Centennial at the poverty of our fathers. I cannot call to mind a single church in this city that has not had a great struggle, either with debt, or its untoward circumstances and poor environments, or all combined. The peril of poverty, with two exceptions, faced every enterprise in its beginning. The sheriff has threatened and has sometimes appeared to sell the church property, but God has raised up friends. Even St. Paul's, because of her position and pewed system which was called the "silk stocking" church, and Grace, her queenly daughter, have had to toil and sacrifice, ecomomize and deny themselves as we had never suspected.

It stirs our hearts to hear of their early deprivations, even the mothers toiled in factories during the day and cared for their churches at night. We are not all rich now, nor will we ever be in this world's goods; but thanks be to God we have the victory over the hardships which our fathers endured. A young lady who complained that she could not have a piano, said: "Never shall I forget my mother's gentle tone as she simply replied: 'Never mind if you cannot have a piano on earth, you may have a harp in heaven.'" Said the young lady: "From that moment my feelings changed and the current of my life was changed." So while our fathers were poor, "they esteemed the reproach of Christ greater riches than the treasures in Egypt, for they had respect unto the recompense of reward." Rich in faith. "Seeking a city whose builder and maker is God." Denied the treasures of earth but long since received not only their harp in heaven but a crown of glory also.

2.—*Victory over persecution.*

In this city the Methodist church has had her full share of persecution. Her aged members recount with unfailing memories the heroic days, when in this, the old mother church, the congregation had to meet early in the evenings so as to close their services before dark in order to reach their homes in safety. Stones were often thrown against the building with violent force during service; sometimes through the windows. There are those living who speak of the old pulpit which had a panel knocked out of it by a missile thrown from the hand of a ruffian. Many of her daughters have suffered in a like manner, for Methodism has not been nor is she now a temporizing church. Her motto "Holiness to the Lord" signifies no compromise with evil. Therefore she attacked sin in its strongholds. "From the first she has been outspoken. Bold in her allegiance to the right, she has invariably taken highest ground and the front rank. From the first she recorded her protest against slavery and incorporated it in her organic law. Her testimony and her laws have ever been unequivocal against the theatre, the dance, and all gaming. Against intemperance she has been a burning wrath. No public or private sin has ever escaped her scourge.

Mere formalism she has unsparingly denounced. She has demanded a thorough-paced spiritual experience, and a consistent and holy life. Her habit in all these respects has branded her as extreme and even Puritanical, not to say fanatical, and the straightest of the sects. It is her glory that intense religiousness, separation from the world and self-denial have always been branded as "Methodistic." She has been persecuted for her peculiarities, for her zeal, for her doctrines, but over all God has given her the victory. It is no longer said of Methodism, "Can any good thing come out of Nazareth?"

For others have seen her good works and have glorified our Father in Heaven. "No weapon framed against her has prospered. One has chased a thousand and two have put ten thousand to flight."

4.—Victory over sin.

Of all enemies of the human race, and of the Church of God, sin is the greatest. It has cursed the whole race; entered every home; polluted every heart. "With chilling breath extinguished the light of our households, unsheathed the sword, bathed it in blood." It has dug every grave in the bosom of the fair earth; but for sin we had not known the name of widow or orphan, tear or sigh, sorrow or death. Sin the fell destroyer, the arch fiend of the pit, has done its worst against Methodism, but through Him that loved us and gave Himself for us we are more than conquerors.

During this whole week of Centennial services we have stood with our faces toward the past. Now let us turn to the future and contemplate the duties of the present that we may make the victories of the future as glorious as the triumphs of the past.

1.—By being steadfast.

The word from which we translate steadfast signifies a seat, therefore this word would teach us to be settled in doctrine. It may be that the Apostle had seen the Corinthians wandering from place to place seeking peace and finding none. They had listened to Greek speculation and Atheistic argument. All the while their sins multiplying in number and accumulating in burdens upon their souls. They wandered, weary and worn. The Apostle preached to them Christ and his resurrection the true doctrine. They accepted it; believed it. Being justified by faith they had peace with God. They had found the true doctrine, and the Apostle said to them, be steadfast, or in other words you are tired and worn, take a seat; sit down; rest your souls.

Be firm in the conviction of the truth; be settled in the faith; be rooted in love; be steadfast. That is, do not move yourself from the doctrine of the word. The greatest calamity that ever befell Methodism in the Mother Church has not been her poverty, her ignorance, nor her persecution, but her disaffection in doctrine. Well do many remember how the wolf in sheep's clothing entered this peaceful fold. How the poor sheep were left scattered, bleeding, dying. Now in order that a similar calamity may be avoided, be ye steadfast in doctrine. There are three conditions of stability: the grace of God, a fixed faith, and a determined purpose. Concerning the first: "Being justified by faith, we have peace with God through our Lord Jesus Christ, and access into that grace wherein we stand, and rejoice in the hope of the glory of God."

2.—*"If ye will not believe ye shall not be established. Doubt disturbs, faith settles.*

Doubt darkens, faith illumines. Doubt looses Christian moorings and sets the soul adrift lining the shores of time with spiritual wrecks. Faith and hope are as anchors to the soul sure and steadfast having entered within the vail. Abide by the doctrines of Methodism, tried and true, the doctrine of God's word. Do not move yourself from them. Believe the word, believe it all. Doubt will unsettle you, faith will make you strong that you shall never be moved. The Chautauquan, one of the finest literary magazines of this country, published this story which belongs to natural history. A little fish called the kite which makes it home along the shore among the water-covered rocks; when feeding sometimes seizes a sweet morsel on the fisherman's hook, if it is out in the channel it is helpless and is soon taken by the angler; but if it is near the rock and can settle down upon it, nature has provided it with power to expel all the air from between itself and the rock, so that it clings fast to the rock. The angler may tear the hook from its mouth and leave it torn and bleeding, but he cannot separate it from the rock. So it is with the Christian, God has given him power to stand. The foundation is sure. The doctrines of His word are sound. The "Rock of Ages" is secure and so is the Christian who trusts in Him. The stars might more easily be removed from the heavens, the mountains raised from their foundations and hurled into the sea, than a child of God plucked from His hand.

3.—A determined purpose.

Joshua said, "As for me and my house we will serve the Lord," and expressed a purpose and a determination that saved Israel from idolatry. David saw and felt the persistent efforts of the world to move him from the foundations of his faith, but said, "O Lord my heart is fixed." He set his face like flint and turned his feet to the testimonies of the Lord.

Perhaps I cannot better illustrate the power of a determined purpose than by the following incident. A few years ago in a rolling mill in this city, a laborer was rolling iron, a very hard and difficult work; the bar had been heated and drawn from the furnace and by two men was to be passed back and forth between the rolls. The bar was brought to the proper position but it was with difficulty that the rolls were made to take hold of it, and in the struggle and haste the workman's foot was caught and drawn between the rolls, which crushed and burned him almost to the knee. He threw up his hands, seized a rod of iron suspended above him, held on and cried for help. Help came and he was saved from a horrible death. He determined by all his power of soul and body to hold on, for he saw and felt it was life to hold on but death to let go. So in this world, we are sometimes caught between the upper and nether millstones and are in danger of being ground to powder, but by the side of all such the cross of Christ is planted with extended arms so that all may lay hold on eternal life, "and nothing shall be able to separate them from the love of God in Christ Jesus." Again, as God has given us the victory through our Lord Jesus Christ, we should abound in the work of the Lord.

The fields are white unto the harvest and laborers are still comparatively few. The world's need appeals to us. Doors stand open before us. Evils are rampant. Intemperance is destroying its millions. Worldliness is a great maelstrom swallowing up precious souls. The subtle influences of rationalism are doing their deadly work. The youth are being corrupted. Manhood destroyed. Old age deprived of the joys of religion. The heathen are perishing. God is calling. Who will go unto the field? Who will enter these open doors? Who will lift his voice against intemperance, worldliness, gambling, theatrical performances and the ball room? Who will cry out and spare not?

Let us try how much we may do, not how little. Let us abound, always abound in the work of the Lord. There is work for all. Let every one do whatsoever his hands find to do with his might. Let the heroic deeds of our fathers, the self-sacrificing labors of our local preachers, the devoted services of the laity as rehearsed in our hearing during this Centennial occasion, inspire us to undertake great things for God, to expect great things from God. There is work for the least as well as the greatest. This affecting incident occurred in the M. E. Church at Mt. Vernon, N. Y., a few Sabbath evenings since: A little girl, frail, but very bright, came with an elder sister to the altar for prayers. Her father, a highly respected lawyer, sat in his pew. After a brief prayer, the child rose from her knees, went to her father, put her arms about his neck and whispered: "Papa, I can't stay there without you." The father was deeply moved and permitted his little one to lead him forward as a penitent seeker. The effect on the audience was wonderful. Many rose and asked the prayers of God's people. It was the turning point in the work, and more than fifty have since been happily converted. This but illustrates the truth of His word, "A little child shall lead them."

Let us abound in the work of the Lord because we know it is not in vain in the Lord.

We know that the work of Methodism is not in vain. First, Because of its success in our country at large.

The general summary published in our year book for 1889, gives the number of Episcopal Methodists in the United States as follows:

Itinerant Ministers	27,741
Local Preachers	42,335
Lay Members	4,413,836
Total Lay and Ministerial	4,441,567

Non-Episcopal Methodists in the United States:

Itinerant Ministers	4,072
Local Preachers	1,702
Lay Members	201,314
Total Lay and Ministerial	205,386

Grand total Methodists in the United States:

Itinerant Ministers	31,813
Local Preachers	44,037
Lay Members	4,615,150
Total Lay and Ministerial	4,646,953

This summary shows that our numerical progress reaching through the entire period has been nearly five times as great as that of the population.

We have under the blessing of God seen that our labor is not in vain in the Lord. "Methodists, much less other people, have no idea what has been done. We must endeavor to bring into our view the present working of this vast army. Thirty thousand preachers every Lord's Day, preaching sixty thousand sermons to millions of hearers; a Sabbath-school force much larger molding as many millions of youths, other officers working in their appropriate spheres—the whole permeating the land, working in the pulpit, and by the press, and in educational halls, all to build the age in intelligence and virtue, working against vice, against intemperance, against false doctrine, against oppression, against all manner of wrong and sin-working to lift humanity towards God."

Second, Because of its success in our city. This is shown in my paper "Then-Now" as read during the Centennial services, which may be found among the historical papers published in this book.

Has any church in this city ever failed? Did a sinner ever trust and perish?

It is also shown on this beautiful arch under which I stand, and upon which we have been looking all the week. In the days of Rome's glory, when her generals returned from victorious fields triumphal arches were erected in conspicuous and suitable places in honor of the victorious general. The general himself came quietly into the city, lodged with his friends or in privacy until a day of triumph was appointed. On that day gates were thrown wide open, snow-white horses bore the trophies of many battles, the streets were strewn with roses; tablets showed the battles fought, the victories won. Captive kings followed the triumphal car. The whole city witnessed the procession. Coins were thrown broadcast among the people. Great feasts were provided, and the triumph continued for days.

So this Centennial service has been a week of triumph. We have celebrated the victories of a hundred years. We have fought on more battle-fields than either Pompey or Cæsar, and have contended with greater and more difficult foes. The powers opposing them were visible, ours invisible. Theirs the strongholds of Europe, Asia and Africa, ours the strongholds of Satan. We have greater reasons to rejoice than they. Our arch means more than theirs. Our rejoicing is over men made alive; theirs over men put to death. Ours is a triumph over sin: theirs a triumph in sin. Their victory came by the sword; ours through our Lord Jesus Christ, "who led captivity captive and gave gifts unto man."

"Now unto Him that is able to do exceedingly abundant, above all that we ask or think, according to the power that worketh in us, unto Him be glory in the church by Christ Jesus throughout all ages, world without end. Amen."

The Transitory and the Permanent.

By the Rev. Jacob Todd, D. D.

Text: Hebrews xii: 26-27. "Whose voice then shook the earth: but now he hath promised, saying, Yet once more I shake not the earth only, but also heaven. And this word, Yet once more, signifieth the removing of those things that are shaken, as of things that are made, that those things which cannot be shaken may remain."

The idea in this passage seems to be that we are living in a world of change—that all things in nature are moving like a panorama before us and are passing away. This truth, within the narrow circle of observation and experience, is one with which we are all familiar. From our childhood we have seen the bursting buds of springtime disappear to make room for the flowers of Summer; and the flowers in turn vanish to give place to the purple fruitage of Autumn; and the fruit pass away to leave the bare branches a sobbing harpsichord for the bleak winds of Winter.

We do not pass far along life's pathway before we become aware that this law of change is broader than the circle of the seasons. Let a young man leave his home and be absent twenty years and then return. He remembers all things as they were when he left, but he never finds them thus again. The trees have grown larger, the ivy has spread farther over the walls of the old home and the moss is much thicker upon its roof. Father and mother are either in their graves or are gray-haired and wrinkled old people now. Brothers and sisters with whom he romped in childhood are staid, middle aged persons now with homes and families of their own. He looks around for his playmates of former years, but they have all either passed away or moved away. He seeks his old time haunts, but scarcely recognizes them. The school is not the same. The scholars are all different and another master is behind the desk. There is a new miller at the mill and the old blacksmith is no longer at the anvil. Slowly and sadly the truth dawns upon him that the past has moved forever out of sight—that life means moving forward ever and that there is no return to former scenes.

Beyond the circle of our observation and experience history teaches on a broader scale the same solemn lesson. Take up any account of our own country a hundred years old and you will be startled to find how antiquated it is. It will describe log cabins, bridle paths and Indian trails where now we find the great cities and steel railways of the West. Where now the steamship on the ocean and the steamboat on our rivers churn the waters into foam, then vessels with sails or oars crept slowly and lazily along. Where now the lightning flashes thought along the wires across a continent in a second of time, then the old post-chaise came lumbering along with the news at the rate of seventy-five miles in a day. Then people carried tin lanterns along the streets at night and went to bed by the light of a tallow candle, where now our cities blaze with electric light and our homes are radiant with saffron jets of gas. Then the farmer whetted his scythe, and swung his cradle, and plied his flail for weeks, where now the mowing, and the reaping, and the threshing machine cut down and thresh out a harvest in a day.

Take a wider range of vision and go back to the splendid civilizations of ancient times. Read how Egypt, Assyria, Persia, Greece and Rome in turn dominated the earth with their armies, and how their literature and art made their capitals centres of wisdom and beauty that dazzled the world; and then go search for their greatness to-day. Where are Thebes and Babylon and Ninevah now? A heap of ruins on the banks of the Nile or a mound of earth on the Euphrates or the Tigris is all that is left of them. A few rolls of papyri, a few monuments covered with hieroglyphics and a few cuniform inscriptions engraved upon the rocks are all that remains of their literature. The people themselves have vanished, leaving nothing behind them but their mummies which are being utilized to-day as fuel to run locomotive engines. Even Athens and Rome, of more modern date, are rapidly moving out of sight. Pericles and Cæsar, could they rise from their graves, would not recognize these modern cities as their ancient capitals. The marble of the Parthenon is black with age and its inimitable sculptures are gnawed away by the tooth of time. The Colliseum, gutted of its magnificence, is only a colossal, naked wall, and the palace of the Cæsars is now but a subterranean labyrinth. Greek and Roman literature, though still alive, is fading slowly away and now shines only in the libraries of the learned. The nations of the past are gone or are going, and soon only the owl hooting from some moss-covered tower or the bittern screaming among the wild grass and reeds will tell where they once stood.

The text under consideration, however, carries us farther than history can go, and declares that this same chorus of continual change was sounding through the prehistoric ages to the same solemn measure as now, and that its last note has not yet been heard. Modern science, groping around among the laws of nature with its dark lantern, has just thrown the light upon the face of this truth of revelation and waked it up from its slumber of ages. Science teaches that our globe was not always what it now is. In the beginning (whenever that was) we are told that the matter of which our earth is composed was so intensely heated and expanded that it floated in space as a vapor, lighter than hydrogen gas. As the ages rolled away this glowing star dust radiated its heat and slowly cooled. As it cooled it contracted its bulk and became more dense until at length the vapor became a liquid. For ages more our earth swept its fiery course around the sun as a red hot ball of molten matter. In course of time the surface had sufficiently cooled for a crust of rock to form, like the shell of an egg, around the liquid core. Still cycles rolled away, the earth's crust growing thicker all the time, while its outer surface, swept by fierce storms, seathed by wild lightnings and corroded by an acid atmosphere, was being pulverized into soil. The vapors in the atmosphere at last condensed into water and formed rivers and lakes and oceans while the dry land grew green with the lowest forms of vegetable life. By-and-by a temperature was reached which made animal life possible, and at once the coral insect began to build his strange masonry in the deep, and fishes splashed their finny oars as they started to explore the ocean. Age after age new forms of life appeared and old ones disappeared on land and sea, until finally man steps upon the stage of action and calls himself lord of creation. During all these periods the surface of our globe has been rising and falling like the waves of the sea. Vast ranges of mountains have been upheaved and continents have sunk beneath the ocean. Our earth at times has poured out floods of lava to relieve her internal fever and at others has shuddered in earthquakes from a sudden chill. We talk of the solid earth and think of the ground beneath our feet as something fixed and stable. But the earth's crust is now not more than a hundred miles thick—the merest shell around a molten core, seething and heaving with internal fire. In consequence, this crust is never at rest, but is constantly slowly rising in one place and falling in another, while at times an island suddenly rises in the sea and then as suddenly disappears; and occasionally, as we have reason to remember, an earthquake jars a continent and shakes a city into ruins. There is nothing permanent and stable here. Eternal change has kept creation's cradle rocking until now and will continue to shake the earth for ages yet to come. The final catastrophe, foretold in Scripture, when our globe shall be wrapped in a winding sheet of fire is rendered very probable by the discoveries of physical science. A time must come in the future from the process of cooling and contraction when another gigantic crushing in of the earth's crust will take place. Whenever that occurs it were easy for the continents to be submerged beneath seas of boiling lava, whose fiery waves will burn up every green thing and leave our globe a blackened, smoking slag.

I do not claim that the teaching of science and the Bible are identical. But while they differ widely in details there is a marked general agreement. Both teach that through evolutions and revolutions the earth and man have reached their present state, and that the process is not yet complete. Science digs out of the rocks the evidence that our globe has been shaken and shattered in the past and that it will be again, and Revelation looks up to God and cries; "Whose voice then shook the earth, but now He hath promised, saying yet once more I shake not the earth only but also heaven."

Again the passage implies that this change is a real progress from lower to higher forms and is in obedience to God's great law of creation. Just as a scaffolding is erected and within it the edifice is reared, and then, when the building is complete, the scaffolding is torn down and removed, so in the plan of unfolding creation as any form has served its purpose and become useless it is shaken down and disappears. Evolution is no discovery of science. It was taught in Scripture long before science dreamed of it. It was an inspired pen that wrote "First the blade, then the ear, and then the full corn in the ear." This regular progression from lower towards higher forms marks all the works of God. If we go back to the Mosaic account of creation we shall find that in general the scientific order obtains. Creation did not spring into being all at once at the fiat of God. First God created the heavens and the earth. But they were without form, and void and darkness was upon the face of the deep. It was simply a creation of the elements in a chaotic state. Next God said "Let there be light," and the darkness disappeared. Then came the gathering together of the waters and the division of the earth into land and ocean. Next came the creation of vegetable life—grass, herbs and trees. Then in due time came the creation of fishes in the sea and fowls in the air. Next in order came cattle and wild beasts and creeping things, and finally to crown the series God created man in His own image.

The record of the rocks and that of the Book are in strict harmony thus far. Dig down into the mountains and you shall find that the oldest fossils are vegetables, then comes marine animals, next birds, then beasts and then man.

Moreover the rocks will show that the unfolding of each type of being has pursued the same order. In the beginning God commanded each species to multiply, *i. e.*, unfold into all the varities and forms of which the species was capable. Just as to-day the oak is enfolded in the acorn, so originally God locked up the species with its endless varities in a single pair. From that primal pair the species was to be evolved, not haphazzard, but by a law of regular progression. Go ask the geologist if the oldest forms of life were not the lowest, and whether each in turn has not been succeeded by a higher and better form. The first plants upon our globe were flowerless ferns and rushes, and from these step by step the flora has unfolded until the earth to-day is covered with a robe of blossoms and the air is burdened with their perfume. The oldest animals were fishes with cartilaginous skeletons and without eyes, as much inferior to a salmon or trout of to-day as Noah's ark was to an ocean steamer of the White Star Line. The rocks are paved with animal and vegetable forms which are now extinct, but in every case the form that has vanished was succeeded by another of a higher order. The fossils in the mountains are the garments which nature has outgrown and has laid aside and they serve to show the humility of her origin and the progress of her growth.

Scientific evolution and Scriptural evolution are wide apart in details but in their general trend there is substantial agreement. Science starts with dead matter and supposes that it organized itself into some lowest form of life, and that from this first form were developed by natural law, without any creative act, in regular gradation, one form out of another until at last man was reached. It teaches that a plant produced a polyp, and a polyp a fish, and a fish a reptile, and a reptile a bird, and a bird a beast, and a beast a monkey, and a monkey a man. Scripture, on the other hand, starts with a separate creation for each class of creatures and then leaves the class to unfold under natural law into many branches, and perfect itself by passing through many forms. God created plants, fishes, fowls, creeping things, cattle, beasts and man, and endowed them with capacities to multiply varieties and improve their condition until the multitudinous species and endless varities of flora and fauna should be reached which people the earth to-day.

I submit that until the missing links between widely different species are found, the Scriptural theory is more scientific and rational than the Darwinian.

But while the two theories clash in regard to their teaching respecting the orign of living forms, they agree perfectly in teaching that from the beginning until now there has been a constant evolution and steady progress and improvement. Science expresses its faith in this truth by the phrases, "The struggle for existence" and "The survival of the fittest." Scripture epitomizes its teaching upon this subject by the declaration, "And this word, yet once more, signifieth the removal of those things which are shaken as of things which are made that those things which cannot be shaken may remain."

But the one great and all important teaching of this passage is that this system of change is not only a progression from lower to higher and better forms, but that it is steadily working towards a final result which shall be changeless and eternal.

Thus far science and revelation have marched side by side, but just here they part company. Science sees no purpose in nature but only a process. It recognizes no directing intelligence and knows nothing of a final end. Nature is only a system of endless mutation, evolution and revolution, with no God at the beginning and no outcome at the end. Science starts with a cloud of star dust floating in space and traces it until it becomes the solid ball which we call our earth. It follows matter then through countless transformations, each rising higher in order of being than its predecessor. It sees successively rising above the ground ferns, and flowers, and polyps, and fish and reptiles, and birds, and beasts, and at last man, highest and grandest of all. But then it sees man die and beholds his body decompose into its original elements. He who was the outcome of all the progressive changes of all the ages and to whose production all lower forms of life have contributed, science sees go back to dust to fatten the soil and nourish grass and grain and thus in turn himself become food for fish, and fowl, and reptile, and beast. It is as if nature should labor through millions of ages to give birth to a child and then turn round and devour it as soon as it was born.

Human reason revolts at such teaching and demands that for all this plowing and planting, and reaping, and threshing, there shall be some harvest garnered. It will consent to change through countless ages if at last something permanent shall be the result. It will agree that life shall pass through a thousand deaths and have as many resurrections if at last an immortal being shall emerge from the grave to die no more. But it utters an unmistakable and uncompromising protest against endless change to no purpose, and against living only for the sake of dying. If materialism can discover nothing which survives the death of man, then the deepest and strongest instincts of human intelligence must turn away from it disappointed and disgusted.

What science cannot discover, but what human nature craves and human reason demands, revelation comes to supply. It tells that "the earth [at first] was without form and void, and that darkness was upon the face of the great deep;" it tells of a deluge and of God's voice shaking the earth in the past, and that other convulsions await her in the future. There is a fiery baptism coming in which "the elements shall melt with fervent heat; the earth also and the things which are therein shall be burned up." But it does not stop there. There is a method in nature's madness. She has some worthy end in view. The transitory is to be succeeded by the permanent the temporary by the eternal. Listen to the bugle notes of revelation as they ring out over a world on fire. "Nevertheless according to His word, we look for new heavens and a new earth wherein dwelleth righteousness." Paul from the summit of inspiration lets his eagle vision sweep over the ages of the past and down the centuries to come, and then shouts in the ear of a bewildered world God's ultimate design: "Whose voice then shook the earth, but now he hath promised, saying, yet once more I shake not the earth only, but also heaven, and this word once more signifieth the removing of those things which are shaken as of things which are made that those things which cannot be shaken may remain." When the lightning and thunder are past we are to expect a purer atmosphere. When the blossoms fall we are to look for the fruitage. When the scaffolding is taken down we are to behold the edifice. When the chrysalis bursts its cerements we are to look for the butterfly rising on golden wings above its tomb.

The microscope and the telescope will make discoveries much farther than the unaided human eye can see, but science with all her instruments can behold only the physical. Beyond the power of the microscope and the telescope, beyond the power of the crucible and the subtle agents of the laboratory, inspiration discovers the spiritual rising like a Phœnix from the ashes of the physical. Man is the outcome of all natures working. He is the summit of the long and ascending plane of life. But the human body is not the man, and when it falls in death the man does not die. The body was only the crutches with which the immature spirit supported itself; but when the spirit can stand and walk alone you may bury the crutches out of sight. Don't look in the grave to find your departed loved ones. The disciples made that mistake more than eighteen hundred years ago; and an angel sent by God whispered to them loud enough for all succeeding ages to hear "Why seek ye the living among the dead? He is not here, he is risen." No human eye ever saw a man nor ever can. We see his features and his form, but these are only the house in which he resides. That something within which thinks and feels and loves and wills, is the real man, and him no microscope can discover, and over him death has no power. When the body falls in ruin he does not go down into the grave, but rises into a new and higher state of being. The physical is temporary and transitory, the spiritual is permanent and eternal; God has not wrought through all the ages for naught. "The mills of the Gods grind slowly, but they grind very fine." The material chaff and successive hulls which enclosed the precious kernel, one after another have been separated and removed, until at last the grinding is complete—this last covering of flesh and blood is stripped off—and there comes forth the fine flower of a spiritual existence as invisible as ether and as imperishable as God.

Not only does God through successive stages of perishing creations at last reach a stable and everlasting result, but human labor also, doomed to disappointment all through life, has the promise of imperishable guerdon at last. Our life work is not to travel round a tread mill and end just where we begun, though to the eye of sense this seems to be the only result of living. "We brought nothing into this world, and it is certain we can carry nothing out." So far as material possessions and worldly honors are concerned, we leave the world just as naked as we entered it. But be not deceived by appearances. While much of our life work can be shaken, and will be removed by death, something that cannot be shaken will survive and remain. If we acquire wealth in houses or land, flocks and herds, gold and silver, it will take to itself wings and fly away. If we win honor and fame, office and influence, power and place, they will slip through our fingers and soon all be gone. We may subdue and govern nations and build up splendid civilizations, but they, too, will pass away as a dream fades from memory. We may spend our lives in founding vast charities and cover the land with hospitals, asylums and colleges, and these also will crumble to dust as well as the people who are benefited by them. We may dig deep in science and literature and amass the treasures of mind. We shall thus secure something which death cannot destroy; but we shall find it a useless possession in the land to which we are going. The wisdom of men is foolishness with God, and future discoveries will render our present knowledge foolishness with man also. Hence it is written, "Whether there be knowledge, it shall vanish away." But all does not perish. The grave is greedy and devours much of human achievement, but there are somethings which even death cannot swallow.

Send a boy to school, and after he has mastered all the studies of the course, the institution may be burned down, the books may all be destroyed, even the knowledge acquired may be of no practical use to him whatever in his life work, but the thought power and mind discipline acquired are indestructible and will be his invaluable possession forever. So man's untiring search after truth all his life and throughout all ages, may or may not be rewarded with clear discovery. All his efforts and sacrifices to establish truth and right on the earth may be defeated, and over his failure error and wrong flaunt their black flag in triumph. But in his search after, and his labors for the true, there has been developed in him a love of truth which the crash of the universe cannot eclipse or destroy.

So also a life of righteousness may seem to be overwhelmed by injustice and hypocrisy, but above the dark waves of fraud will float like a white albatross the love of justice which is indestructible. Carlisle, the most rugged thinker of the nineteenth century, has said, "The great soul of this world is just. With a voice soft as the harmony of spheres, yet stronger, sterner than all thunders, the message does now and then reach us through the hollow jargon of things. This great fact we live in and were made by." Our life work is to get ourselves in harmony with the spirit of the universe. By lives of strict justice we create a hungering and thirsting after righteousness, so that it becomes our meat and our drink to do our Master's will. This love of justice once born can never die; it is one of the eternal verities in the life of the mind.

A man may spend his life in seeking after the pure and the good and never find them in the world nor realize them in himself. Holiness is a flower of rarer bloom than the century plant. Our best motives are seldom perfectly pure, but are almost always mixed with some dross. But though we struggle after holiness till death, and never reach it in its fullness, the effort has not been in vain. We have caught glimpses of the beauty of holiness and have fallen in love with it. That passion once kindled in the soul neither time nor death can extinguish. The love of holiness is the bed rock in all right thinking minds, so that to shake it would be to wreck the moral universe. And so of every other moral principle; right living begets in us a love for it which is stronger than death, and which remains untouched by the dissolution of the body and must be as eternal as mind. These several loves make up what we call moral character, and this is what remains unharmed of our life work when everything else is shaken to pieces. Not what we do, but what we become in the doing, is stamped with immortality. All that we have wrought out will crumble, perish and vanish, but what has been wrought in us is an "inheritance that is incorruptible, undefiled, and that fadeth not away."

Just as the loves in us of the true, the just, the right, the pure and the good make up moral character, so the ensemble of the objects of these loves constitutes our God. All that we know of God is that he is the embodiment of all that is just and true and good and holy. He is to us the focal point in which all moral principles meet, and the fountain head whence all virtues flow. And the loves which make up moral character are therefore none other than the love of God.

Let death with vandal hand strew all the universe with wreck and ruin, but let God and man and the love of God survive, and heaven is eternally secure. No matter where heaven is, God is everywhere; and wherever moral character can feast its love upon truth and justice, goodness and holiness, there is heaven as unshakable as the throne of the Eternal.

Let that which is perishable fall and vanish. That which cannot be shaken will remain. When the cities of earth in the last conflagration are tottering to their fall, above the fire and the smoke which envelope them will rise the gilded domes and glittering spires of the "city that hath foundation whose maker and builder is God." Death and darkness are not the end of all human existence. "Dust thou art, to dust returnest," was not spoken of the soul. Above earth's vast necropolis, over the graves of all the ages, spiritual man shall walk through the gates into the city and be forever with the Lord.

No honest labor in this universe is ever lost. Apparent failure and defeat, no less than success and victory, are chiseling character into the Christ-like. Death only ends the toil but cannot touch the finished work. "Blessed are the dead which die in the Lord. They rest from their labors and their works do follow them." Out of all this withering, dying foliage, comes at last a flower of fadeless, deathless bloom. Light after darkness, and life after death, is the song both of nature and revelation. Forward, brother, and be not dismayed. "Look not behind you, neither stay in all the plain. Escape to the mountain." "Unter die graben, oben die sterne." Beneath us are graves, above are the stars. "Here eyes do regard you in eternity's stillness. Here is all fullness ye brave to reward you. Work and despair not."

The Heroic Element in Christ's Sympathy.

By the Rev. W. Swindell, D D

Text —Luke xix : 7: "He was gone to be guest with a man that is a sinner."

The land of our Lord's birth, as it stands in the history of His life, impresses us as a great infirmary. As we follow the footsteps of Jesus through the streets of the cities and towns, or along the public highways of His native land, we feel as though we are walking through the corridors of a hospital. Wherever we go there are sick people— the blind, the lame, the halt, the withered, the leprous and the fever-stricken. We visit the Pool of Bethesda, and the steps of the pool are crowded with suffering people, who are waiting for an angel to trouble the water. For whosoever steps in first after the waters are troubled, is healed of whatsoever disease he may have. We go down to the pool of Siloam and a man approaches with his eyes bandaged with clay. He reports that a man named Jesus, spat upon the ground and made clay of the spittle, and annointed his eyes, and bade him go wash in the pool of Siloam and his sight should be restored.

The Saviour no sooner enters a house in Capernaum than the house is thronged with people, who implore him to heal their sick friends. The dwelling is crowded to its threshold so that a few tardy friends bringing a sick man upon a cot are compelled to climb the outside staircase to the roof. Tearing up the tiles they lower the man down through the roof into the presence of Jesus and implore Him to exercise His beneficent power and heal him.

The population of Palestine in the time of Christ seems to have been divided into two classes, people that were sick and people that were possessed with devils. As a matter of fact this was not its condition. The office book of a physician contains only the names of invalids, and if we follow the physician in his round of daily visitation, we discover that he stops only at houses in which there are sick persons. The explanation is simple and explicit. It is the business of the physician to prescribe for the sick, either to restore them to health or to alleviate their sufferings. In like manner we must reflect upon the fact that Christ came to this world on a mission of benevolence. He was dedicated to humanity. A great many questions that were unsettled when He came were not settled when He left the world. They did not belong to His mission. He came not to determine for us the antiquity of the universe, to furnish us with an exact chronology, or to construct for us any of the natural sciences that interpret to us the composition, relations or movements of matter. He came to seek and to save that which was lost.

On a visit to Wharton Street Methodist Episcopal Church, Philadelphia, Dr. Hanlon stood in the presence of five hundred little people and asked this question, "What did Christ come into the world for?" A child of six years of age lifted her hand in readiness to answer, when he repeated the question and she replied, "To help people along, sir." Was not that His work when on the earth, a man among men; has it not been the mission of Christ ever since, to help people along?—to help them along from sin to holiness, from darkness to light, from bondage to freedom? Work among the troubled in spirit or such as are engaged in a very great moral struggle requires large sympathy. The heart must be quick to receive the photograph of other people's sorrows and joys. There never was a heart that responded more promptly to human appeal than the heart of Jesus. But it is not the general question of His sympathy that I wish to discuss, but its staunchness or the heroic element in it.

However deaf others might be to the cry of the needy, none ever cried to Him in vain. The outcast, the forlorn, the oppressed, found in Him an instant and unfailing friend. This element of His character is nowhere more evident than in the incident of which the text forms a part. First, in the character of the man He befriended, "a sinner." A man is a sinner in one of two senses, either by the omission of a duty, or by the direct violation of a law. The mass of mankind are sinners in both senses. It is written "The soul that sinneth it shall die," and as all men have sinned, all are lost sinners. Christ died for all men, "that whosoever believeth in him should not perish but have everlasting life." But it was not in this generic sense that He used the term lost, He employed it in a special sense. For instance, some men are lost sinners by force of strong passions. Strong feelings and convictions are included in God's best gifts, but like many of His gifts they may be a blessing or bane as we use or abuse them, as we control them by reason and conscience or permit them to control us. If we throw the bridle upon the neck of our passions they will speedily ruin body and soul for time and eternity, but if they are curbed by intelligent judgement and strong moral sense, they will be powerful allies in achieving success, and be the support of hope and courage in the stress and peril of life. Take for example, Judas. He was born with the lust of gold in him. He loved money but not for the sake of the good that money would enable him to do, but for its own sake. As he laid shekel of silver upon shekel of silver, or shekel of gold upon shekel of gold, they furnished him with more satisfaction than an epicure could derive from the richest banquet.

On the occasion of the Saviour's visit to the house of Simon, Mary purchased a box of spikenard, and breaking it poured the contents upon the Saviour's head ; the precious odor soon advertised itself and her deed through the house. When Judas came in he detected instantly the value of the perfume and churlishly complained, saying "Wherefore was this waste, for this might have been sold for much and the money given to the poor?" But one who was present and wrote of it in this book has said of him, "Not that he loved the poor but because he loved the bag," while another said of him, "Judas was a thief." This inordinate greed of money so consumed every virtue in him, that at last he was induced to barter away the life of his Lord and Master for the paltry sum of thirty pieces of silver. When he could not retain the money but returned and threw it upon the table in the presence of the chief priests and elder saying, "I have betrayed the innocent," they ruthlessly turned to him and said "What is that to us? see thou to that," and he went out and hung himself; a lost sinner by force of the strong passion for money. With Absalom the case was entirely different. He had an inordinate love of power. He was born in a court, the son of a king. Shekels of silver and gold were the toys of his childhood. Alienated from the court and reconciled to his father by the kindness of the Prime Minister, he spent his idle time at the king's gate. As the people went out or came in he said to each man that had a controversy and whose case remained unheard "Oh that I were made judge in the land that every man which hath any suit or cause might come to me. All wrongs should be redressed and all rights secured." And so he stole the hearts of the people away from his father, and out of a great mob he organized a formidable army. He drove his father from the palace, and David became a fugitive, pursued by an ambitious and malignant son. Absalom would have gladly purpled his hands in the blood of his own father, if by stepping over the body of David he could have ascended the throne of Israel and heard the shout of the people "Long live King Absalom." He staked his ambition upon a battle in the neighborhood of the wood Ephraim. The day was lost. He fled through the forest on the back of a mule. In some mysterious way his head became entangled in the boughs of a tree, and as he could not release himself, he remained suspended in mid-air. When Joab learned of his plight he hastened to the spot, and finding the helpless rebel, he took three darts and thrust Absalom through, and the epitaph of Absalom was then as now. "He died as the fool dieth." He was a lost sinner by force of the passion for authority and power.

How many there are who are lost sinners by force of the strong passion for drink. The awful thirst for intoxicants, cultivated and strengthened by frequent indulgence, corrupts every noble attribute, weakens the human will, destroys all natural affections, until the sense of manhood or womanhood utterly destroyed, the helpless victim becomes a lost sinner by force of this awful appetite for drink. Have you tasted your first cup? Let it be your last. Now you may resist, but repeated indulgence may make you the sport of this dreadful passion.

Some men are lost sinners by force of worldly entanglements. While it is true that by the bias of our nature we are in constant jeopardy, yet there is frequently added the peril of circumstances in business, political and social life. They constitute a great net work in which multitudes are snared. A giant might laugh at any attempt to bind him by a spider's web, but let spider's web be added to spider's web, and enough of such flimsy threads will bind him as securely as though he were held by cords of steel. So in business partnerships, in domestic fellowships, in social and political clubs, in the countless relationships by which we are bound to each other in human society, men are the slaves of custom or opinion. They have not the courage, the spirit of self-denial or the defiance of worldly usage that are necessary to run the gauntlet of worldly criticism. Many who would turn to Christ and accept as imperative the ethics of the New Testament, are ashamed of ridicule. Many a young man, caught in the snare of a social club, feels himself too weak to resign from its membership or endure the scoffs of his associates.

Others are lost sinners by force of social laws. David preferred punishment by the hand of God rather than to fall into the hands of man. His verdict is that "The tender mercies of the wicked are cruel."

When once society has put its ban upon a man or woman how hardly can they be saved.

God made us to need human as well as divine sympathy. Many bereft of kindly encouragement from those about them, as leaden weights drop to the bottom of the sea, so they sink into sin, guilt, misery and death.

I stood in the jail in Allentown at the close of a religious service, and observed a man leave one of the upper cells with a bundle of clothes under his arm. I suspected that his term of imprisonment had expired, but his face was sad and his steps heavy, so that when he reached me I said "Has your term of imprisonment expired?" and he answered "Yes." I further inquired "How is it, then, that you feel so badly about it? you look more like a man going in than one coming out." I never can forget his answer: "Ah sir," he said, "You don't know what a world I am going into. When it is known that I have been in this jail I shall be received in contempt and suspicion by every one, I shall not be able to get a night's lodging in this town except in connection with some low bar-room."

How true his words. Suppose he had come to your house or mine and informed us that he had just been dismissed from prison, but wanted a night's lodging and a chance to begin a better life. What would we have done. We should probably have told him that the station house was erected for his benefit; or if we had entertained him, we should have put him in the uppermost story in the back room, locked the door, put the key under our pillow and then laid awake all night, afraid lest he should by some trick unlock the door and burglarize the house before morning.

The criminal classes are lost sinners by the very hostility of of society to their existence. The Saviour said, "How hardly shall they that have riches enter into the kingdom of heaven," and we may simply change the direction of his interrogation and say, how hardly shall they whom society has branded with its curse be saved.

It is stated that a man who now wears Episcopal robes and has attained to much literary distinction, was in an Illinois prison for six months. There he resolved that at the expiration of his term, he would live a true life. The day of his release he secured employment, but before twenty-four hours had elapsed some one informed his employer that he was an ex-convict, and he was instantly dismissed. He obtained work again in a few hours, for he was willing to take any honest task however lowly it might be, and again some one informed on him, and again he was sent adrift. Time after time he secured a position that would have afforded him an honest living, and each time some one was malignant enough to betray him. He one day answered an advertisement and found that the inquirer was a lady who owned a large factory. He said, "Madam, I might as well make a clean breast of it, I have been in prison and have obtained work several times and some one has secured my discharge each time, I want to be a true man, won't you give me a chance?" She replied, "Come to-morrow morning." He returned at the appointed time and she said, "I have concluded to give you a chance and hope you will not be false to my confidence." She gave him the lowest position in the factory and he was faithful in things that were least and finally came to things that were greatest, for she made him superintendent of her works. He soon obtained money enough to support him in college where he graduated with honor, then entered the ministry, and few occupy a higher rank among his brethren.

But we can see that where one rises to virtue and honor hrough such an awful struggle, multitudes sink in hopeless despair under the frown of society. Indeed, it is even true that society lays its fierce hand, not always an iron hand, frequently a gloved hand, on the poor struggling sinner, and holds him under the curse of his own sin until he is lost to all sense of honor, susceptibility and truth. But Christ came to save the lost. He is their friend. Let them cry to Him. He will not turn them away.

Second. The heroic element in the sympathy of Christ is further manifest in the circumstances under which Christ became this man's friend. Friendship frequently costs us no more than the formal salute by which we recognize a neighbor on the street. It means no more than the mere vibration of the air by which we hail in the morning or evening the faces that are familiar to us. But there are times in almost every man's life when friendship requires courage, patience and self-sacrifice. When to stand by a friend is to endure with him neglect, scorn, calumny and bitter persecution. This man was isolated from public sympathy, he was a tax collector but not unpopular on that account, though tax collectors have never been popular under any form of government. He was a Jew, but not hated on account of his race or nationality. The offense that he had committed lies in the fact that he was a Roman officer and as a Jew had consented to occupy an office under a powerful but detested empire.

The Roman government had planted its iron heel upon the Jewish nation and stamped out its national existence, for there was no Hebrew king in Judea or Gallilee. Herod was king. When a Jew therefore forgot his loyalty to Abraham and Isaac and Jacob and so far abandoned the God of his fathers as to accept an office under an alien empire, he brought down upon himself the contempt and hatred of every loyal Jew. No patriot Jew would walk with him on the same side of the street or sit down to eat with him at the same table. The Jews taught their children to spit in the very tracks of his feet. This man, by the office he occupied, was an outcast from Jewish society. His life only was sacred because guarded by the sword of Cæsar. Again the Saviour became this man's friend at the time when He was universally popular. We well know His life was not uniform, one day they would take Him and make Him a king, the next day they would cast Him from the brow of a hill headlong that they might destroy Him, but at this time He was in favor with all classes. He left the city of Cæsarea Philipi, at the foot of Mount Hermon, for the city of Jerusalem proceeding along the highway which forms the backbone of Palestine. His fame had preceded Him. The people came out of the hamlets and villages, down from the mountains and up from the valleys, hoping to see His mighty works or hear His wonderful sayings. The citizens of Jericho concluded to extend to Him a royal reception. It was then the metropolis of fashion. Jerusalem was the seat of religion. The preparation for His visit was so enthusiastic, that a special anthem was adopted with which to welcome Him. The children were trained to sing it. The excitement attracted the attention of Zaccheus. I fancy that as an old surly Jew visited the receipt of custom to pay his taxes, Zaccheus said, "I have seen groups of people throughout the city and evidently there is an unusual stir among all classes, why is it?" Then the old Jew deigns to answer him by saying "The Messiah is coming. He who has given eyesight to the blind, cured the leprous and even raised the dead, and whom we hope will restore the glory of Israel." On the eventful day Zaccheus emerges from the city gates before the crowd pass out and climbs a sycamore tree or Egyptian fig tree that stands by the wayside. He went out before the rest, for he knew they despised him and that on such a day the mob might turn against him and rend him. He sought the fig tree both because he was little of stature and to escape the observation of the crowd. Hiding himself in the leaves he must have said, "I can see and not be seen." Yonder comes the Messiah, and the children herald his approach waving palm branches and singing, hosanna. It is a great gala day and religious jubilee. The Saviour advances with the happy procession until He stands in the shadow of the overspreading tree and looks up into its boughs. Zaccheus says, "I am discovered and the Messiah is about to upbraid me even as others. He will arraign me for my disloyalty." The Master calls him, calls him by name, and the tax gatherer says, "Why He knows my name, some one has told Him all about me." But there is a tone in the Saviour's voice that reassures the heart of this wayward Jew. In it perhaps the first kind tone that had fallen upon his ear since his mother died, when as he laid his hand in her withered hand she said, "Zaccheus, be true to the God of your fathers," and he had pledged her his loyalty to those triple names that constitute the federal head of the Israelitish race. The Master says, "I shall abide at thy house." The tax gatherer instantly descends and joins himself to the Lord's company. Yonder they go, Jesus and Zaccheus. The elders of the church have silenced the happy voices of the children and tearing the palm branches from their innocent fingers have trampled them in the dust.

Yonder they go, the Saviour and the sinner. Passing through the gates of the city and pursuing one narrow street after another, at last they reach the home of the hated Jew and enter it. The crowd gathers without the door and murmurs. Murmurs as the wind murmurs through the pine forest before the wild blast leaps from its lair. Murmurs as the sea murmurs before the fermenting storm lashes its calm bosom into savage rage. They say, "It is too bad, too bad, we hoped to have given him a magnificent reception in the home of one of our loyal citizens, but he has gone to be the guest of a man that is a sinner."

I have no doubt that Zaccheus spread a rich banquet for Jesus. But as I look in upon the scene: Zaccheus reclines upon a divan there and Jesus rests his weary body upon a luxuriant couch here. The feast between them has not been touched, no pomagranate eaten nor a grape plucked from the stem. Both had meat that the world could not provide or relish. The sinner had found a sufficient Saviour. The Saviour whose one mission was to save men had found one soul weary of the world and wrong doing and willing to be saved.

The penitent sinner confessed his sin saying, "Lord I give half of my goods to feed the poor, and if I have taken anything from any man wrongfully I will return him fourfold," and Jesus answered, "This day is salvation come to this house for thou also art a son of Abraham." He was a son both by blood and faith descent.

We learn here not only the heroism of true friendship, but that the hardest heart may have one tender spot, that touched with Christian sympathy, may yield a fountain of penitence. This man had waited for a kindly word and touch. Jesus had touched the one spot that could be responsive to the claims of truth and righteousness.

I think of a day when I stood in a great garden. It was adorned with the works of the great masters in sculpture. A statue of a woman, fresh from the artist's chisel, had just been put upon a pedestal. The figure was life size, and the face shone with a joy that was without a shadow. Out of the rude block the sculptor had carved a face that was the embodiment of human satisfaction. Life mantled with eloquent fullness on her lips and sparkled in her glance. I gazed for an hour wondering at the great achievement of the artist, then turning aside in a by-path I cast one more look at an image that I might never see again, when, to my surprise, the face that I had looked upon was but a marble mask and behind the counterfeit was the real face. He who had made the marble gleam with the realization of the proudest hopes had made the real face so dark with sorrow and despair that not a ray of light could be seen on brow, or cheek, or lip. The eyes were lightless and every line of the countenance had fallen.

Oh, how many pass us on the street each day, some of whom sit in the evening at the same fireside wearing some disguise to shield an awful sorrow or dreadful struggle, longing again and again for a little sympathy, yet too proud and self-willed to ask for it. Why should we dole out our sympathy as a miser contributes to charity, even though much of what we bestow is wasted? If we were more bountiful in our kindness, here and there a human heart would receive it, and encouraged and strengthened by it, would feel that we are but the medium through which the love of God reaches them and be led to the feet of Him who never breaks the bruised reed or quenches the smoking flax.

Third. The heroic element in the sympathy of Christ is also indicated in the overflowing kindness that Christ bestowed upon this man. He went to be his guest, not to lend sanction to his sin, but to save the sinner. It is the Christ attitude toward every transgressor.

It was reported with great pride, that as the train lingered a few moments one day in Philadelphia, General Grant called an apple girl to him, and after purchasing some of her fruit, printed a kiss upon her brow. It was published as a mark of the great commander's generous nature and real sympathy for humanity. But infinitely above this is the gracious visit of Jesus to the house of this sinner. The King of Kings accepts the hospitality of a penitent rebel. He not only absolves him but abides in his house and assures him of His love and confidence.

The Saviour left the city next day, and as He looked upon it from the crest of some neighboring hill, it was a sweet satisfaction to Him to know that there was one sinner less in Jericho than when He entered its gates.

He who came to save men could only be supremely happy on earth in saving men.

8

When does a Christian strike his highest note of joy? Some one says it is when kneeling before the mercy seat, guilty and undone, in darkness and sorrow and despair, he receives the evidence of his pardon in the whisper of the Spirit, "Thy sins which are many are all forgiven thee." The rapture of that hour few, if any, have ever been able to describe. But it is not then. Another one replies it is in that moment when dissolving nature releases the immortal spirit from this house of clay, when the world recedes and heaven rises into view, then, victorious over death and the grave, the soul attains its highest joy. The dying hours of Christian people have been so glorious as to astonish beyond all expression the watchers who have seen their departure. But it is not then. But still another says it must be when the ransomed soul has passed through the gates of pearl, and realizes for the first time that heaven is secured. The battle of life is over. The journey ended. Temptation, sin, care, pain, sorrow, disappointment, disease and death, are no more. We have no language that can fully set forth the ecstacy of the first moment in heaven. But it is not then. Then it must be when the saint of God appears before the King eternal, arrayed in garments that reflect the lustre of the great white throne, then as he receives a harp of gold, a palm of victory and a crown of glory, honor and eternal life, it must be then. As he joins the choirs of heaven in celebrating the praise of the Redeemer, it must be then that he touches the highest note of finite joy. But it is not then.

Bear with me until I answer the question. A friend of mine, in passing down the road that skirted the bay, heard the cry of a man for help, and plunging through the foliage, he saw an upturned skiff and a man struggling for life. Looking up the beach he saw a boat; running to it, he found it loose and two oars in it. Pushing the boat into the stream and thrusting the oars into the water, he pulled for the drowning man. As he drew near to him he heard once more the gurgling cry of the man for help, and knew that he was sinking for the last time. Bearing with all his power upon the oars he drew them into the boat, ran quickly to the bow, but the man was gone. Thrusting his hand down among the bubbles he seized him, and succeeded in getting his helpless body into the boat. The form of the man was limp, his eyes set, and his lips livid. Hastily conveying him to the shore, he applied proper restoratives and was soon gladdened by signs of life. The eyelids dropped, the color of the lips began to change, and the man began to breath, but with great agony. After laboring with him for an hour the man opened his eyes, and with unspeakable gratitude slowly articulated these words: "You saved me." "At that moment," he said, "there came to me a feeling to which I had been an utter stranger. I had saved a man. It was a new joy and one that I cannot describe." Do you yet ask me when does a Christian strike his highest note of joy? I answer, it is when he finds a human soul sinking in sin and misery and he brings him to the foot of the Cross. When such a one with joy unspeakable and full of glory says, "By the blessing of God you were the instrument of my salvation," then the Christian reaches his highest note of joy. That was the joy set before Jesus, and the apostle Paul said of those brought to Christ saved under his ministry, "Ye are the crown of my rejoicing in the day of His coming."

Letter from the Rev. Joseph C. Mason.

OCEAN GROVE, N. J., October 30th, 1889.

REV. JOHN D. C. HANNA.

Rev. and Dear Sir:—Please accept my thanks for your kind remembrances, in regard to your late Centennial Services in Old Asbury. It would have given me great pleasure to have been with you and participated in the services, but my own precarious health and sickness in my family prevented. I am happy to learn that you had a good time, and that you intend to embody the proceedings in a volume which will, no doubt, be of great interest to the coming as well as the present generation. It is a very happy thought, and I wish you great success in the enterprise. I can hardly imagine that any thing I can say will add to its interest.

Permit me, however, to say, that I have always had a particular attachment to Old Asbury, indeed, to Wilmington Methodism. It was there, in 1838, that I was admitted into the traveling connection, having traveled Dover Circuit the whole of the preceding Conference year, under the direction of the Rev. David Dailey, Presiding Elder. Of the grand men who formed the Conference at that time but few remain, nearly all of them have been transferred to the church above.

At the Conference held in Asbury, 1842, I was ordained Elder by Bishop Waugh.

At the Conference of 1854 I was appointed to St. Paul's, Wilmington; at the succeeding Conference, 1855, I was appointed pastor of Old Asbury, succeeding that grand man Rev. Robert Gerry, who at that Conference, owing to failing health, was compelled to retire from the effective rank. He soon after passed to his heavenly home; his remains, with multitudes of God's saints, sleep in the graveyard connected with the church. Time would fail me to name the glorious men and women who then rallied around the a'tars of Old Asbury and made her walls rings with their shouts and songs of praise, the great majority of whom have been called from labor to reward.

REV. JOSEPH MASON,

Pastor of Asbury Methodist Episcopal Church, 1855-57.

At the Conference of 1861, after an absence of four years, I was appointed by Bishop Janes as Presiding Elder of Wilmington District. During most of the term of my Presiding Eldership I resided in the vicinity of old Asbury, thus renewing the pleasant associations of the past.

Suffice it to say, that as Pastor and as Presiding Elder, my relations with old Asbury, indeed, with Wilmington Methodism, were always of the most pleasant character. Among the pleasant reminiscences of those days was my acquaintance, indeed, I may say, intimacy and fellowship, with Bishop Scott, who then resided in Wilmington, one of the purest and best men who ever graced the Episcopacy of the Methodist Episcopal Church.

A hundred years of church activity, who can tell its results? What a beacon light Old Asbury has been! What thousands have been saved through her instrumentality! May her future be even more glorious than her past! Very truly yours,

JOSEPH MASON

Letter from the Rev. G. Oram.

2124 North Thirteenth Street,
Philadelphia, Pa., November 13th, 1889.

Dear Brother:—Hope you will excuse my tardiness in replying to your kind letter. My health at present will not permit me to go out any distance, consequently, I am unable to have a picture taken, and enclose one taken several years ago, and considered a good likeness. I feel great pleasure in the success of your Centennial celebration, and pray that the future of Asbury may be still more glorious than the past. Memory often calls to mind the pleasant days I spent at Asbury, the kind friends, many of whom have long since passed to their home in heaven.

As to myself, I can only say I am waiting the will of the Master for my dismissal to my eternal rest. But I know whom I have believed, and am persuaded He is able to keep that I have committed to His charge against that day. Remember me kindly to enquiring friends.

Sincerely yours,

G. ORAM.

REV. GASSAWAY ORAM,
Pastor of Asbury Methodist Episcopal Church, 1857-'59.

HISTORICAL PAPERS.

REV. W. L. S. MURRAY, PH. D.,

Presiding Elder of the Wilmington District, Pastor of Asbury Methodist Episcopal Church, 1883-'86.

"Then—Now."

By the Rev. William L. S. Murray, Ph. D., Presiding Elder of the Wilmington District.

Perhaps I cannot better bring before you the condition of society, the influence and teachings of existing churches, the difficulties under which Methodism was introduced, the doctrines it taught, the opposition it met, and the profound impression it made one hundred years ago and more, than by giving you a few extracts from the life of Benjamin Abbott, who, in 1779, ten years prior to the building of Asbury Church, resolved to visit the four weeks' circuit embracing Wilmington, Del.

On this circuit, as nearly as I can find out, there were at least twenty-eight preaching places, and it took twenty-eight days to reach all the appointments, preaching once or more every day.

Said Abbott: "Having been pressed in spirit for some time to visit Pennsylvania, and in the love and fear of God, with my life in my hand, it being a time when war was raging, I left my home in New Jersey. I crossed the Delaware at New Castle, and that night at early candle light preached at R. F.'s to a pack of ruffians assembled in order to mob me. One stood with a bottle of rum in his hand swearing that he would throw it at my head; but Mr. F. stood in the door and prevented it. If ever I preached the terrors of the law, I did it then."

"Two days after," he says, "I went to J. H.'s, where I preached chiefly to Baptists. There were two or three sheep here, but they were afraid to hold up their heads. As soon as I was through, I was attacked by several of the Baptists. I told them if God had foreordained such a certain number for salvation, and pre-ordained the remainder to damnation, it was vain for them to try to persuade me to renounce my principles, for let me do what I would, I was certainly as well off as they were, and laid before them the absurdity of such anti-scriptural doctrines."

On his way to another appointment, being a stranger, he stopped to inquire the way. The man of the house told him he was going to that place, for there was to be a Methodist preacher there that day; "and our preacher," said he, "is to be there to trap him in his discourse." A constable coming up, we set off and soon fell into conversation about the preacher, having no idea of my being the man, as I never wore black. The constable, being a very profane man, swore by all the gods he had, good and bad, that he would lose his right arm from his body if the Methodist preacher did not go to jail that day. My mind was greatly agitated. The more so because I was a stranger in a strange place where I knew no one. When we arrived at the place appointed, I saw about two hundred horses hitched. I also hitched mine and retired to the woods where I prayed and covenanted with God on my knees; if he would stand by me in this emergency, I would be more for Him, through grace, than I had ever been. I arose with a perfect resignation to the will of God, whether to death or to jail.

"When I entered the house, the man took me into a private room, and desired me to preach up war as I was in a Presbyterian settlement. I replied I should preach as God should direct. He was very uneasy and before the sermon renewed his request, but I replied as before. I followed him out and he said: 'Gentlemen, this house is my own and no gentleman shall be interrupted in my house in time of his discourse but after he is done you may do as you please.' I took my stand. The house was so crowed that no one could sit down. Hundreds stood about the door. The constable was only two or three feet from me who had sworn so bitterly. When he saw I was the man he had so abused on the way, his countenance fell and he turned pale. I gave out a hymn but no one offered to sing. I sung four lines and kneeled down and prayed. I arose and felt such power come over me that I was above the fear of either men or devils, not regarding whether death or jail should be my lot. I preached with great liberty. I gave them my authority for coming to them by telling them of my conviction and conversion; the place of my nativity and place of residence, also my call to the ministry. I told them I spent my own money and found and wore my own clothes, and that it was the love I had for their precious souls, for whom Christ died, that had induced me to come among them at the risk of my life, and then I exhorted them to fly to Jesus. No one offered me any violence, but they committed the next preacher that day two weeks to the common jail.

"At Father Boehm's meeting house the Lord wrought wonders, divers fell to the floor and several found peace. In family prayer the power of God came upon me so wonderfully that I lost both the power of my body and the use of my speech, and I cried in a strange manner. The people also cried aloud. Here I thought I should frighten them, being among a strange people of a strange language; but it turned out to the contrary. At my next appointment I found a large congregation. When I came to my application, the power of the Lord came in such a manner, that the people fell all about the house and the cries might be heard afar off. This alarmed the wicked who sprung for the doors in such haste that they fell one over another in heaps. The cry of mourners was so great I thought to give out a hymn to drown the noise, and desired one of our English friends to raise it, but as soon as he began to sing the power of the Lord struck him and he pitched under the table and there lay like a dead man. I gave it out again and asked another to raise it; as soon as he attempted it he fell also. I then made the third attempt and the power of God came upon me in such a manner that I cried out and was amazed. Father Bohem said, 'I never saw God in this way before.' At a late hour we went to get some dinner. About five o'clock a messenger came from the preaching house requesting that I would go there immediately for there was a person dying. We went without delay. People lay all over the house, up stairs and down. I went to the person said to be dying; she lay gasping. I kneeled down and prayed and immediately she was converted, arose and praised God. My next appointment was in a large store house, but the most dirty place I had ever been in. I had no stomach to eat, they were so monstrous filthy, and when in bed I was ready to be devoured with fleas and bugs. Here there seemed but little good done.

"After preaching at my next appointment, where the Lord laid to His helping hand, divers fell to the floor and some cried aloud for mercy, an old Presbyterian gentlemen attacked me and told me that it was all the work of the devil; that God was a God of order, and this was a perfect confusion. 'Well,' said I, 'if this be the work of the devil, these people, many of whom then lay on the floor as dead men, when they come to, will curse and swear and rage like devils; but if it be of God their notes will be changed.' Soon after one came to and began to praise God. I said to my old opponent, 'Brother, do you hear them? This is not the language of hell but the language of Canaan.' My Presbyterian opponent followed me for several days, until one day I was so exhausted from constant service and there was still a great opportunity to speak for God, that I said for God's sake if any one can speak for God, say on for I can say no more. My old Presbyterian opponent arose and began by informing them that he was not one of this sect, that he had never seen the power of God in this way before, and gave a warm exhortation for about three-quarters-of an hour.

"A young man was converted in one of our meetings. I turned to his mother and said, 'Thank God that you have this day a son born again.' His mother immediately cried out: 'Away with you; I want no more of you here. Whitefield was here, like you, turning the world upside down; I want no more of your being born again.' 'Mammy,' said I, 'were you ever born again?' 'Yes,' said she. 'When?' said I. 'When?' replied she, 'why when I was christened, and besides, I took the sacrament when I was fourteen years of age and was made a member of Christ's mystical body.' 'My dear mother,' said I, 'you were born blind and are so to this present moment.'

"The Quakers also took a great interest in my meetings, often marveled and wept under the power of God. They invited me also to speak in their school-houses. I was sometimes called an enchanter. At one of my meetings the power of the Lord struck a woman who owned the house in which we were worshipping. She cried to the Lord for mercy, but she was soon tempted that it was witchcraft and that she was bewitched, and must now leave her husband and children and follow me through the world. This she did for a few days, attending the meetings. At last the power of God came upon her. She fell to the floor and cried out: 'Lord, I have called Thy servant an enchanter; now I know it is of the Lord.' She arose and said: 'Now I can go home in peace;' and departed.

On his return after twenty-eight days' labor, he says: "I set off or home and went to Wilmington and preached in an old store house on the wharf. Some people went through the town and said there was an old sailor cursing and swearing at a terrible rate. This brought the people together from every quarter, and the house and wharf were crowded. Some wept, some laughed, and others mocked; some were awakened and came to me and inquired what they should do to be saved.

"During this round on the circuit twenty-four professed sanctification and how many more were justified I know not, but at Father Boehm's they informed me there were twelve. I left Wilmington and went to New Castle, crossed the Delaware, and returned home so much broken down that my friends thought I would never be able to preach again." But in the year 1789, the year Asbury dedicated the first Methodist church in Wilmington, Benj. Abbatt entered the itinerancy and continued therein until 1795, when he retired from the active work.

The foregoing extracts which I have read in your hearing from the life of Abbatt show,

First. That great wickedness prevailed in Wilmington, Del., when Methodism was introduced; that rum, rowdyism, profanity and evils of every kind were rampant.

Second. That Presbyterians, Episcopalians, Baptists and Quakers were leading denominations in the field. None of these, however, believed or taught the doctrine of the new birth, and all except a few Quakers bitterly opposed the doctrine of the witness of the Spirit and called it the heresy of Methodists.

Third. That Methodist ministers were opposed by both clergy and layity as well as by the civil authorities.

Fourth. That Methodism was hard to plant in Wilmington, and with this Bishop Asbury's statement at the dedication of Asbury Church agrees for he said, "Thus far have we come after twenty years' labor."

What hath God wrought? The little one has become a thousand. The leaven hidden in the meal has leavened the whole lump. "The seed truth which was shaken from invisible wings a century ago lodged in human consciousness and has become a bread-bearing tree for the nations." Then in the United States Methodism stood among the existing denominations number eight, but through the blessing of God it has advanced to the first place in this country, and far exceeds in numbers any denomination in this city. In the beginning Methodism was suspected, criticised, and opposed, but it has shown itself such a blessing to humanity that it is respected, honored and commended.

Then the diary of Ezekiel Cooper, June 13, 1786, states that a profane man claimed that it was not so much harm to swear as it was to take the Methodists' part. He also states that two Calvinist ministers appointed a day for fasting and prayer that God might remove falsehood and error from among them, looking upon the Methodists as guilty of both. Now many of the opinions published by sister denominations are flattering and complimentary. Chalmers said of us: "Methodism is Christianity in earnest," which has been translated, "Christianity with its sleeves rolled up." Another has said: "The Methodist Church, more nearly than any other, is representative of the nineteenth century American religion, not only by its moral earnestness, by its democratic spirit and its aggressiveness, but also by its directness and business-like methods."

Then Wilmington existed under Governor Penn's Charter. In January 31, 1809, the Legislature passed an amendment to it by which the borough boundaries were defined as follows:

"Beginning at the mouth of the Brandywine Creek, on the east side of the same, thence along the eastern and northeastern side of the same about two and a half miles to the Old Ford, above the head of tide-water; thence crossing the Brandywine westwardly and passing along the Old King's Road according to the several courses, then to the State Road leading from Wilmington to Lancaster; thence in a direct line southeasterly passing over the mouth of the riverlet called Stallcups Gut to the opposite side of the Christiana, west of the lower point of the mouth of the Brandywine; thence northeast to the place of beginning." Now the city contains about nine square miles. The only streets laid out were those from Water street to Mill (street,) and from Walnut to Pasture, now called Washington street. Then the inhabitants numbered about 2,335 (1790), now there are between sixty and sixty-five thousands. Then many broad and fertile acres yielded wheat, corn, and other produce which are now covered with palatial residences, fine churches and humming machinery.

In 1789 Wm. Jessop, a deacon brought up from Dorchester where he had served as junior preacher, was appointed first pastor of Asbury Church. Now we have twelve regular pastors and one missionary. Then the itinerancy was pure and simple, with no time limit removing pastors either in six months or in six years; now pastors are appointed for one year at a time, with the privilege of five years if deemed wise.

Then we had in Wilmington, Del., one little church 35 feet x 35 feet. Now we have twelve churches valued at $956,100.

Then no carpets were used, and the worshippers sat at night and heard the word of the Lord in the dim light of candles; now our churches are well furnished and lighted with oil, gas, or electricity.

Then we had no parsonage property; now we have six parsonages, five of them well furnished and valued at $17,250. During this year Mrs. Ann G. Perkins, a worthy and liberal member of Asbury Church, who had already given Scott Church a parsonage requiring only a small annuity, has also given Epworth Church a parsonage, also on the same conditions, valued at $2,000; making the total value of parsonage property now in our possession $19,250.

Then the great majority of colored people in the United States were slaves. The agency of the Methodist Episcopal Church in abolishing slavery has never been duly estimated and set forth, nor can it be in this paper; but a few extracts may be given to show how early she sought the liberty of the colored race.

In 1780 the Conference Minutes, under the form of questions and answers, presents the following: Question, Ought not this Conference to require those traveling preachers who hold slaves to give promises to set them free? Answer, Yes.

Question, Does this Conference acknowledge that slavery is contrary to the laws of God, man and nature and hurtful to society, contrary to the dictates of conscience and pure religion, and doing that which we would not others should do to us and ours? Do we pass our disapprobation on all our friends who keep slaves, and advise them? Answer, Yes.

In 1783 appears the following: Question, What shall be done with our local preachers who hold slaves contrary to the laws which authorize their freedom in any of the United States?

Answer, We will try them another year; in the meantime let every assistant deal faithfully and plainly with every one, and report to the next Conference. It may then be necessary to suspend them.

In 1784 the following questions and answers are given:

Question, What shall we do with our friends that will buy and sell slaves?

Answer, If they buy with no other design than to hold them as slaves, and have been previously warned, they shall be expelled, and permitted to sell on no consideration.

Question, What shall be done with our traveling preachers that now are or hereafter shall be possessed of slaves and refuse to manumit them where the law permits?

Answer, Employ them no more.

At the organization of the Methodist Episcopal Church in 1884 the following was enacted:

Question, Are there any directions to be given concerning the negroes?

Answer, Let every preacher, as often as possible, meet them in class. Let the assistant always appoint a proper white person as their leader. Let the assistant also make a regular return to the Conference of the number of negroes in society in their respective circuits.

We conjure all our ministers and preachers by the love of God and the salvation of souls, and do require them by all the authority that is invested in us to leave nothing undone for the spiritual benefit and salvation, and for this purpose to embrace every opportunity of inquiring into the state of their souls, and to unite in society those who appear to have a real desire to flee from the wrath to come, to meet such in class and to exercise the whole Methodist Discipline among them.

One hundred years ago we had forty-three white members and nineteen colored. Now we have no colored members belonging to white churches in this city, the colored members having withdrawn and built Ezion Church, founded 1805, one of the best church buildings in this city, valued at $45,000. They pay their pastor $1000; Presiding Elder $210; Bishops $20. Total for salaries for pastors $1230. They have a parsonage valued at $1800. This church is doing a grand work not only at home in establishing missions in this city, viz., Haven and Whittington, both of which are now strong churches, but she is also contributing liberally to the benevolent interests of the church abroad.

From forty-three white members we have increased to 3,506 full members and 945 probationers.

Then we had no Sunday-schools in Wilmington. Bishop Asbury, however, had organized the first Sunday-school in the United States in Virginia in 1786; but its influences had not yet reached Wilmington.

Now we have thirteen schools with 617 officers and teachers, and 6,088 scholars of all ages.

Then we had no Sunday school libraries, now each school has supplied itself with a library, some of which are very valuable.

Then Ezekiel Cooper and the early preachers lined the hymns and were very much attached to this method. So much was Bro. Cooper attached to it, that he gave his consent reluctantly to the first request to sing without lining. He writes in his diary: "I read off the Psalm and they then took it and sung it through, but I do not know that I was ever so beaten out by singing before; it almost put me out of order for preaching and I am afraid it hurt many in hearing; it was so light and airy that I thought it looked more like a place of vanity than of worship." In the society in Wilmington after the Tuesday night prayer meeting closed, a singing meeting was called to practice Methodist tunes dating from February 13, 1798. But these singing meetings did not always meet with the approbation of the pioneer preachers. Ezekiel Cooper writes concerning these meetings: "Such singing is strange to me—four parts all going at one time, and each part on different words. This is what they call the new mode of singing, and my opinion is, it was instituted more to please the ear than anything else." Now the new mode triumphs and there are but few congregations where all the four parts are not distinctly heard.

Then there were no musical instruments in the churches, and many remember the oppositions they met by many of our early ministers and laymen, but if this or the new mode of singing should seem to be a reflection on the wisdom and foresight of our fathers, let it be remembered that long before Methodism arose ministers of other denominations did not show superiority in many other things. In 1611 an English gentleman traveling in Italy, made this entry in his journal: "I observe a custom not used in any other country. They use a little fork when they cut their meat." He purchased one and carried it to England, but when he used it was so ridiculed by his friends that he wrote in his diary: "Master Lawrence Whitaker, my familiar friend, called me Furcifer for using a fork at feeding." That little two-tined article of table furniture brought about a fierce discussion. It was regarded as an innovation unwarranted by the customs of society. Ministers preached against its use. One minister maintained that as the Creator had given men thumbs and fingers, it was an insult to Almighty God to use a fork. Some of our fathers believed the organ to be satan's instrument, and left the church when it was brought in ; but now every church and chapel and mission school as well are all supplied with organs, and this is not all, for we have carried out the request of the Psalmist as expressed in the one hundredth and fiftieth Psalm :

> "Praise God in His sanctuary.
> Praise Him for His mighty acts.
> Praise Him for His excellent greatness.
> Praise Him with the sound of the cornet.
> Praise Him with the psaltery and harp.
> Praise Him with the timbrel and pipe.
> Praise Him with stringed instruments and organs.
> Praise Him upon the loud cymbals,
> Praise Him upon the high sounding cymbals,
> Let every thing that hath breath praise the Lord."

Then William Jessop, the first pastor of Asbury Church, received perhaps 20 £. or less than $100, for his year's service. The general minutes of 1788 state that many of the preachers did not receive more than 18 or 20 £. and several not more than 15 £ per annum.

Asbury Church one hundred years ago paid less than her youngest daughter, Cookman, pays, whose first Quarterly Conference has been organized since the last annual Conference when she promised her pastor $260. The largest salary paid by the Methodist church in this city is paid by Grace, $2,700 with parsonage. While the Methodist church in Wilmington one hundred years ago paid less than one hundred dollars salary, she now pays $14,007 in salaries to her pastors alone.

Then, as the following question and answer will show, donations and presents were all counted in to make up the salary :

"Question. What shall be done to get a regular and impartial supply for the maintenance of the preachers ?

"Answer. Let everything they receive, either in money or clothing, be valued by the stewards at quarterly meeting and an account of the preacher's deficiencies given in to bring to Conference, that he may be supplied from the profits arising from the books and the Conference collections."

Now no such law or custom prevails, and stewards who would

estimate a donation, and credit a preacher's salary with the same would be deemed worthy of being stewards no longer.

Then the whole church in the United States only contributed to the fund for the superannuated preachers and the widows and orphans of preachers 65 £, 5s. or about $325. Now Asbury Church alone contributes to this fund $150 annually and Methodism in this city $1,007 per annum.

Then we had no societies especially for the young ; now there are quite a number of societies, associations, lyceums, Chautauqua circles and Christian Endeavors, and last of all and largest of all, has been organized the *Epworth League*, under whose broad wings it is proposed to give all young people's societies a place and a representation through delegates in the board of control. Then in this country we had neither railroads nor steamboats. Bishop Asbury said: "I have ridden (on horseback) rapidly two hundred and thirty miles in six days, to redeem a day to write." Now we have railroads, steamboats and street cars run by steam and electricity, so that our Bishops often ride a mile a minute and have no difficulty in making two hundred and thirty miles in as many hours as it took Bishop Asbury days. Then the term Presiding Elder was first published in the minutes in 1789, and it would seem not without opposition in as much as it does not again appear until 1797, and he was appointed for one year at a time for a term of four years, now he is appointed one year at a time, and a whole term includes six years. Then the districts were without names. Wilmington stood at the head of a list of eight appointments which formed a district to which two Presiding Elders were appointed, namely, Henry Willis and Lemuel Green. Now the Wilmington district has forty appointments or charges. Then the Presiding Elder found his way to his appointment by Saturday and spent the whole Sabbath in one place, preaching and presiding over all the services of the quarterly meetings; now I am compelled to average three sermons each Sabbath and sometimes preach four times at as many appointments, and am compelled to ride in order to reach them sometimes twenty or thirty miles. It often seems to me that I am more of a riding Elder than a Presiding Elder.

Then none of the seven benevolent collections were organized and consequently no monies were collected or reported for them. The only effort made in the way of collecting money seems to have been for bringing up the deficiencies of preachers' salaries and for the conference claimants. *Now* we give to the Sunday-school Union $86 ; Tract Society, $85; Bible Society, $115; Domestic Missions, $210; Education, $197 ; Freedmen's Aid, $390 ; Church Extension, $521 ; Missions, $6,286. Then we had no Woman's Foreign Missionary Society, nor had we any W. H. M. Society, but now, like Ruth, the former gleans among the sheaves $709 annually, the latter, like Dorcas, provides for the poor to the extent of $612 per annum. The total amount given by our Wilmington churches to benevolences and published in our minutes annually is $8,511.

Then our preachers raised their voices against dram drinking, but there were no temperance societies ; now they abound. The best organized and most influential is the Woman's Christian Temperance Union which we heartily endorse and with which we actively coöperate, furnishing a large per centum of their membership. While there is great difference of opinion concerning methods, all agree that the only safety for the individual is in total abstinence ; for the State, total prohibition of the sale of intoxicants as a beverage by legal enactment. To secure the latter many methods are proposed. There is agitation everywhere. The earth trembles under the tread of approaching armies. The press publishes daily the victims of drink. The platform rings with the utterances of temperance advocates. The pulpit hurls its anathemas against this iniquity. In a thousand ways the sum total of the people's wrath is increasing against the day of wrath, for

> "There's a fount about to stream.
> There's a light about to gleam ;
> There's a warmth about to glow,
> There's a flower about to blow ;
> There's midnight darkness changing into grey.
> Men of thought and men of action clear the way.
>
> "Aid the dawning tongue and pen,
> Aid it, thought of honest men ;
> Aid it, paper, aid it, type,
> Aid it for the hour is ripe ;
> And our earnest must not slacken into play.
> Men of thought, men of action, clear the way."

We believe, while evil opposes truth, disputes her rights, crosses her track, impedes her progress, that truth has the right of way. One morning early I landed at the wharf in Philadelphia, and being in a hurry to get up town, elbowed my way through the crowd, and finally succeeded in reaching the street car, which was so surrounded by carts, wagons and footmen that it was difficult to see how we should proceed. However, when the driver gave the signal, the track was hurriedly cleared for we had the right of way. So the truth has the right of way. The liquor traffic may dispute it, but when the hour strikes, God will speak and prohibition's car will go forward. " It may not be in your way. It may not be in my way, but in God's own way" he has promised to answer prayer and watches from heaven's throne that the labor of His people shall not be in vain.

In the early days of Methodism our preachers were greatly persecuted.

Asbury was concealed, in time of the Revolution, at his friends, Judge White's, where he spent five or six dumb Sabbaths. Joseph Hartley was imprisoned in Easton, Md.; Freeborn Garretson was beaten and imprisoned in Cambridge, Md.; Gatch was tarred by a mob; Abbott and others were threatened at New Castle and in Wilmington. At Newport, Del., they were compelled to lodge with people of color, and were glad to find such accommodations. "But they choose rather to suffer affliction with the people of God than to enjoy the pleasure of sin for a season. Esteeming the reproach of Christ greater riches than the treasures of Egypt, for they had respect unto the recompense of reward. They, through faith, subdued kingdoms, wrought righteousness, obtained promises, quenched the violence of fires, escaped the edge of the sword, out of weakness were made strong, waxed valiant in fight, turned to flight the armies of the aliens. Some were tortured, not accepting deliverance, that they might obtain a better resurrection, and others had trials of cruel mockings and scourgings; yea, moreover, of bonds and imprisonment. They wandered about, being destitute, afflicted, tormented; in perils of waters, in perils of robbers, in perils by their own countrymen, in perils by the heathen, in perils in the city, in perils in the wilderness, in perils in the sea, in perils among false brethren, in weariness and painfulness, in watchings often, in hunger and thirst, in fastings often, in cold and nakedness; besides those things which were without, there was that which came upon them daily—the care of all the churches."

Once our church was poor, her hands were hard, her garments coarse and plain, her face soiled with the sweat of manual but honest toil her children came from the lanes and highways, from the field and workshop. Now she is rich. The cot is changed for the palace, the homespun for the purple, the rigging-loft for marble churches. She has money and social standing. She sits among the rulers of the land; she lives at court; she is in honor; her colliers and cobblers have become merchant princes, and her rustic converts have grown up families of refinement and culture. And with all, and best of all, she retains the old time power. Penitents still bow at her altars and rise rejoicing. The old doctrines are still faithfully proclaimed. Great as the success of Methodism has been there is yet a great work for her to perform.

I urge upon you the necessity of personal piety, the importance of united efforts in your home church work. Stand by your pastors, doing all possible to carry forward the work of the home church.

I also recommend a union of effort upon the part of all the Methodist churches of this city, for the purpose of extending Methodism in Wilmington. I do not believe that any city in the United States has greater reasons to boast of the spirituality and liberality of her Methodist laymen than Wilmington, Del. My almost seven years' experience as pastor and Presiding Elder in this city enable me to speak with knowledge of the facts. For during that time about $30,000 have been expended in extension, repairs and in the payment of debts on Asbury, St. Paul's, Brandywine, Scott and Epworth. About $20,000 have been expended in building Sweedish Mission, Silverbrook, Edgemoor, Wesley and Cookman. Besides the addition of two new parsonages and improvements in our preachers' homes to the amount of at least $5,000, making a total of $55,000. While our laymen have spent this amount and more on church property in the city, they have been frequently called upon by the regions round about. The requests by personal appeals and by letters for help have been so frequent, that they have become a great tax upon the time, patience and means of our laymen who give and give, (doubtless never turning any away representing a good cause without regret.) They do not give more than they ought, nor do I believe they have reached the limit of their ability, but their benevolence, in my judgment, could be more wisely and more effectively used, if, instead of diffusion, there should be system and concentration. For instance, every Methodist believes in the extension of Methodism, and especially do Wilmington Methodists believe in the extension of Methodism in Wilmington; therefore, let the city Methodism combine and resolve to concentrate their means, and help the neglected parts of this city to build one Methodist church a year. It can be done. It ought to be done. You have averaged for the last seven years about $3,000 annually in new church buildings without system, with it you could average $5,000 which would put a small church on a self-supporting basis, which would furnish a grand opportunity for young men who are now graduating at our theological schools, who would help solve the problem of reaching the masses. It might be well to set apart a day to be observed by the churches, when all might be informed through their pastors of the locality needing help, when they could make their contributions and be saved much time and annoyance. As Kingswood has already resolved to build, why not begin by concentrating our efforts first of all to aid her in securing a church. There are five other places already spoken of by different persons as proper locations for building Methodist churches. Bro. Joseph Pyle spoke on Monday of the needs of the district lying between Market street bridge and Wesley. There ought, also, to be a church near West Eighth Street

Park, one in the neighborhood of Cookman, one Thirteenth and King, and the improvements, new houses and Children's Home make a Methodist church a necessity in East Lake Park. $5,000 a year for the next six years will enable these communities to build six Methodist churches which will become centers of influence and power. In my judgment no wiser investment of capital for the extension of Christ's Kingdom and the salvation of souls, could be made by Methodist laymen. I plead for the poor. Extend to them a helping hand. Neither pauperize nor pension them, but help and trust them. Put upon them the responsibility. There is nothing like it to strengthen and build up. God trusted the fathers when they were poor. Many of their sons and daughters have grown rich. So that there are individual members of the Methodist church in this city who could do the work I have pointed out in the next six years if life should be continued with God's blessing upon their business, and be richer in spirit and happier in their life work. The generations to come would bless their memory. There is no higher tribute paid to man in the Gospel than that given by loving hearts, which said He hath built us a synagogue.

Standing between the century past and the century to come, I close this paper with the eloquent words of Bishop Foster as appropriate to Asbury Church as to the Methodism for which he wrote them:

"There is a glorious future for her of long and hallowed successes. Her brilliant morning is but the harbinger of a resplendent day. The marvels of her first century we may believe are but the precursors of the hallowed wonders she is to witness in the long march of the coming ages. If to-day suggests retrospect, it is no less a Pisgah of prospect. If it thrusts upon us memories of the struggles and victories past, it also beckons us on to the contemplation of the future. The *has been* is linked with the *will be*. As the old century recedes, the new advances. With grateful tears we wave farewell to the one and hold up signals of welcome to the other."

History of Asbury Methodist Episcopal Church.

BY THE REV. JOHN D. C. HANNA, PASTOR.

The century's history of Asbury Methodist Episcopal Church, of the heroic efforts for her establishment, of the sacrifices endured for her advancement, of the magnificent results of her endeavors, is written in glowing characters on high, but cannot be fully betrayed at these services. It is a thrilling record of long preparation, mighty struggle, glorious victory. Whose soul is so dead as not to be stirred by the associations of this place, by the memories of the heroic days that now crowd upon us. From the pulpit of this church have spoken pastors whose voices have been the most powerful of the century, and whose saintly ministrations among the people have comforted the broken-hearted, raised the lowly, and encouraged the desponding. Thomas Ware, Ezekiel Cooper, Joseph Rustling, Levi Storks, Lawrence Laurenson, Henry White, Joseph Lybrand, Matthew Sorin, Solomon Sharpe, Robert Gerry, Anthony Atwood, Thos. J. Thompson, Wm. Cooper, Geo. Quigley, and many other equally great men, living and dead, have made these walls resound with their mighty appeals to men to be loyal to Christ. The church records bear the names of such men of God as Edward Worrell, Samuel Saffington, James A. Sparks, Henry J. Pepper, Miller Dunott, John Hagany, Thos. Young, Samuel Wood, John Taylor, James P. Merrihew, James Guthrie, Charles Farra, Wm. R. Cotter, Wm. Beggs, and a host of other godly men and saintly women, who long since have answered the roll on high; while in the tombs about us, beside these already named, sleep Jeremiah Dodsworth, John Bosler, Edward Kennard, Wm. Torbert, Jr., John Guyer, Lewis Ashton, James Simpson, Jr., Charles Sanders, Edward H. Bonsal, George Young, David Webster, Curtis Rudolph, and other noted men and women of early Methodism who will have a triumphant resurrection when the trump of God shall sound. It is a great privilege to be permitted to gather here to-day to trace the feeble efforts of this society before this church was built, and review the dealings of God in century past.

Wilmington Methodism was born in 1766 or '67. At this time Capt. Thomas Webb, an officer in the British army, came from Philadelphia to Wilmington and preached under some trees near the corner of King and Kent streets (now King and 8th). This remarkable man, wherever he went, must have attracted great attention. Clad in the uniform of King George, but owning a higher allegiance to King Jesus, described by John Adams as "one of the most eloquent men he ever heard," still in the prime of life, preaching the heart-moving, all-embracing Gospel of the Methodists, no wonder he had earnest listeners whenever he preached, and stirred the souls and fortified the courage of the followers of Wesley in these days of constant strife. It does not require a vivid imagination to see him more than a century ago, within a few squares of this place, preaching the first Methodist sermon ever heard in Wilmington. The crowd gathered under the trees, study with curious interest the peculiar preacher delivering his strange truths: one eye blind, covered with a green shade, the other flashing fire or melting into tenderness as he presents the many-sided Gospel, his voice ringing out over the commons, his mien martial, his soul fearless, his form dilating under the marvelous power of the matchless truth, he is a fit messenger of God, and a man of whom we may well be proud as the founder of Methodism in our city. In these services John Thelwell, who kept a public house near the Lower Market, officiated as clerk and set the tunes to the hymns given out by Capt. Webb.

After these meetings had been held under the trees for a while, the first assemblage of Methodists worshiped in an upper story of Capt. Joseph Gilpin's storehouse on King street wharf. Here they remained a short time, until invited by John Thelwell to occupy his school-room. This staunch Methodist and unswerving friend of the church, and his daughter Deborah, or Miss Debby as she was called, had commenced teaching at the foot of Quaker Hill, but were soon promoted to the little Senate Chamber over the Market House. To this building, on the southeast corner of King and Third streets, afterwards used as a chair manufactory, where the office of the Daily Republican now stands, the Methodists accordingly moved. Meetings were also occasionally held at the cedar cooper shop of Mr. Geo. Witsill, on Water street below Main (now Market). Sometimes the preachers administered the word in the upper and lower Market Houses.

It was in Mr. Thelwell's school-room, however, that the society obtained its first formation. John Thelwell, Deborah Thelwel, his daughter, Henry Colesbury, Betsy and Sarah Colesbury, John Miller, Thomas Webster, William Wood, I. Jaquet, George Witsill, David Ford, Samuel Foudry, James Bell, and others, were among the earlier members.

At this time the society was connected with Chester Circuit, and persons as distant as Bethel held their membership at Wilmington. The preachers appointed to Chester Circuit preached at Wilmington in their regular tour of their work. Many men of note preached Christ with power to this small society in those early days. John King, in 1769, was appointed to labor in and about Wilmington. In 1772 Francis Asbury preached for the first time at Wilmington to a few persons. In 1780 Benjamin Abbatt, in his regular monthly round of a circuit of more than 28 appointments, and extending from the Delaware to the Susquehanna, and from New Castle far up into Pennsylvania, found his second appointment at Wilmington. He preached at the dwelling of J. Stidham to a small but attentive congregation, some of whom were very happy. One woman lay under the Divine power for three hours, and said God had given her a clean heart. She continued to cry, "O, Daddy Abbatt, how can I live! O that I could go to Jesus." The rejoicing was continued all night. On his second round he preached in the old storehouse of Joseph Gilpin's, on the wharf, to which reference was before made. Mr. Abbatt says in his journal: "Some people went through the town and said there was an old sailor cursing and swearing at a terrible rate. This brought the people together from every quarter, and the house and wharf were crowded. Some laughed, some mocked, and others wept; some were awakened, and inquired what they should do to be saved. I told them to look to Jesus."

Celebrated among the pioneers of Methodism was Harry, the black traveling companion and servant of Francis Asbury. "He was small, very black, keen-eyed, and possessing great volubility of tongue. Although so illiterate that he could not read, he was one of the most popular preachers of the age." Harry preached once, at least, to the Methodists of Wilmington. On the occasion of one of Asbury's visits to this charge, it was announced that the Bishop would preach. Methodism was most unpopular here in that day, and many would have felt much more disgraced at being seen at a Methodist meeting, than to have been caught in a bar-room or on the race track. But as the Bishop was to preach, a number of citizens, who did not usually attend the meeting-house, concluded to go at least this once. When they arrived, the room was crowded, and many stood outside. They were compelled, therefore, to take a position from which they could not see the speaker, though they could hear distinctly every word. For some reason, Harry was put up to preach, and these visitors standing outside, were carried away with what they supposed to be the Bishop's eloquence. Before they left the place they complimented the speaker by saying with much enthusiasm, "If all Methodist preachers could preach like the Bishop, we should like to be constant hearers." "The Bishop," exclaimed a by-stander, "why, that was not the Bishop, but the Bishop's colored servant that you heard." This only served to raise the Bishop higher in their estimation; "for," they reasoned, "if such be the servant, what must the master be." The fact is, Harry was a much more popular speaker than the Bishop, and could always attract as large audiences as the Bishop, and frequently larger.

Besides Bishop Asbury, who always took a great interest in this struggling society, and often preached here, Dr. Thomas Coke, Richard Whatcoat, and other distinguished men of the early times, made them occasional visits. Indeed, Richard Whatcoat was Presiding Elder of the district in which Wilmington was included in 1790, the year after the church was built.

In 1785, a few days after the organization of the Methodist Episcopal Church, a revival of religion blessed the Methodists of Wilmington. Thomas Coke visited the Peninsula after the adjournment of the Christmas Conference, and records in his journal that when he visited Wilmington, a revival was in progress. Doubtless, the addition then made to the membership, crowded the humble room in which they still held their meetings, and led them to discuss the propriety of having a Methodist meeting house in this city.

In the period from 1766 or 1767, when Captain Webb first preached at Wilmington, to 1789, when the church was built, there was a small but heroic band of men and women, who, in spite of opposition and persecution, maintained the faith as preached by the Wesleyans. The history of their struggles to continue their society, of the trials they endured and the shame they suffered, of the devoted men, who, without home, comforts, or salary, ministered to them in holy things, would, no doubt, make a thrilling story, but no complete account has been left of these early times. Enough light comes from the general history of early Methodism to show us that the fathers and mothers of this church, were no less heroic than were those whose names are more conspicuous in history. On our mind is imprinted the picture of a little band, numbering 10 or 12 at one time, and never more than 40, toiling against the enmity of the world about them, facing the malice of men and devils, regardless of sneers, obloquy, and shame, until at last their faith is rewarded, and one Sabbath morning, a hundred years ago, they sit in their own church, with their beloved Bishop before them preaching the dedicatory sermon, and their hearts all aglow with gratitude to God for his goodness, while they sing,

"Here I'll raise mine Ebenezer,
Hither by Thy help I'm come ;
And I hope by Thy good pleasure,
Safely to arrive at home."

On May 12, 1789, a lot of ground near the south east corner of Walnut and Third streets was purchased from Caleb Way and Sarah, his wife, for the sum of £105, for the purpose of erecting thereon a house of worship. It was conveyed to the following persons as trustees, viz: H. Colesbury, John Miller, Thos. Webster, John Thelwell, Samuel Foudry, Richard Sneath, Geo. Witsell, James Bell and John Jaquet, Jr.

In 1823, the society bought from William Simmons, through Edward Worrell, who afterwards made a liberal gift to the church on this purchase, a house and lot on the south east corner of Walnut and Third streets for $405. The church lot was further enlarged in 1838 by the purchase of a piece of ground south of the church property for $675. The cemetery then had the same dimensions as at present. The Rev. J. Rustling says in 1834: "The ground at the corner of Walnut and Third streets, after furnishing a situation for the church, the school-house and the sexton's house, serves as an eligible place for interment for the different families connected with the society. It lies eastward from the buildings, (enlarged, as we have seen in 1838,) and gradually declines toward a small stream that winds its way to the Christiana River." Subsequently a sewer took the place of the stream, and a stone wall was extended along the east and south boundries, and the ground graded. "In this ground," continues Mr. Rustling, "repose, under their respective grassy hillocks, the ashes of many who were the original members of the church, as well also as of many who have since occupied their places. Here liethe Colesburys, Thelwells, |Witsills, Woods, Whalers, McLanes, Joneses, Worrells and many others. The mortal remains of I. Jarrell, once a distinguished itinerant minister, rest in this field of the tombs. Here, likewise, are portions of the families of several ministers, who from time to time officiated in the church. Miller, Kendale, Smith, McCombs, Wiggens,

Rustling and other names are here represented. Several of those last mentioned lie near the east end of the church, and some of the former lie under it, the building by enlargement extended over their graves."

It was on this lot of ground that in 1789, less than four years after the organization of the Methodist Episcopal Church, the society proceeded to rear a house for the worship of God according to Methodist usages. It was a plain and unpretending structure. No one then dreamed of the future glory of Methodism, but what a harvest has resulted from this timely planting! The building which stood back 10 feet from the building line, fronted as now on Walnut street, and was about 35 feet square, with a gallery in the west end, and a peculiar old-fashioned, high pulpit at the east. This pulpit was about 4 feet wide, with its floor 5 feet above the main floor. On the north side was a door to which five steps led, and the preacher shut himself in after mounting to this elevation. The south side of this box-pulpit was closed, and there were no steps on that side. Edward Worrell said, because of its one-sided appearance: "That it reminded him of a crab with but one leg," and offered, if permitted, to put steps on the south side. The preacher had a kind of inclined shelf in front of him, 4 feet high, so high that if he stooped, he could not be seen, and yet not high enough to prevent him pounding the Bible while he expounded the truth. Below the pulpit floor, it was open to the floor of the church, making a sort of open cupboard. In this the leader of the singing sat, and when the hymn was announced from above, after the hum of his tuning fork had died away, he came out from this retreat and led the music; when the hymn had been sung, he retired to the same quarters until needed again. John Thelwell was the first who thus literally sat at the preacher's feet, and Samuel Sappington enjoyed the same honor for many years. It was not till 1840 that a modern pulpit was introduced. The seats were simply a board bench with a single-rail back. A partition 4 feet high ran down the center of the church to divide the men from the women. When services were in progress the members of one sex were completely hidden from the members of the other. This partition was even continued through the front yard, where a fence 7 feet high extended from the church to a brick wall of the same height, that then stood in front of the church. A lady and gentleman coming to church together separated on the pavement, and entered through their respective gates the church yard, nor did they see each other again until, the service being over, they met again on the pavement.

In the Summer of 1789 the corner-stone of the church was laid. John Lednum, in 1860, met Mr. Harris, then 84 years old, who said he well remembered the laying of the corner-stone of the first Asbury. "The preacher," said he, "knelt upon the stone, which was laid in a large deep hole prepared for the purpose, and offered up prayer. This, with the singing of a hymn, constituted the religious services of the occasion." Wm. Jessup was the stationed preacher at that time, and Henry Willis and Lemuel Green were the Presiding Elders of the district, which then extended from the Delaware to the Ohio Rivers. It was probably one of these brethren who laid the corner-stone.

It was here that 100 years ago to-day Francis Asbury came to dedicate the first Methodist church of Wilmington. It was a time of thrilling import to that little band of early Methodists, it is a time of great interest to us, their sons and daughters, who look back over the century. There were gathered the men and women who for 20 years and more had struggled with open enmity, secret slander, vile abuse, sneers and persecution to preserve the faith delivered to them by Capt. Webb. There were the men who, because they taught that all men might be saved by the atonement of Christ, were derided as free-willers; because they declared that man could be saved from all sin in this life, were ridiculed as perfectionists; because they testified that a man might know his sins forgiven, awakened the bitter enmity, the wicked revilings, and the unjust violence of the formalists about them, and because they dared defend these great doctrines of Methodism that are now preached from all the pulpits of the land, their lives were put in jeopardy every hour. On the lower floor most of the 43 white members were gathered, thrilled with the eloquence of the occasion, scarcely believing that the church was really theirs, while up in the little gallery, not less interested and perhaps more demonstrative, were the 19 colored members who had cast in their lot with the despised Methodists. Here, under the pulpit, sat John Thelwell, older in years, of course, and older far in experience and faith than when he pitched the tunes for Capt. Webb under the trees twenty years before. At this time his voice is heard performing the same office for Bishop Asbury, while the voices of the little company, blending in sacred song, sound out upon the solemn stillness of that Sabbath morn a prophecy of the song almost unceasing that should be heard in the coming century. On the right and left of the pulpit, in the old-fashioned amen corner are the oldest members of the church, the mothers of Israel, in plain garb and peaceful faces upturned on one side of the pulpit, and the fathers with words of encouragement for the preacher and gratitude to God in their souls, on the other side. Long before the hour of service, a throng of people, some drawn by curiosity, some by love, might be seen wending their way to this spot on which stood the unpretending meeting house, until when the services commenced it is filled in every part.

But the center of this humble scene is Francis Asbury, standing to deliver the first gospel message heard in these walls. It would be delightful, could we draw the likeness of this great man as here a century ago he stood. It is known that in life he was very shy of having his picture taken. "Only by his good friend, Mr. Cannon, was he trapped into it, and then he fell a victim to his compassion. Mr. Cannon offered to make of a fine piece of velvet which he possessed, a vest for each of his preachers if Mr. Asbury would sit for his portrait. Asbury could not refuse such terms, and to this pleasant trick of the good Methodist tailor, are we indebted for the best, if not the only, reliable, original likeness of our great and good bishop." There he is as he looked as he stood in the little pulpit here a century ago, "erect, sinewy, with flesh of iron firmness, and nerves of steel; his countenance open, his head ample and well poised, eyes steady and mildly expressive, lips compressed, chin well set, his hair cut square across his forehead, and flowing gracefully behind his neck, he stands before us in the prime of manhood, just in his 44th year, thoughtful, religious, self-contained," a born leader of men. Let us pause a moment to look upon another picture of this great man, drawn in part by the pen of Prof. Little at the Centennial Conference of 1884: "He had a robust figure, a face of blended sweetness and severity, an eye that saw far more than it revealed, a voice steadied by an iron will, but tremulous with feelings that sometimes shook his soul as a reed is shaken by the wind. He had none of Robert Williams' wild earnestness; he was without the charm of Robert Strawbridge, or the gentle harmlessness of Richard Whatcoat. He had not the thorough humanness of Jessie Lee, nor the mystical tenderness and strength of Freeborn Garrettson.

> 'Thy soul was like a star, and dwelt apart;
> Thou hadst a voice whose sound was like the sea,
> Pure as the naked heavens, majestic, free,
> So didst thou travel on life's common way
> In cheerful godliness, and yet thy heart
> The lowliest duties on herself did lay.'"

The son of an English gardener, he came to America when 26 years of age, to do the work of a missionary among his own race on this side of the water. Coke crossed the ocean eighteen times, but Asbury never went back home again, not even "to see his aged mother for whom he would have sold his last shirt, and parted with his last dollar." He had but one work—to win America for Christ. "He traversed this land for nigh a half century amid heat and cold, rain and sunshine, often destitute of food and clothing and shelter, and could often say with Wordsworth's wanderer,

'Homeless near a thousand homes I stood'

He was not a hater of beauty, much less of beautiful women, whose refined sense and affection render home the fairest and happiest domain of earth. But he was homeless, wifeless, like Paul, the apostle, for the kingdom of heaven's sake. Methodism was his second mother, his only wife, his riches, his home, his inheritance, his legacy, his all. He refused to bind a woman to his life of sacrifice, and the man whom little children ran to kiss and hug, was buried in a childless grave. He never shrank from danger or hardship, but his life was one of continuous toil, until at last rest itself could yield him no repose. A sort of spiritual Cromwell, compelling obedience at every cost to himself as well as others, Asbury could have broken his mother's heart to serve the cause for which he died daily."

This was the man who stood here one hundred years ago preaching God's word to the little flock, and who, as he dedicated in his Master's name their modest church, looked back over the struggles of these heroes, and said: "Thus far have we come after more than twenty years' labor." What an auspicious beginning! Do you wonder that this man stirred the infant society into a closer walk with God, and increased fidelity to Methodism? Who doubts that the imprint of that hand is felt upon the church to-day.

Though the Methodists now had a meeting house of their own, still the difficulties against which they had been contending for twenty years, were not removed. They seem, indeed, from the time of the building of the church to many years subsequent to have increased. The fluctuations of the membership show the struggles through which the society was passing. The 43 white members found upon the church-roll in 1789, though they had become 93 in 1791, when Thomas Ware was pastor, were reduced to 40 in 1796, during the pastorate of John Vanneman, and, though in several previous pastorates, there were over a hundred white members, yet as late as 1808, in Wm. Bishop's pastorate, but 99 were reported to the Conference. After that the society with a few fluctuations grew steadily.

In 1811, in consequence of this continuous increase, it was deemed necessary to make the first enlargement of the church. The wall where stood the old-fashioned high pulpit, was taken down, and moved 20 feet eastward, making the church 55 feet long by 35 feet wide.

During the 22 years between the building of the church in 1789, and its first improvement in 1811, despite the bitter opposition to the Methodists from all classes of people, the business of the society was transacted in a most careful manner. From the time the meeting house was erected to at least 1800, it was almost at the risk of their lives that our fathers and mothers repaired to this place to worship God. Thomas Ware, a great and good man, was pastor here in 1791, two years after the church was built. In his autobiography he refers to his work at Wilmington in these not very complimentary words: "This was my first station; but I sighed for the back-woods, which was paradise to me compared with this suffocating borough, infected with a mystical miasm on the subject of religion, which had a deleterious effect on many, and especially on the young. They had imbibed this moral poison until it broke out in supercilious contempt of all who were by one class denounced as hirelings and will-worshipers, and by another as free-willers and perfectionists. Hence, the house in which we worshiped was surrounded by hundreds of these sons of Belial night after night, while there were scarcely fifty within; and such were their character and conduct that females were afraid to attend our meetings at night, and we had no alternative but to commence service in time to dismiss the congregation before dark. Gladly would I have exchanged this, my first station, for the Western woods. I had, however, the pleasure of numbering among those of my charge some of the excellent of the earth, and much satisfaction in marking their growth in grace."

On September 23, 1800, the male members of the church were called together to take steps to prevent the further depredations of this mob. Because this gathering enables us to get a clear picture of the times, and because we may thus see the advancement in public sentiment in 80 years, I record in full the minutes of this meeting. Can it be possible that less than a century ago, in a country enjoying unusual freedom, in this our own city, such a meeting was a necessity? The proceedings are as follows:

"WILMINGTON, September 23, 1800.

"At a meeting of the male members of the Asbury Church in the borough of Wilmington, convened for the purpose of consulting what means would be best calculated to prevent in future the collecting of mobs and disorderly persons, from disturbing our public and private worship, which has been a growing evil since the year 1790, at which was present Caleb Kendall, preacher; Samuel Wood and George Jones, stewards; Allen McLane, John Thelwell, James Osborn, William McClung, Henry Witsel, James Payne, and Edward Worrell. After appointing Caleb Kendall to the chair, and Edward Worrell clerk, the following resolution was entered into:

"WHEREAS, We have been long and grievously persecuted, and often interrupted in our public and private worship of Almighty God, we deem it highly expedient that some method should be adopted to protest against the insults of a relentless mob, and prevent in future the disorder that is often occasioned by the more decent part of the congregation.

"*Resolved*, That it is necessary that there be a committee of three persons appointed whose business shall be to take such measures as they (with the advice of a counsel) may think best calculated to prevent in future the evil complained of.

"*Resolved*, That Allen McLane, Edward Worrell, and James Payne, be a committee to carry into execution the foregoing resolution.

"In consequence of the foregoing meeting, the following notice was published in the newspaper called the Monitor:

ADVERTISEMENT.

"The male members of the Methodist Episcopal Church who worship in the borough of Wilmington, assembled last evening to take into consideration the necessity of adopting such measures as may in future deter the infidel rabble from disturbing them in time of worship, which they have been in the habit of doing for some time back, by breaking the windows, stoning the preachers, casting nauseous reptiles, insects, and other filth in at the windows among the female part of the congregation, and otherwise intruding on the order of their church, in violation of the most sacred laws of a free people, which privilege all persons to worship Almighty God agreeable to the dictates of their own conscience.

"After maturely weighing every circumstance, and duly considering their repeated grievances, it was determined that, should they hereafter meet with any interruption at their place of worship, from any person whatever, resort will be had to the laws of the state, and prosecution commenced against the offenders."

What effect this action had cannot be determined by the records, except by their silence. Nothing more is said about the society being persecuted. The only actions in regard to order after this time, are such as might be passed by the church to-day, such as the preventing of standing in the vestibule, crowds upon the sidewalks, occasional rowdyism, and such like. We judge, therefore, that after this resolute action in 1800, our church enjoyed comparative quiet, and was not seriously molested.

While, however, these unpleasant demonstrations on the outside were thus quieted, others on the inside were yet to be quelled. In 1805 Asbury Church had upon her records about one hundred colored members. The classes were held on the floor of the church, sometimes two or three classes being held at the same time in the same room. Among others who were thus privileged were the one hundred colored members. That they did not believe in an undemonstrative Christianity may be gathered from an action of the trustees on June 19, 1805, when a resolution was passed which in few words brings before us the noisy scenes enacted here in these primitive times. It reads as follows:

"WHEREAS, In consequence of meeting the classes of the black people on the lower seats of this church, a number of the benches have been broken, and the house so defiled by dirt, &c., as to render it unfit to meet in, and if any longer tolerated, more injury may be sustained; wherefore it was

"Resolved, That no black classes shall hereafter meet on the lower floor of Asbury Church, and if they refuse to meet in the gallery, the sexton inform them that the door will not be opened for their reception, and furthermore, the leaders of the same are requested to respect this resolution and govern themselves accordingly."

On Sunday, April 28, 1800, Dr. Thomas Coke convened the male members of Asbury Church to draft an address to the General Conference, soon to be held at Baltimore, to adopt some plan to secure pecuniary aid for the married preachers, to prevent in future so many leaving the traveling connection. On Monday evening John Thelwell, Samuel Wood and Edward Worrell, who had been appointed a committee to draft the address, reported the following, which was read to the society by Dr. Coke and signed by all the male members:

"WILMINGTON, April 29, 1800.

"To the members and preachers in General Conference assembled at Baltimore:

"As a small part of those composing the family of which you are the stewards, feeling in common with you and our lay brethren in general, an earnest desire for the prosperity of Sion, and seeing her often linger for want of help, it is with the deepest concern that we have seen for a considerable time so many of our aged, and some of the most useful married laborers, are no longer working in their Lord's vineyard for want of pecuniary aid.

"The evil we sincerely lament, and view it as one in magnitude next the greatest that could come upon us. But while we deplore the evil it is not in our province to devise the remedy, or the mode of preventing it, but leave it to the wisdom of those who have the care over us, and hope they will dictate a system of finance calculated to prevent in future as much as possible the thing complained of, by acting in aid of former establishments to give present relief to those who otherwise may be under necessity to recede from their labors.

"From these considerations, (though we are as but the drop to the ocean both in number and circumstances), we feel willing to contribute our mite in promoting any plan which may in the wisdom of conference be adopted. This address Dr. Coke took with him to the General Conference of 1800."

Asbury has always been decidedly in favor of free seats, and in the early days of her history, while nearly all other churches made a stranger feel that he received a seat only as a personal favor, Asbury opened wide her doors to all, and gave to all men an equal right to a place in the church during Divine worship. There is no prospect to-day that this policy will be changed. What the sentiment of the early church authorities was, may be inferred from the action of the trustees, on June 21, 1809. It reads thus:

"WHEREAS, It is contrary to the order and rules of our church to erect pews, or place other obstructions to entering the seats in the said church; and

"WHEREAS, An obstruction has been placed by some unknown person at the entrance of a seat in the gallery; therefore,

"*Resolved*, That the sexton be hereby authorized and required to remove as soon as convenient the said obstruction, and suffer no more such obstructions to be placed to the entrance of seats in the said church during his continuance to be sexton."

It is said that this proceeding of the trustees was occasioned by a number of singers determining they would sit together and lead the singing. They erected doors to one of the seats to exclude all others. This wise action of our fathers in making the seating free to all, has doubtless, been one cause why such vast crowds attended Asbury to-day and for years past, while many other churches are rarely filled.

In the year 1802 the church was incorporated, and on the 25th of May of that year, the first corporate trustees were elected. They were Henry Colesbury, Isaac Hews, Samuel Wood, Henry Metz, George Jones, Maurice Williams and Caleb Kendall.

At the very first meeting that they held, on June 17th, 1802, steps were taken to build a dwelling-house for the preachers. It was built during that year on the southwest corner of the church lot, very near the southwest corner of the church. This building was a small, two-story, frame structure, very well remembered by many of our older members of the present day. In its erection a debt was contracted that the small society could not pay, and, on June 21, 1800, it was surrendered to the mortgagee, Edward Worrell, in satisfaction of his claim, on condition that it should be removed at once. It was removed to the other side of the church, on the southeast corner of Walnut and Third streets. In 1823 the trustees bought it and the lot on which it stood, as we have already seen, and until 1853 the building was used as a sexton's house. In that year Chas. Moore was authorized to sell it for $00. This he did, and it was removed to Seventh and Church streets where it still may be seen. In 1826 another effort was made to build a parsonage, but it was not successful. A house for the preacher was rented in different parts of the city for many years. At one time the parsonage was on High street, (Sixth) between King and French, at another time on the corner of Walnut and High. In 1843 the church owned two houses, one on Market street occupied by the preacher, the other on Shipley which had been the parsonage. On March 10, 1843, the house on Shipley was exchanged for a three-story brick building on King street, above Seventh. This was sold to Allen Vane in 1846 when the present parsonage was erected. The stewards paid to the trustees $150 annual rent for this house for several years.

Though considerable repairs were made in 1818, in consequence of damages from a great storm, the second improvement on the church, in which the walls were changed for the enlargement of the building, was in 1828, when Thomas Young, Richard Williams, John Guyer, James Simpson, and Edward Worrell, constituted the building committee. It is probable that a great revival blessed the church in the first pastorate of J. Rustling, 1819-21. In his first year he reported 215 white members, and in his second 305. A subscription paper was put in circulation to build a school-house, but it failed. Enough money, however, had been collected to repair and paint the church. In 1828, during the pastorate of Solomon Higgins, in consequence of another great revival, which increased the white membership to 344, the work of enlargement could be no longer delayed. On March 11, 1828, therefore, it was determined to extend the north wall 30 feet toward Third street. At a subsequent meeting this was reconsidered, and it was decided to enlarge 15 feet toward Third street and 15 feet eastward. This was accordingly done and the church, which was originally 35 feet square, was, in 1828, 50 feet by 70 feet with galleries on the south, west and north sides, but was still a one-story building.

In the early history of the society there was great opposition to the holding of a Sabbath-school in the church. Some of the officials said they did not so much mind the girls coming in, but the boys were rude and unruly, and cut the benches with their knives. Still the Sabbath-school was popular and continued to grow. In 1822 it was decided to provide suitable quarters for the children and a school building, about 18 feet by 25 feet, was erected next the church at the southwest corner of the lot. In this building several who are still among us attended Sabbath-school. A day-school was conducted here, the building being rented from the trustees for this purpose, and a Young Men's Beneficial Club debated great and weighty matters within its walls. It stood here till 1846, when better arrangements were made for the comfort of the Sabbath-school.

By members of Asbury, Sabbath-schools have been organized in various parts of the city. Some of these were apparently not successful; others have developed into strong churches. The infant department of the school purchased a lot on Shipley street on which they erected a two-story brick building in which to conduct a school. At first they met with great success but reverses came, and because of a mortgage of $900 they were compelled to surrender their property to the trustees of the church, on condition that the trustees would assume the debt. The property accordingly was taken by the trustees in 1832 and the building was so altered as to make it a comfortable parsonage.

Other schools were commenced by Asbury Church which have developed into independent societies. Seventh street school became Scott Church, rivaling in earnestness and fidelity her mother. A school in Brandywine village grew until to-day we have the flourishing Brandywine Church. Mt. Salem school is now but one of the many enterprises of Mt. Salem Church. Madeley began in Sabbath-school work by Asbury toilers, who surrendered when Grace was willing to provide according to their usual liberality for the infant society. Wesley, Silverbrook, and Cookman of a later day, date their incipiency from the labors of Sunday-school workers from the old Asbury hive.

In all institutions supported by the voluntary contributions of the members, there are always a number who shirk all financial responsibility, and are perfectly satisfied to let some one else pay what they themselves know to be their due. In most churches to-day, one-half to two-thirds of the members bear these burdens, and the remainder thank God for a free gospel. It was so at Asbury in 1826, but our fathers decided that every one must pay, or they should not enjoy the privileges of the society. One of the rules of the church was that all persons not members of Asbury must pay for graves in the churchyard.

but to members graves for their own family were free. In 1826 it was enacted by the trustees that no members who could not show by the books that his quarterage accounts were square for the preceding three months, should have the privilege of interring his dead free; but, since he did not support the church, he must pay for his grave like one who was not a member. According to this resolution, a member was refused by the grave-yard committee permission to bury one of his family. On August 14, 1830, he appealed to the board of trustees, but they unanimously sustained the committee. As late as 1841 these resolutions were read and explained from the pulpit by Robert Gerry, and their enforcement pledged. Many a church financier has bothered his brain to concoct a plan by which church delinquents might be compelled honorably to take their share of church burdens, but it was for an earlier age to use such determined efforts.

For us who stand in the full blaze of the modern electric light, it is hard to conceive the day when this church was lighted by nothing better than the flickering and dim candle light. Yet 65 years ago all the light that illuminated this building when the sunlight had disappeared was the tallow candle. They hung from the walls in little brackets high enough to be out of the reach of the heads of the people. About every fifteen minutes the sexton had to pass all around the church and snuff them. This operation, especially when the sexton was a short man, was a delicate piece of work, and afforded great amusement at times to the young and ungodly part of the congregations, while even the saints could not forbear to smile, when the little sexton, losing his uncertain equilibrium, snuffed the candle out. On December 2, 1824, after mature deliberation, Lewis Ashton, Miller Dunott, Richard Williams and Henry J. Pepper were appointed a committee to take into consideration the comparative merits and expense of candles and oil. At the succeeding meeting of the trustees, their report having been heard and maturely considered, and as it demonstrated the superiority and cheapness of oil, it was decided to procure lamps, and a barrel of the best sperm oil was purchased. It took five years to discuss the next change, from oil to gas, and it was not till 1851, when John A. Roche was pastor, that gas was introduced into the church.

The third improvement made upon the church by which the building was enlarged, was in 1838, when, after a revival under Wm. A. Wiggins, the membership had increased to 420 white and 110 colored. Miller Dunott, John Flinn and Richard Williams were appointed the building committee, and John M. Turner did the work. The old brick wall that stood in front of the church was then removed and the church was extended ten feet westward to the building line. The old west wall of the church was not torn down, but the ten-foot space between the old wall and the new was used for a vestibule. In this vestibule the stairway ascended, and over it, in the back part of the gallery were two class rooms, the first the church possessed, in which some of these old men and women about me to-day met for years. The church was then 80 feet by 50, with a gallery on three sides, but still one-story.

Many of our fathers delighted in late meetings, and often the songs and shouts of the people were heard till midnight and beyond. There were some, however, who thought this was not letting all things be done in decency and order; so on January 16, 1829, the trustees, after discussing the many evils arising from this disturbing practice, especially, as they state, the "unnecessary waste of fuel and the means of lighting the house," directed the sexton, "to extinguish the lamps at 10 o'clock, unless there are mourners in the house engaged in prayer, and some prospect of good being done."

Previous to 1830 it would have been considered the grossest impropriety for men and women to enter by the same door into the church. One side of the church and one door were exclusively for men, the other for women, while, as we have already noted, down the center of the church was a high partition, running the whole length of the church where seats extended, and effectually barring off the one sex from the other. By 1832 this gave rise to many complaints. If a husband desired to escort his wife home, he must pass out his door, and out his gate in the brick fence, and around to the other gate and door in search of her, or else he must stand out on the pavement to meet her her upon her exit, not a pleasant duty if the weather were inclement. It is quaintly said in the trustees' record that this man's difficulties were made all the greater by the fact that one of the doors was usually surrounded by a crowd. Which door this was I leave to the judgment of our sisters, with the single suggestion that the mothers were just as fond of a little social chat at the close of the service as the daughters are to-day. On August 20, 1832, therefore, it was decided by the trustees, in order to silence these complaints and promote the comfort of the worshipers, that the men and women should enter by the same doors, the men to take seats on the left hand side of the aisles, and the women on the right. The idea of promiscuous sitting even then would have aroused the indignation of the church. This custom was not introduced until 1845, when Chas. Moore moved to this effect in the trustees' meeting.

In 1835 and 1836, when J. Rustling was serving his second

term at Asbury, he had a long spell of sickness, and was unable to perform the work of the charge. To assist him, junior preachers were employed, whose names do not appear on the usual list of Asbury preachers. During Mr. Rustling's first year Levi Storks was his assistant, and during his second William Urie occupied the position. Matthew Sorin followed Mr. Rustling, and, of course, needed no helper.

It is sometimes supposed that the custom of the church in inviting a special preacher to be their pastor, is of very late origin, and that our fathers would have been horrified at such a procedure. This is a mistake. The fathers were no less anxious to secure the man of their choice than the sons are to-day. After a general meeting of the society on December 30, 1835, to consider what steps should be taken to secure a desirable preacher, it was resolved that the trustees use all proper means to secure from the Philadelphia Conference, the appointment of the Rev. Chas. Pitman as the pastor of Asbury for the next year, and Thomas Young, Miller Dunott, and Henry Hicks were appointed a committee to carry out the wishes of the church. Like many other committees, this one failed in securing their choice. Surely, however, they had no cause of complaint when the bishop read the name of Matthew Sorin as their preacher.

The fourth improvement, and, perhaps, the most radical of all, was made in 1845, when Anthony Atwood was pastor. No change was made in the linear dimensions of the building, but the church at this time was transformed into a two-story structure. The floor was lowered two feet, and the walls were raised seven feet six inches, and, of course, a new roof was put on. In the basement, which was nine feet high in the clear, four class-rooms, two on each side of an eight-foot entry, were laid off at the Walnut street entrance, back of the vestibule. The rest of the basement was used for a lecture-room, fifty feet by thirty-eight, with the desk changed from the east to the south end, and a door on the Third street side. The auditorium had a gallery eleven feet six inches wide on the north and south sides, and over the vestibule on the west; the seats were placed in two blocks with a four-foot aisle in the center, and a three-foot aisle on each side of the church; doors opening into the vestibule were placed at the end of each aisle, and two small windows were put in over the pulpit. The building committee consisted of Anthony Atwood, pastor, Richard Williams, Chas. Moore, and George Magee. When this work was completed, for the first time, in many years, the congregation had accommodations for the varied work of the church. From this time the Sabbath-school occupied the lecture-room, and the school house was soon after removed. The next year, 1846, part of the roof of the church was blown off, but the repairs needed were soon made. The membership a year before this improvement was made was eight hundred and eighty-four, the largest the church has ever had.

In 1839, one hundred years after Methodism was organized in England, and just fifty years after the dedication of Asbury, pursuant to a resolution passed by the Philadelphia Conference at its preceding session, interesting centenary services were held in this church. On September 2, 1839, the centenary committee met in its first session. The following members were present: Rev. Joseph Lybrand, preacher in charge, Rev. David Daily, Presiding Elder of the Chesapeake district which included this station, Richard Williams, Chas. Moore, Miller Dunott, Asa Poinsett, George Magee, John Flinn, and Thomas Young. Upon motion of Rev. David Daily, all the other official members were added to the committee. The following persons were thus added: John Hagany, local elder; Samuel Wood, local deacon; Solomon Prettyman, Samuel H. Higgins, and Wm. Kirkman, local preachers; James Thomas and Robert Thompson, exhorters; and James Lane, John M. Turner, John Guyer, Jarrett Magaw, John Quinby, Isaac M. Connell, Jacob M. Garrettson, and Barney Harris, class leaders. The committee appointed September 16th as the day for holding the general centenary services. When the day arrived, at 3 o'clock in the afternoon Joseph Lybrand took the chair, and explained the purposes of the meeting, after which the Revs. Jas. H. McFarland and John Kennaday delivered addresses. The secretaries of the meetings, Solomon Prettyman and Dr. S. H. Higgins, have left well-written and interesting minutes of the meeting. Of Mr. McFarland's address, the secretaries say: "He was introduced to the audience and proceeded to address the assembly in a very pertinent and forcible manner for the space of thirty minutes. Mr. Kennaday followed with a short address which he intended should be very brief, in view of the fact that he had been appointed to address the meeting in the evening. He enlarged somewhat upon the views of the first speaker, and exhibited some interesting facts and some amusing occurrences illustrative of several interesting positions previously stated, demonstrating the benefits of the Methodist itinerancy in stirring up and animating the zeal of other Christian communities." In the evening Joseph Lybrand was again in the chair.

After prayer by the Rev. Edward Kennard, Mr. Kennaday delivered a very interesting address, exhibiting the design of the centenary celebration in relation both to the temporal and spiritual prosperity of the church. "The matter of the address," says the secretary, "was well chosen, and the speaker was happy in the manner of its delivery.

He brought forward some interesting examples as well as arguments to show that piety and benevolence go hand in hand, anticipated and answered many objections made by those who would excuse themselves when benevolent enterprises should call to action, and argued that the objects for which the centenary fund is designed are ever worthy and noble." A collection was then taken for the fund, when 156 persons gave $581.56. On Sunday, October 25, the religious observances of the centenary took place. A large congregation met at 6 o'clock in the morning and held a general prayer meeting, which was characterized by the most devotional feelings and sentiments. At 10 o'clock the pastor, Rev. Joseph Lybrand, delivered a discourse based on I Samuel, vii: 12.—"Then Samuel took a stone and set it between Mizpeh and Shen, and called the name of it Ebenezer, saying, Hitherto hath the Lord helped us." The sermon was admirably calculated to excite feelings of pious gratitude to God for his wonderful preservation of that form of Christianity, called Methodism, during the first century of her progress, and of the most lively hopes of the part she has yet to act in the conversion of the world to God.

It was in the centenary year, 1839, that the trustees first selected a secretary for the relief of the chairman of the board. Chas. Moore, now in his 83rd year, who still moves among us to prove the sustaining power of God in old age, was chosen for this position.

Considerable agitation was caused in Asbury Church by the action of the General Conference in 1844, and the formation of an independent church by our southern brethren. Discussion ran high, and some advocated joining the southern church, or at least suggested the propriety of such a course. But, as on many other occasions, the wisdom of the officials asserted itself, and the following action was entered upon the Quarterly Conference records for November 4, 1844: "Some conversation took place in reference to the division of the church, and the proceedings of the General Conference in the case of Bishop Andrew. But it seemed to be the general opinion that, owing to our geographical position and the quiet that prevails throughout this congregation, it is prudent for us to take no action in the case."

The fifth general repair of the church was in 1872, when the Rev. Enoch Stubbs was pastor. Charles Wood, Jacob Webb, Charles Heald, J. J. McMullin and R. Heisler were the building committee. No change was made in the walls of the building except in a small recess to enlarge the pulpit at the east end, but improvements were put upon the interior costing $12,000. The church was dedicated on January 19, 1873, when the dedicatory sermon was preached by the Rev. C. N. Simms, D. D. LL. D. of Syracuse, N. Y.

There are indications in all the records that the cause of temperance has always occupied a warm place in the affections of this church. Often were the most noted temperance lecturers invited to speak from the pulpit at a time when temperance work was not popular. John B. Gough and other distinguished leaders have thrilled large audiences within these walls as they depicted the evils of the drink traffic, and laid upon the church its duty. As early as 1853 a resolution was introduced into the Quarterly Conference that antedated more than twenty-five years similar action by the General Conference. After referring to the growing evils from the use of intoxicants, it was resolved by the Quarterly Conference "to advise our people to abstain from signing petitions for license to sell ardent spirits, and that the preacher, Robert Gerry, be requested to read this action from the pulpit." It was not till 1880 that the General Conference included under "Imprudent Conduct" the signing of a license to sell intoxicating beverages. Thus was our church far ahead of the church generally, and this interest in temperance work continues to the present day.

In 1861 the division of our conference territory was agitated. The Philadelphia Conference referred the matter of division to the several Quarterly Conferences of the Peninsula. On October 5, 1861, the officials of this church, in Quarterly Conference assembled, decided that, as the country was so greatly excited by the civil war then in progress, it would not be wise to divide at that time. The wisdom of this action is apparent now, as a severing of our connection at that time from Philadelphia and the northern work would have greatly injured our standing on the Peninsula, and built up the other Methodist churches.

In 1866 Asbury had the misfortune to lose by death its much beloved pastor, the Rev. George Quigley. He was a faithful man, a boanerges in the pulpit, constantly at work in his pastorate, full of the Holy Ghost. He was advised some weeks before he died to take a rest, but he replied that there were sick in his membership who needed pastoral care. He would not leave them. He was soon after stricken down with typhoid fever and died on June 25, 1866, at the Asbury parsonage, a victim of over work. He was the only minister that died while pastor of this church. His body lies in the Wilmington and Brandywine Cemetery, awaiting the resurrection of the just. I. Mast filled out the unexpired term.

Asbury has always been conservative, slow to introduce innovations upon established usages, devoted to the records of the past. Retaining many of the customs of earlier days, she looks upon it as no reflection upon her standing that she is regarded as nearer primitive Methodism in her modes of worship, than any other church in the Conference. It may easily be imagined what bitter opposition was aroused when, during the civil war, the question of the introduction of an organ into the church was agitated. On June 3, 1864, the trustees received a communication from the choir, asking permission to introduce an instrument of music into the church. They were about to settle the question, but, proving too weighty for them, it was referred to a joint meeting of the trustees and stewards. This meeting was held and the matter was debated with interest, but it was too large for even this meeting. Upon motion of Alexander Kelly, it was decided to appoint a committee to wait upon all the members of the Quarterly Conference and secure their vote, yea or nay, for the government of the trustees in their action. When this committee had completed its work it was found that eight had voted yea, fourteen had voted nay, and the others had shown the white feather and would not vote at all. The trustees accordingly deemed it inexpedient to grant the request. On November 3, 1865, it was again brought forward upon motion of Bro. Kelly, but negatived. During the strife the choir refused to sing, and for some time the church was without its assistance. On May 4, 1866, however, the trustees appointed a committee to raise the money for an instrument of music, and in the fall of that year, the organ was introduced into the church. Mr. C. Wells, at a salary of $100, was the first organist, and Mr. Ashley Simpson the leader of the choir.

During the latter part of the term of Enoch Stubbs, and during the pastorate of John A. B. Wilson, and the last pastorate of Chas. Hill, the Sunday-school suffered greatly for want of proper accommodations. The main school was unpleasantly crowded, and the infant department had no proper place to hold its sessions, being compelled to use the gallery of the church for this purpose. After many discussions, in the board of trustees and among the members, relating to the building of a large chapel in the northeast corner of the church lot, the problem was finally solved during the pastorate of W. L. S. Murray. At this time the sixth and last improvement was made upon the church, David S. Truitt, John Gray, Benjamin J. Downing, Charles F. Welch, and George Rickards, being the building committee. The outward appearance of the building was radically changed, and no one who looks upon the church to-day, can imagine the little one-story church, thirty-five feet square, from which this structure arose. In this improvement the lecture-room was extended twenty feet to the building line on Third street, the church being thus converted into an L-shaped building. The floor of the lecture-room, in order to give greater height to the room, was lowered two feet. This improvement added fifteen feet to the lecture room, and provided space for an ample library, and a large vestibule on the ground floor. In the second story, on a level with the floor of the auditorium, it provided a room 50 x 20 feet for the infant department, and in a third story, on a level with the gallery, is another room of the same dimensions now used as a church parlor.

On November 8, 1885, when this much needed improvement had been completed, the church was re-opened with appropriate services, including a collection. The Rev. C. N. Simms, D. D., LL. D., Chancellor of the Syracuse University, preached in the morning, Bishop H. W. Warren in the afternoon, and the Rev. J. Richard Boyle, D. D., of Grace Church, Wilmington, in the evening. The day was very inclement, yet nearly $5,000 of the $10,000 needed were raised in cash and subscriptions. During the pastorate of the Rev. J. E. Bryan, whose indefatigable efforts to complete the payment of this debt will long be remembered, the debt was nearly cancelled, the last dollar being paid during the present pastorate, October 6, 1889.

In 1875, at a time when Asbury was on a high tide of prosperity, the Rev. Geo. R. Kramer was appointed pastor. This appointment seemed at first to promise great beneficial results, but soon the pastor began to promulgate doctrines antagonistic to the Methodist faith. The brother, without doubt, had a perfect right to his opinions, but he had no right to use a Methodist pulpit, as a Methodist preacher, to attack Methodist doctrines. As soon as a preacher of any church feels impelled by his conscience to preach doctrines out of harmony with his vows there is but one honorable step left for him to take—resign his pulpit at once. The preaching of Mr. Kramer, who was a man of great eloquence, greatly disturbed Asbury Church, and, when in 1877 he retired from our communion, many useful and honest but mistaken members went with him. A church was established by them, entitled "The Household of Faith," which had but a brief existence. Their pastor received a call to a better position in Brooklyn, and accepted it. The members, left shepherdless, struggled againt debt and disappointment for a while, and finally succumbed. A few still believe the doctrines of "The Household of Faith," some have drifted clear away from all Christian moorings, a number have returned to Asbury, and Mr. Kramer himself is now a preacher in the Baptist church. It was thought at first that great and lasting damage had been done to Asbury by this schism, but the old church quickly recovered, and advanced in her career of prosperity more rapidly than ever.

Thus after a century and a fifth of history we stand to-day within these sacred walls to thank God for his never-failing care over this people. As we look about us how different are the surroundings from a century ago! Then we were persecuted, now we are in honor; then we were reviled for preaching salvation for all men, now everybody preaches it; then we were a little, obscure company, now a mighty host. Of the old church only a small part remains. On the south side about 35 ft. from the east end, 10 ft. from the west, and 7½ from the eaves, and on the west side in the partition that divides the vestibule from the rest of the church, part of the original wall still remains. The rest, like our fathers who founded the church, is gone. The alterations in the building are but an emblem of other and equally important changes constantly being made in the membership. There have been many vicissitudes, a few discouragements, some schisms, yet the church to-day has upon her record 840 full members and 52 probationers. St. Paul's, Union, Scott, Brandywine, Mt. Salem, Silverbrook and Cookman, as will be seen from the papers read here from these churches, have gone directly from this family circle, and many more sons and daughters of old Asbury have departed with the mother's blessing upon them to work for Christ in church-homes of their own choosing. To change the figure, the old hive is still full. Though swarm after swarm has gone forth in search of a hive of its own there have always been hundreds more of busy workers to take its place, and to-day the old hive is in good condition to swarm again.

We begin our second century with a bright outlook. Our services are soul-thrilling; often the saints of God shout aloud the praises of the King. Our classes have the old time fire still resting upon them; our lecture-room, on Friday evening, is usually well-filled with earnest souls, verifying the promise of Christ to meet with them, as they renew the vows of fidelity to Him; the Sunday morning prayer meeting is of the primitive type, no man there is afraid to tell what the Lord has done for his soul; old-fashioned revivals are frequent, in which nothing better than a Methodist altar for a sinner to seek Christ is wanted, and cries of penitence mingled with the shouts of rejoicing of the converted, and the triumphant songs of the saints, are often heard; at the ordinary Sunday services often hundreds, who would gladly worship with us, are turned away, and we are well assured that God is in our midst.

The work of the church is varied. A Sunday-school doing work that will be felt in eternity; a Ladies' Aid Society, caring for the comfort of the parsonage inmates and the beautifying of the church; a Woman's Foreign Missionary Society and a Murray Band of young ladies, sending the gospel to the benighted women of the Orient; a Woman's Home Missionary Society and Home Circle attending to the work at home; a King's Daughter's Society, ever ready to assist in any good work; a Young People's Christian Endeavor Society, building up young Christians, and saving the unregenerate youth about us; twenty classes meeting weekly for testimony and prayer; these represent some of the energies of the church; while trustees, leaders, stewards, faithful men of God, watch and forward every interest of our Zion.

From our church have gone forth the following men into the traveling connection of the Methodist ministry: John B. Hagany, Samuel H. Higgins, Edward Kennard, Thos. L. Poulson, Jas. McLaughlin, A. T. Scott, Jacob Dickerson, Wesley Johnson, T. B. Killiam, T. J. Cochran, W. W. Sharpe and Asbury Burke.

The following Annual Conferences have been held at Asbury:

CONFERENCE.	DATE.	BISHOP.	SECRETARY.
Philadelphia,	Ap. 11-19, 1832.	McKendree and Hedding.	G. G. Cookman.
"	Ap. 4-12, 1838.	Hedding.	W. A. Wiggins.
"	Ap. 6-14, 1842,	Waugh.	"
"	Nov. 25, Ap. 3, 1857.	Waugh,	P. Combs.
"	Mar. 9-16, 1864.	Ames,	R. H. Pattison.
*Wilmington,	Mar. 17-23, 1869,	Simpson.	Samuel L. Gracy.
"	Mar. 5-11, 1884.	Harris.	John D. Rigg.

In the 100 years of our history 62 men have officiated as pastors. Of these one died while pastor, George Quigley, in 1866; six served two pastoral terms, viz: John M. McClaskey, Ezekiel Cooper, Joseph Rustling, John Kenneday, Joseph Lybrand and Robert Gerry; to Chas. Hill alone belongs the honor of having occupied this pastorate three times. Of the 62 pastors, one, Geo. R. Kramer, is now a minister of the Baptist church, and 51 have gone to their eternal reward. Of the ten who are still in the ranks of the Methodist ministry, Joseph Mason and Gassoway Oram are on the retired list of the Philadelphia Conference, John A. Roche is an active member of the New York East Conference, W. C. Robinson and Enoch Stubbs are serving churches in Philadelphia, John A. B. Wilson and W. L. S. Murray are Presiding Elders in the Wilmington Conference, Chas. Hill and J. E. Bryan are pastors in the same Conference, and the writer is the present pastor of Asbury.

*This was the first session of the Wilmington Conference.

The following is a list of the pastors that have served Asbury in the last hundred years:

TIME.	PREACHERS.	WHITE.	COLORED.	PRESIDING ELDERS.
1789	William Jessup,	43	19	Lemuel Green.
1790	John McClaskey,	40	20	Richard Whatcoat.
1791	Thomas Ware,	93	48	Lemuel Green.
1792	Silvester Hutchinson,	83	41	John McClaskey.
1793	Robert Cloud, 6 mos.,	82	55	" "
1793	Evan Rogers, 6 mos., On Chester Circuit.	90	55	Freeborn Garretson.
1794	Wm. Earley, James Smith,			Valentine Cook. " "
1795	Fredus Aldridge,			John Merrick.
1796	John Vanneman,	40	30	Thomas Ware.
1797	Ezekiel Cooper, Wilmington & Newport.	61	37	" "
1798	Ezekiel Cooper, Wilmington.	69	48	" "
1799	Daniel Fidler.	73	46	" "
1800	Caleb Kendall.	87	47	Joseph Everett.
1801	" "	157	85	" "
1802	James Lattomus,	125	117	Thomas Ware.
1803	Thomas Jones, On the Circuit.	113	98	Christopher Spry.
1804	Wm. Hunter, Jos. Osburn, J. Stephens,			Wm. Colbert. " " " "
1805	Wm. Hunter, D. James. James Moore, Wilmington a station again.			Solomon Sharp.
1806	Joshua Wells.			" "
1807	John McClaskey,	112	96	" "
1808	William Bishop,	90	104	Wm. Chandler.
1809	Ezekiel Cooper.	126	145	Wm. Hunter.
1810	Wm. M'Lenahan,	132	134	" "
1811	James Sanders,	137	137	" "
1812	James Bateman,	142	178	" "
1813	George Sheets, Chester and Wilmington.	138	46	Henry Boehm.
1814	Geo. Sheets and Thomas Miller to change once a month.	123	71	Henry Boehm.
1815	John Emory,	127	72	Robert R. Roberts.

TIME	PREACHERS.	WHITE.	COLORED.	PRESIDING ELDERS.
1817	John Goforth,	190	67	" "
1818	Samuel J. Cox,	212	67	" "
1819	Joseph Rustling,	215	68	" "
1820	" "	305	74	James Bateman.
	Wilmington and New Castle.			
1821	Lawrence Laurenson,	325	70	"
	Wil..N. Castle and Newport.			
1822	John Potts,	339	77	" "
	Wilmington a station again.			
1823	John Potts,	203	88	" "
1824	Solomon Sharpe,	319	78	Joseph Lybrand.
1825	Henry White,	279	42	" "
1826	L. M'Combs,	288	55	" "
1827	Solomon Higgins,	290	104	" "
1828	" "	344	101	Lawrence Laurenson.
1829	David Dailey,	347	90	L. M'Combs.
1830	John Kenneday,	334	98	" "
1831	" "	360	98	" "
1832	Joseph Lybrand,	385	100	" "
1833	" "	437	131	Matthew Sorin.
1834	J. Rustling; Levi Storks,	439	134	" "
1816	Wm. Williams,	130	57	Daniel Hitt.
1835	Jos. Rustling, W. Urie,	382	130	Matthew Sorin.
1836	Matthew Sorin,	363	173	David Dailey.
1837	William A. Wiggins,	348	90	"
1838	"	420	110	"
1839	Joseph Lybrand,	558	119	"
1840	"	505	136	Henry White.
1841	Robert Gerry,	580	136	"
1842	"	700	140	"
1843	John Kennaday,	750	150	"
1844	"	884	163	Daniel Lambdin.
1845	Anthony Atwood,	840	170	"
1846	"	594	192	"
1847	Thomas J. Thompson,	693	256	"
1848	"	694	260	James Smith.

Previous to 1849, no report of probationers was made in the general minutes.

TIME	PREACHERS	WHITE MEM.	WHITE PROB.	COLORED MEM.	COLORED PROB.	PRESIDING ELDER
1840	Wm. Cooper,	622	121	277	29	James Smith.
1850	"	550	70	235	32	"

After this colored people are not reported in Asbury minutes. They are independent.

TIME	PREACHERS	WHITE MEM.	WHITE PROB.			PRESIDING ELDER
1851	John A. Roche,	529	185			James Smith.
1852	"	621	100			Anthony Atwood.

TIME	PREACHERS	WHITE	COLORED	PRESIDING ELDERS
1853	Robert Gerry,	637	90	Anthony Atwood.
1854	"	640	90	"
1855	Joseph Mason,	584	70	T. J. Thompson.
1856	"	502	64	"
1857	Gassaway Oram,	570	42	Wm. Urie.
1858	"	550	62	"
1859	Wesley Kenney,	568	20	"
1860	"	580	120	"
1861	Charles Hill,	661	46	Joseph Mason.
1862	"	663	33	"
1863	W. C. Robinson,	592	25	"
1864	"	589	160	"
1865	George Quigley,	664	75	James Cunningham.
1866	" died, and I. Mast filled out the year.	670	102	"
1867	J. D. Curtis,	639	144	"
1868	"	640	30	"
1869	Charles Hill,	572	40	J. D. Curtis.
1870	"	569	87	"
1871	"	628	119	"
1872	Enoch Stubbs,	631	63	"
1873	"	612	62	T. J. Thompson.
1874	"	620	170	T. J. Thompson, died Nov. 29, 1874, John B. Quigg.
1875	Geo. R. Kramer,	675	105	John B. Quigg.
1876	"	690	238	"
1877	Geo. R. Kramer, tell, T. B. Killiam, remainder of year,	764	63	"
1878	J. A. B. Wilson,	618	14	"
1879		575	65	L. C. Matlack.

TIME.	PREACHER.	WHITE.	COLORED.	PRESIDING ELDERS.
1880	Charles Hill,	604	19	
1881	"	594	27	
1882	"	587	49	
1883	W. L. S. Murray,	593	52	Charles Hill.
1884	"	650	101	
1885	"	750	50	"
1886	Jas. E. Bryan,	720	80	"
1887	"	813	45	W. L. S. Murray.
1888	"	700	90	"
1889	John D. C. Hanna,	720	126	"

At the present time the members of the Quarterly Conference, upon whom rest the responsibilities of the church, are as follows:

Charles. Moore, Dr. J. H. Simms and John Simmons, local preachers; John Wise, Matthew Megarvey, Andrew J. Dalbow, Robert Humphreys, Chas. A. Foster and A. Sergeant, exhorters; Chas. M. Leitch, recording steward, Wm. T. Groves, district steward, Chas. Moore, J. C. Johnson, John Wise, Chas. Wood, John T. Mortimer, Wm. F. Maclin, H. A. Roop, H. H. Ferguson, Chas. Heald, Wm. F. Johnson, and Geo. S. Hagany, stewards; David R. Truitt, president of the board of trustees; David Whitsell, secretary; John Gray, Benj. J. Downing, Augustus Dennis, Chas. F. Welch, Jas. H. Floyd, Wm. B. Wharton, and T. A. D. Hutton, trustees; Chas. Moore. John Banthrum, Wm. B. Genn, Jas. E. McKay, Louis Maxwell, A. Sergeant, John Wise, Mrs. Chas. Moore, Wm. Pennell, Jacob Ellwanger, Chas. F. Bordner, Chas. A. Foster, Wm. T. Houpt, Andrew J. Dalbow, T. B. Ridgway, B. F. Leonard, Noah Cunningham, Robert G. Humphreys, Geo. Heisler, and the pastor, leaders. Jas. E. McKay is superintendent of the afternoon school, and the assistant, Wm. J. Johnson, has charge in the morning. Miss Sallie Shaw and Miss Ella Marvel are also assistants in the main school. The infant department is in charge of Mrs. M. A. Taggart, assisted by Mrs. Chas. Moore and Miss Georgia Carver.

Thus most imperfectly have we traced the century's history of our beloved church. The forty-three white members have become four thousand four hundred and sixty-one members and probationers, the nineteen colored members are now seven hundred and forty, and both white and colored people have given off many more to assist in building other folds. We are standing together and looking back during this centennial week. Yet we are not so much concerned with the past as with the future. How are we building for the generations to come?

God of our fathers make us faithful to our goodly heritage. Make the next century more glorious in heroic endeavor and magnificent results even than the one now closing. Make the children of to-day faithful, determined, persistent, self-sacrificing, victorious. And when the generations to come review our work, may they pronounce upon us the encomium, "They did what they could."

History of Asbury Methodist Episcopal Sunday School.

By Charles F. Bordner, Esq.

In the year 1818, three noble Christian women, one by the name of Elizabeth Cable, who afterwards became the wife of a man named Yeager; the second one was Anna McClees, who afterwards married a man by the name of Ford; the name of the third one we have been unable to obtain; but while we are unable to record her name here below, we feel safe in saying that her name is registered above. These women of God were deeply impressed with the thought that a Sabbath-school should be organized in connection with Asbury Church for the purpose of instructing the children in the nurture and admonition of God, and thus fit them for a life of usefulness in this world, and prepare them for the world to come. Through the persistent efforts of these women, the school was organized in Asbury Church. Though the school was organized in the church, they were only allowed to meet there on condition that they would take no boys as scholars. The objections raised against the boys by the board of trustees was, that the boys would cut the benches with their knives.

It will be remembered that knives were not so plentiful as they are nowadays. Not every boy was the owner of a knife, and those who were favored with this very useful article were determined to use it, if even the furniture at times would have to suffer. These restrictions, however, did not suit the broad philanthropic ideas of the originators of the school; but determined in their minds that the boys should not be excluded if they could help it. After some effort they secured a place to hold the school in the house owned by John Taylor, on the S.

W. corner of Second and Walnut streets. Here they continued the work of instructing both boys and girls in the words of eternal life. From Second and Walnut streets the school was removed to a loft over David Bush's storehouse, known as Nos. 6 and 8 East Front street. From Front street the school was removed to Sixth and King streets to a frame building which stood on the site where Hanover Presbyterian Church now stands, from which place the children, in company with the officers and teachers, could be seen every Sunday morning marching down King street en route to Asbury meeting-house (as it was called in those days) where they would attend preaching services.

Through the persistent efforts of the few who organized the school the good work grew in interest to such an extent that it drew the attention of the officiaries of Asbury Church, and they resolved to take hold of the new enterprise and thus help and encourage its growth.

On the 5th of July, 1819, a meeting was called by the Rev. Joseph Rustling, the preacher in charge, for the purpose of organizing a Sabbath-school, on which occasion a constitution was formed and adopted and an election of officers was held. The pastor, Rev. Joseph Rustling, was elected as president; Benjamin Fred and Samuel Sappington were elected as secretary, treasurer and superintendent for the first quarter.

The funds of the school were provided for according to the provisions presented in Article II of Constitution, viz: That each member upon signing the constitution shall pay the sum of twelve and one-half cents, and quarterly the same sum to the treasurer.

Article VII, relating to duties of teachers and officers. This article provided that the superintendent should see that promptness be observed in opening the schools, and also to see that the school be closed fifteen minutes before Divine service commenced, then to have the children conducted by their teachers to the Methodist meeting-house, and see that they behaved well and kneel in time of prayer. In case either of the superintendents being absent they were required to furnish a substitute or be fined twelve and one-half cents.

Section II of By-laws provided for the classifying of the scholars, as follows: The first class were to recite from the New Testament, and commit to memory a portion and answer questions from the catechism. Class No. 2 were to commit to memory hymns and small lessons out of the spelling book. The third class were to be taught the alphabet and words of one syllable.

Section 2nd, By-Laws, Rewards. First class for every six verses of Scriptures, or each lesson in the Catechism, should receive one blue ticket.

Class 2nd, For being present at roll call one blue ticket, and for every lesson or hymn they recited one blue ticket.

The third class for punctual attendance, and for good behaviour during day, one blue ticket.

Punishment, Section 3rd. Children absent at roll call, or neglecting to recite, would forfeit one blue ticket, for bad behaviour one, and for general bad behavior during the month should receive no tract. A teacher absenting him or herself, would be fined six and one-fourth cents; under these and similar rules, the school grew in numbers and interest.

The 25th day of April, 1822, the board of trustees of Asbury Church decided to build a school house on the southwest corner of the church, and appointed as building committee, Bros. Richard Williams, Miller Dunott, and Edward Worrell. On August 2, 1822, the committee reported the building completed at a cost of $375.58½. Week day school was held in this building also. In the fall of 1822, the Sabbath-school moved from Sixth and King streets to their new quarters in the school house, which had just been fitted up for their accommodations, where the school remained until 1835, when the objections against boys as scholars had ceased, and they were admitted into the church proper.

At a meeting of the Sunday-school Association held March 13, 1827, it was decided to procure a library of such books as would suit the capacity of the children belonging to the school. The books were to be loaned to such scholars only who distinguished themselves as learners, and for good behaviour in and outside the school. On September 25, 1837, the board of managers of Asbury Sabbath-school presented the following interesting report:

There are at the above date sixty-six male and one hundred and twenty-six female scholars on the roll, with an average attendance of one hundred and fifty three scholars. Recited during the past year, eight thousand one hundred and fifty-nine verses of Scripture, and two thousand eight hundred and seventy-one verses of hymns. In this year the school sustained a great loss, in the death of Bro. Edward Worrell, who from the first organization of the Sabbath-school worked for its best interests. Under the management of various superintendents the school increased in numbers and interest to such an extent that it was necessary to have two schools, known as No. 1 and No. 2.

The sessions of No. 1 were held in the lecture room, and the sessions of No. 2 in the auditorium of the church.

During the year 1866 the officers of No. 1 School were as follows: superintendent, Alex Kelley; assistant superintendent, Rebecca Matlock; secretary, William Moore; treasurer, Bennet Matlack; librarian, H. A. Roop.

Officers of School No. 2 were: superintendent, John C. Thomas; assistant superintendent, Virginia Robinson; secretary, William Loyd; librarian, Elisha Cole.

As separate bodies these two schools were carried on successfully until September, 1869, when, by the action of the Sunday-school board, they were consolidated. On January 23, 1872, the Sunday-School Association adopted the Berean lesson system, which system is still being used.

I can not close this paper without referring, particularly to Sister Rebecca Matlack, who departed this life May 7, 1884. She was a charter member and also its assistant superintendent for many years. Her interest in the school was untiring and much of its success must be attributed to her. Her's too was a nature that poets like to sing of and philosophers moralize upon. So filled was she with the love of God, that she was never satisfied unless making another life happier. She died as she lived the very embodiment of Christian perfection.

To D. T. Hawkins who died in June, 1881, must be also ascribed part of the success of Asbury Sunday-school. His devotion to the interest of the school was untiring and persistent. So examplary was his character, that his memory, wherever he was known, will be cherished.

The school is at present holding two sessions, one at 9 o'clock, a. m. and at 2 p. m.

Number of scholars, 900, with an average attendance of 500; number of books in library, 700; average collections to missions for past five years, $700.

Present officers—superintendent, Jas. E. McKay; assistant superintendent, Wm. Johnson; secretary, A. Fielding; financial secretary, Frank Cannon; librarians, Frank Willing and Elmer Perry; treasurer of Home Missions, A. Dennis; Foreign Mission, Geo. F. Hartman; musical director, W. B. Genn; Superintendent of infant school, M. A. Taggart; assisted by Mrs. Chas. Moore and Miss Georgie B. Carver.

REV. CHARLES MOORE,

Local Preacher and Mission Worker for more than a half century

"Our Local Preachers."

BY THE REV. CHARLES MOORE, LOCAL PREACHER AT ASBURY M. E. CHURCH.

In writing the history of Asbury Church, the Centennial of which is now being observed October 16th, 1889, memories of heroic struggles are awakened, and gratitude to our fathers' God and ours is excited. The services for the Centennial occasion commenced on Sunday, October 13th, and continued till October 20th, the whole affair being a grand success spiritually and financially.

In this report of the labors of the local preachers who were members of Asbury Church, I first give a list of them as my memory calls them up. I notice the names of the Revs. John Hagany, Samuel Wood, Edward Kennard, John E. Simmons, Samuel H. Higgins, William Kirkman, John Quinby, Robert Thompson, A. T. Scott, William L. Taylor, William Zimmerman, Thomas Lamplugh, Charles Moore, David Ricords, David Dodd, William Galway, John M. Simms, Asbury Burke, W. W. Sharp, William Genn and Nathan Genn.

The first named local preacher, John Hagany, was associated with Asbury Church from the year 1808 till the time of his departure for his better home with the saints in glory. He was one of the early helpers in the time when the church most needed men loyal to Methodism. His house was always open to the preachers; and especially was it a home for the young itinerant, who was not only cared for in his temporal needs, but received such instructions and advice as, in the early history of the church, was much needed to protect the young from the errors of false teachers, who often attacked the doctrine and discipline of the Methodist Church. This good old loyal man of God was truly an Israelite indeed, guileless and fearless in the cause of Christ, his Master. He died in a good old age, much respected by the community, and beloved by the church of his choice. One of the sons of Father Hagany, the Rev. John Bishop Hagany, was an itinerant of the first-class, a profound theologian, known throughout the Philadelphia and New York conferences. He was stationed in one of the first churches in Brooklyn, New York, when he died. His remains lie in the Wilmington and Brandywine Cemetery.

I notice next on the list the name of the venerable Father Samuel Wood, another old standby in time of need; he was exceedingly apt in his scriptural quotations during his preaching; a Methodist of the early school, believing fully in the doctrines of free grace, as taught by Mr. Wesley and his followers. He died at a good old age, well known and respected. He and Father Hagany would alternate in their preaching at Asbury Church, and thus keep the pulpit regularly supplied in the absence of the stationed preacher. The local preachers following these old veterans of the cross were generally useful workers in the church. Samuel Hale Higgins, one of the list, was a physician with a good practice, when serving the church as a local preacher; a man highly esteemed for his good social qualities and usefulness in the church of his choice.

All the local preachers named in the list as belonging to Asbury Church, were men engaged in some active business to support their families, and none of them were idlers, but men of good standing in the community where they resided.

Much might be said of their labors in church matters, and of their charity and general good works.

We notice one of them who was also a leader in Asbury for fifty-four years, and who, in looking over his books, found that he had collected from his class during that time $6,700.55 for the support of the gospel, and thinking of the positions he had occupied in the church during that time, discovered that he had served nine years as a trustee ; thirty four years as a steward ; sixteen years as a local preacher ; was assistant secretary of the leaders, and stewards, meeting for forty years, and from 1836, forty years voluntary chaplain of the New Castle County Alms House. During his work in the church, he associated with one hundred and forty-two class leaders up to October 16, 1889. He yet holds the office of local preacher, steward and leader and has a list of the leaders, numbering one hundred and forty-two, since his first leading class in the year 1835. In writing the history of Asbury Church for the past one hundred years, it is impossible to describe the work done through the instrumentality of that church, but in naming some of her working places, some idea may be formed of a great deal of good done in that time.

I would notice here a plan gotten up for the regulation of the work the official members were required to do. This plan was written in 1877 by the leading preachers in the city at that time. It embraced the following named places: Brandywine, Old Academy, Riddle's Banks, Edgemoor, City Mission, Browntown, Richardson's School House, the Alms House, Oak Hil., McDowelville, School House half way to New Castle, Silverbrook, Kingswood, and other places.

The pastors in this plan were T. B. Killiam, W. P. Davis, J. B. Mann, W. G. Stevenson, C. M. Pegg, L. E. Barrett, J. E. Mowbray, and H. Sanderson. There were fourteen local preachers, and twenty-two exhorters. The committee on plan consisted of J. B. Quigg, presiding elder, Henry Sanderson, Charles Moore, Jabez Hodson, and Isaac McCabe. I would here notice the workers sent forth by the committee to work wherever they were ordered; they were as follows: Henry Sanderson, William L. Taylor, Thomas Lamplugh, John Simmons, David Todd, Charles Moore, Bro. Vanhorne, S. A. Young, of the United Brethren Church, W. Rawlins, and John Gray; exhorters, Bro. McKaig, J. Jones, Bro. Bruce, Bro. Shipley, Thos. Moore, A. Thatcher, Bro. Raymond, Bro. McKeever, and Bro. Peters.

These law efforts outside the regular ministerial work, resulted in the building up of eleven other Methodist churches in the city of Wilmington. Asbury to-day is free from debt and in a glorious condition for good work, her success not being second to any other church in our city. The writer of this sketch remembers her seventy-seven years ago, when she was alone, weak and persecuted, her name a by-word and reproach, and her members treated with scorn and derision, but ever true to her Master, and through the instrumentality of the earnest and spirit-annointed preaching of Christ crucified, she stands firm to-day, with the bow of promise above her, and a prospect of noble conquest for the future.

Ezion Methodist Episcopal Church.

By Joseph R. Waters, Pastor.

Mr. Chairman: We come to represent Ezion, the oldest daughter of Asbury. Asbury is the oldest Methodist Episcopal Church in the city of Wilmington, and the mother of us all. Ezion comes next in age, born more than four score years ago.

Ezion, the rather novel, but Biblical name, given to this church, was for a long time a puzzle to the most of us, but to the founders and fathers it was not so; and we may say of them, as it is said of Paul: "according to the grace of God which was given into them as wise master builders. They laid well the foundation, upon which we are building." But when we consider that our fathers were deprived of educational advantages, therefore having little, or no knowledge of words, much less the history of words, the selecting of a name for their church almost a century ago, which name is suitable to be adopted by this generation, is worthy of giving them a place among the prophets. Ezion-Gaber was a very ancient city lying not far from Elath on the eastern arm of the Red Sea. It is first mentioned in the book of Numbers, 33d chapter and 35th verse as one of the stations where the Hebrews halted in their journeyings through the desert. Ezion-Gaber was a seaport and harbor; King Solomon selected it for his navy. Here he built a fleet to go to Ophir, from which country they returned with four hundred and twenty talents of gold. This gold was brought to adorn the temple of the Lord. It is the name of this city that we find inscribed on the corner-stone of our church, having been done by our fathers more than eighty years ago.

The inference which may be drawn from this name is that as Solomon's fleet went forth from Ezion-Gaber in search of gold, so did our fathers go forth from this Ezion, in search, not of the gold that perisheth, but for the golden treasures of heaven which

Pastor of **Ezion** Methodist Episcopal Church.

perisheth not; not to Ophir but to the land of the blessed ; not to return, but to dwell there forever; and nearly all of them have long since reached that country and are to-day walking the golden streets, singing the songs of the redeemed. The meaning of this name Ezion-Gaber, "the giant's backbone," is also very suggestive. In those days, when our race was oppressed and when in many parts it was a crime for our people to assemble even to worship God, it required not a weak backbone, but a giant's backbone to withstand the heavy pressure which was brought to bear against them. Again at this period when the Methodist Episcopal Church was about to be extinguished among the colored people, it took a giant,s backbone to hold up the white flag of the grand old mother church. I am sorry to say, just here, that we will not be able to give you the full and correct history of Ezion, owing to the fact that no records have been preserved, and what we did have were destroyed by the fire of 1886.

According to the date of the church seal, the old stone church was build in 1805. Previous to this date our people were members of Asbury, but of their connection with Asbury as members we have no account. Neither have we any account of them for a great many years after this date. Perhaps Father Jacob Pindergrass was one the first members in the organization. The pastors of Asbury Church supervised the work. Jacob Pindergrass was licensed a local preacher and placed as a sub-pastor over the flock. Under his management the church grew in numbers and power until about 1812, when trouble commenced. Some of the members began to manifest a spirit of independency. This feeling continued until it monopolized nearly all of the young people in the church, so much so, that a dissention was unavoidable. The offices of pastor, presiding elder and bishop, did not come to them as fast as they desired, so they resolved, like Mohammed, to go to it.

The church was now involved in a lawsuit. The church was closed, and the few struggling members who still clung to the old mother, (the Methodist Episcopal,) had no place to worship. The dissenters had now moved on Tatnall street in a barn which was afterwards known as the old pigeon house. Asbury, our mother, seeing the few who were faithful and true to the church, without a place to worship, like a kind and loving mother, said, "Come back and worship with us," assuring them at the same time that she would not leave nor forsake them. The invitation was gladly accepted.

In the meantime the lawsuit was in progress, which was finally settled in favor of the old stone church. The doors of this old church were once more thrown open, and with great rejoicing the members and friends returned. The church was re-organized by the pastor of Asbury, with two trustees, viz: Michael Stirling and Ralph Harding, and three stewards, Jacob Pindergrass, Michael Stirling and Ralph Harding. The membership, consisting of thirty-nine in all, was organized into three classes with Jacob Pindergrass, Michael Stirling and Ralph Harding as leaders. These three men had to fill all of the offices in the church.

Again Father Pindergrass was placed in charge of the flock as speaker or sub-pastor. The church now had peace. The dissenters had organized under the leadership of Rev. Peter Spencer, and denominated themselves the F. C. A. U. M. P. church, which church is known by that name to this day. Ezion, having the Presiding Elder of the district, and the pastor of Asbury at her side, increased daily in membership and influence, but it was not long before the church was called to mourn the loss of their leader, Father Pindergrass, who died in full triumphs of faith. Bro. George S. Hagany, (who is now perhaps the oldest member of Asbury,) informs us that he visited Pindergrass in his death sickness, and also attended his funeral, that he died happy and his funeral was the largest that he had ever seen. But God at this time, as he does in all cases when a good man falls, raised up another full of faith in the person of Rev. Joseph Whittington, who took charge of the flock. Brother Whittington and his cabinet managed the affairs of the church so as to exert a great influence in the community. It was not long before it was found that the old stone church was too small and something had to be done to accommodate the congregation. It was resolved by the officials to enlarge the building which they did by extending it front. This was accomplished in 1844. Soon after the church was re-opened, there was organized what was known as a Local Conference. This Local Conference made our people to feel throughout the states, that a new era had dawned upon them; at this Conference all of the local preachers met once a year, and the Presiding Elders arranged the appointments for the year.

Methodism had spread through the states of Pennsylvania, New Jersey, Delaware, and the Eastern Shore of Maryland, all of the work among our people in these states was under the Local Conference. This new arrangement proved a great incentive to the growth of the church.

Revs. Philip Scott, Benjamin Brown and John G. Manluff were respectfully appointed to Ezion by the local conference. Rev. Scott and Brown each remained but a short time. They then connected themselves with the Washington Conference. Rev. John G. Manluff, who was one of the ablest preachers of his day, remained in charge of Ezion until 1864, when the Delaware Annual Conference was organized. Rev. John H. Pearce was the first pastor of Ezion appointed by a regular conference presided over by a Bishop. Rev. Pearce served one year, Rev. Chas. Wing, three years, he being followed by Rev. Peter Burrows. By this time the membership and Sunday-school had grown so large that is was necessary to tear down the walls and rebuild. Rev. Burrows found several thousand dollars in hand when he arrived. He called the officials of the church and constituted a building committee, and the work was commenced. But before the walls of the new building were up the conference met at Cambridge, Md., and Rev. Burrows was removed, and Rev. Joseph D. Elbert was appointed pastor of Ezion. He found the work in progress with a well qualified official board, and building committee. He had only to begin where his predecessor left off, which he did. The new church was completed in 1870. It reflected great credit on the pastors, and people, as well as the architect and builders, as it was the finest church edifice in the conference. The Sunday-school had now become one of the most prominent features of the church, with Abram Murray as the superintendent, and the splendid new church grew rapidly in members and interest. Rev. J. D. Elbert served the church three years; then followed, Rev. Hooper Jolly, one year; Rev. Solomon Cooper, two years; Rev. L. Y. Cox, two years; Rev. W. F. Butler, D. D., three years; Rev. W. J. Parker, three years; Rev. H. A. Monroe, three years. During Dr. Butler's administration a fine pipe organ was purchased at a cost of $1,100, and some changes were made in the pulpit and gallery.

In Rev. Parker's time a parsonage was secured at a cost of $1,800. Some slight improvements were made in the Sunday-school room during the first year of Rev. Monroe's administration.

The greatest epoch in the history of Ezion occurred on the 6th day of January, 1886, when the church was almost entirely destroyed by fire, just at the time when the church was in the best condition, having only a small debt which the congregation expected in a short time to remove, and perhaps for the first time worship God in a church free from all indebtedness. But all their anticipations were blighted. Imagine the anxiety and grief of this people on this memorable day, when an alarm is sounded throughout the city that Ezion is in flames. Men, women and children left their work, homes and schools and rushed to the scene. The greatest excitement prevailed. Strong men, as well as women and children, wept when they saw their beloved Zion wrapped in devouring flames, and that in the dead of winter they were turned out of doors with no place to worship.

Great sympathy was manifested throughout the city for this sorrow-stricken people. But the people, remembering the promise of God, that passing through the fire they should not be consumed, they came together and decided at once to rebuild. Aid was now coming in from all sides. A building committee was constituted, consisting of the following: B. L. Tomlinson, P. T. Laws, Wm. H. Caldwell, Wm. E. Grinnage, N. B. Waters, James A. Benton, and John M. Kirkman.

The architectural plan was obtained from B. D. Price & Co., of Philadelphia, Pa., and a contract was made with Mr. Archibald Reed. The congregation met in the sister churches, until they could obtain a place to worship, which they did in one of the rooms in the Opera House at fifteen dollars a week. While the work was in progress the people made great sacrifices so that in September of the same year, the beautiful church in which we are now worshiping was completed. Ezion is now one of the most convenient, as well as one of the finest churches in Wilmington. In the spring of 1887 Rev. Monroe was succeeded by the writer. Our church is valued at $45,000. Parsonage at $1,800. We have a membership of five hundred and eighty-one; probationers twenty-two; total, six hundred and thirteen; raising for ministerial support $1,230; for benevolences $513. Ezion, like Asbury, has become a mother, having three daughters, Whittington, Haven and New Castle, under the respective pastorates of Rev. J. A. Richardson, and Rev. J. H. Scott, and Rev. L. W. Deakins. These churches were organized by Ezion as missions, later they were placed under the charge of pastors, and called Wilmington circuit; but since they have become self-supporting, and each church has a pastor, Ezion, and her three daughters, daughters and grand-daughters of Asbury, are Methodist Episcopal, first, last, and all the time. We shall never forget the sheded blood, the scoffs and frowns that our mother has borne for us. We shall never forget 1844, when, on account of our race, she sustained a loss of millions of dollars worth of property, and about one-half of her members. Like Ruth, we say "entreat us not to leave Thee or to return from following after Thee, for whither Thou goest we will go, Thy people shall be our people, Thy God our God."

It has been said that the Methodist Episcopal Church sent more soldiers in the field, and more prayers to heaven, for the country, during the late war, than any other church; also that it was our beloved Bishop Simpson who nerved the arm of President Lincoln to sign the Emancipation Proclamation, by which four millions of poor slaves were set free. We are still looking to our mother for help. No church in this country has done more than the Methodist Episcopal toward solving the race problem in the South. The Freedmen's Aid

Schools of the Methodist Episcopal Church are educating our race in the South intellectually, morally, and spiritually, and raising them from ignorance, immorality, and superstition, so that to-day there is little or no trouble, caused by those under its care. I am of the opinion that this great race question will finally be settled by this great church of the living God, not by the sword, but by Christian education and the preaching of the cross of Christ.

In conclusion, Ezion has a host of living stones in the building, and when Asbury, our mother, with her daughters, St. Paul's, Grace, Union, Scott and others, shall ascend on the beautiful morning of the resurrection to meet the Lord in the sky, Ezion and her daughters will be there to take their part in the great corronation.

History of St. Paul's Methodist Episcopal Church.

By Joseph Pyle, Esq.

In the absence of the Rev. L. E. Barrett, owing to his sickness, and thinking that the historical sketch of St. Paul's ought to be presented on this glad and happy occasion; that the mother church should know how her oldest white daughter had proven her early training and conducted herself generally since setting up house-keeping on her own account, this brief sketch has been hurriedly prepared this morning by one of her members, while knowing that Brother Barrett's would have been more entertaining and instructive, yet he hopes this will prove satisfactory to Mother Asbury.

For some years previous to 1844, there was a feeling amongst some of the leading members of Asbury Church, that the Methodistic field in the city of Wilmington was not thoroughly cultivated, that there was room for at least one more church where the gospel of free grace could be preached with benefit and a rich harvest could be gathered. Old Asbury had been doing a grand and noble work. Since her dedication, in 1789, she had grown so rapidly that her stakes had to be twice extended, her borders twice enlarged, and already her colored members had withdrawn from her communion and established a church at Ninth and French streets, where they could, as they said, enjoy more spirituality and do more good amongst their own race.

Asbury had increased numerically, numbering in her ranks some of the most prominent men in business circles, some leading professional men, and some of wealth and influence. Other denominations were pushing their ranks into popular favor, preaching their peculiar dogmas and extending their influence by building churches and establishing Sabbath-schools, while the Methodists were calmly letting their religious influence be confined to one church and that church embraced within the limits of walls 50x70 feet. This could no longer be tolerated; this state of affairs must be corrected, and, remembering the motto of the founder of Methodism, "The world is my parish," and knowing from happy experience the elastic power and holy influence of the bonds that bind all Methodistic hearts, some members of this mother church, in the year 1844, agitated the project of organizing another society and building another church, if possible in or near the center of the city.

This movement, of course, was opposed by some (I think I am safe in saying by more than one-half) of the members. This opposition was, of course, to be expected, for in all movements for the elevation and betterment of the human race has in all ages of the world been opposed by men; yea, by good men, by pious and God-fearing men — men whose faith, though strong enough to save their souls through the mercy of God's free grace, yet is not strong enough to trust the Almighty power, for the apparent weakening of God's host by withdrawal of a part or a separation of that host under new leaders. But that God who sent Abraham into a strange country, protected and blest him there, also blest and protected the founders of St. Paul's as they left the pleasant associations and holy influences of one who had been their kind and loving mother.

The movement, amid opposition, assumed tangible proportions and soon became a fixed fact, a reality. The first meeting was held at the residence of Hyland B. Pennington, corner of Fourth and Market streets, on the site where Wm. B. Sharp's store is now located. The chairman of the meeting was the Rev. John Kennaday, pastor of Asbury. After the opening by singing and prayer, and a thorough discussion of the subject, in which the hopes and fears were prayerfully considered, a motion was unanimously adopted to organize a society to be known as St. Paul's M. E. Church, of Wilmington, Del. The trustees then were elected as follows: Hyland B. Pennington, Henry Hicks, Wm. H. Calvert, Miller Dunnott, Samuel McCaulley, Jacob M. Garretson and Edward Moore. A purchasing committee was then appointed as follows: Miller Dunnott, Samuel McCaulley, Henry Hicks, Thomas Young, Edward Moore, John Flinn, John M. Turner, Wm. H. Calvert, and Hyland B. Pennington, nine members. This committee purchased a lot on Market street, 50 x 117 feet, above Seventh street, from John McKnight and Samuel Newlin for the sum of $3,000. A building committee was then appointed as follows: Wm. H. Calvert, Samuel McCaulley, Edward Moore, Henry Hicks, and Miller Dunnott, five members. The material and labor were supplied at a reduced figure. Samuel McCaulley, a brick manufacturer, furnished bricks at $6.00 per thousand, and John Flinn, a brick mason, laid them for $2.25 per thousand, while John M. Turner, being equally generous, a carpenter and builder, did the carpentering work for the small sum of $700. It was agreed that the church should have the pew system, and being an innovation in the system of free seats, met with much opposition, both in the Methodist circle and in the worldly opponents, and St. Paul's was known for years under the opprobrious name of " the silk stocking church."

The church was dedicated on Thursday, March 3, 1845, by the Rev. John Kennaday and Levi Scott, and St. Paul's became a fixed power for good in Wilmington. The first pastor was the Rev. John Kennaday, who served from 1845 to 1846; others were Joseph Castle, 1847 and 1848; Pennel Coomb, 1849 and 1850; F. Hodgson, 1851 and 1852; C. D. Carson, 1853; Joseph Mason, 1854; George R. Crooks, 1855 and 1856; Charles Cook, 1857 and 1858; Wm. H. Brisbane, 1859 and 1860; T. C. Murphey, 1861 and 1862; Wm. J. Stevenson, 1863 to 1865; Aaron Rittenhouse, 1866 to 1868; J. F. Clymer, 1869 and 1870; R. W. Todd, 1871 and 1872; J. B. Merritt, 1873 to 1875; Wm. P. Davis, 1876 and 1877, J. H. Caldwell, 1878 to 1880; M. A. Richards, 1881 and 1882; R. H. Adams, 1883 to 1885; W. L. S. Murray, 1886; C. Hill, 1887; L. E. Barrett is now the pastor.

In 1866 some of the most influential members in spirituality and wealth, believing that the cause of Christ would be promoted, and Methodism advanced by more and better accommodations provided for members and strangers, withdrew from St. Paul's and organized Grace M. E. Church. The withdrawal of so many members, amongst which were the pastor, the board of trustees with one exception, the Sabbath-school teachers with five exceptions, and more than half of the class leaders and stewards and all the wealthy members, left St. Paul's in a very weak and almost despondent condition. But the spirit of Methodism could not be crushed by this fearful and almost fatal blow. The members that stayed by St. Paul's with renewed zeal and with a determination that could not be defeated, manfully, and under the blessings of God, and with the spiritual pastor that God sent them, successfully maintained the influence and power of the church, and she arose gradually to her present position in the front rank of the churches in Wilmington. Within six years after the separation she expended $7,000 in the remodeling and improvement of the church, and adding to the choir a pipe organ costing $1,500, and again, in 1882, made alterations in the audience room by taking out the gallery, frescoing the ceiling at a cost of $3,800. This same year the trustees purchased the property next door to the church for $12,200 to protect the church on the right, and again in 1886 extending the school-room to Shipley street, to accommodate twenty-four more classes. This improvement cost $6,000, which was raised on one Sabbath at the re-opening of the school.

The Sabbath-school was opened cotemporaneously with the church and has been in operation to this date. The superintendents, I think, (though I am not certain of being correct in the first ones) were as follows: Henry Hicks, Geo. W. Sparks, Wm. S. Hagany, J. Taylor Gause, Isaac Crouch and Joseph Pyle, the latter being elected to the afternoon school in 1866, and is superintendent at this date. The morning school was opened about the year 1858. The superintendents were W. H. Billany, Charles B. Lore, Joseph Pyle, Z. Pickels, John B. Tribler, James C. Morrow, Noble Hadley, and James W. Robertson, the present superintendent. The afternoon school has a membership of over six hundred scholars and seventy-two officers and teachers with an average attendance of four hundred and sixty. The morning school has a membership of one hundred and seventy, average attendance about one hundred.

The present trustees of the church are Joseph Pyle, president; James C. Pickels, treasurer; Jabez Hodson, Edgar A. Finley, B. Murgatroyd, Wm. Y. Swiggett, S. H. Baynard, Edwin F. Morrow and Wm. Hukill. The secretary is Harvey Hoffecker, who is not a member of the board.

History of Union Methodist Episcopal Church.

By the Rev. Adam Stengle, Pastor.

The Union Methodist Episcopal Church, of Wilmington, Delaware, located on the N. W. corner of Fifth and Washington streets, is chronologically the fourth church in our city Methodism—the order being, Asbury, Ezion, St. Paul's, Union.

Though it is of such comparatively recent origin, yet there is already an error generally prevalent regarding both its founder and the date of its origin. Thus presenting another example of the importance of keeping accurate historic records of our churches, and also of the fact that our Methodism has very generally failed to do so. The error referred to is, that Union Church was founded in 1850, and by the Rev. Andrew Manship, both of which are incorrect.

While the writer would not pluck a single flower from the wreath which adorns the brow of this worthy servant of God, yet fidelity to facts in the presentation of this historic sketch, absolutely require him to correct this error. From the undisputed testimony of many living witnesses, as well as from several "old records," the Philadelphia Conference Minutes, and also from the Rev. Andrew Manship's book, "Thirteen Years in the Itinerancy," it clearly appears that Union Church was founded in 1847 and by the Rev. Edward Kennard, who at that time held a supernumerary relation in the Philadelphia Conference, which Conference at that time included all of the territory now embraced in the Wilmington Conference. Brother Kennard's estimable widow, as well as two daughters and a son, still survive him, the latter is a prominent merchant on Market street, in our city.

It appears that during the year 1847, Mr. Kennard with his family removed from Elkton, Md., to this city. Soon after his arrival a

REV. ADAM STENGLE,

Pastor of Union Methodist Episcopal Church.

house at Third and Orange streets, in which a society of Methodist Protestants worshiped, was sold and he became the purchaser. Immediately he organized a Methodist Episcopal society in this house, preaching regularly himself, and in the following March (1848) reported his work to the Philadelphia Conference as "Orange street," with fifty-three members. That this new society was duly accepted by the proper authorities is evident in the Conference minutes of that year (1848), for in the "list of appointments" made at that session we find "Orange street" connected with St. Paul's under the pastoral care of Rev. Joseph Castle and Rev. E. Kennard supernumerary.

The following year (1849) it appears in the minutes of the above-named Conference as a separate charge, to which the Rev. H. S. Atmore was appointed, with the Rev. E. Kennard as supernumerary. The society seems to have prospered up to this period, for according to the Conference minutes of March, 1849, when Brother Atmore was appointed, it reported seventy-three members, one local preacher, one Sabbath-school with 100 scholars, and also collections for Missions and for Conference claimants.

But during this year (1849) the tide turned, resulting in a complete change of its personnel as well as of its name and location, to which fact doubtless is due the prevalent error regarding its founder and the date of its origin. This change was brought about after the following manner: Early in the year 1849, under Mr. Atmore's pastorate, for several reasons it was decided to build a new and more commodious church, and in a more eligible location. It was to be a two-story brick structure, with lecture and class rooms on the first floor. A lot was soon secured on Second street, near Washington, trustees were elected, and a building committee was appointed, and the work of construction was pushed forward with considerable enthusiasm. On the surface the outlook was promising, but, nevertheless, trouble was brewing. This grew out of two facts which proved disastrous to the young enterprise. The *first* was the very common mistake of building without first counting the cost and securing a sufficient sum to guarantee the success of the enterprise; the *second* was a matter of less frequent occurrence, but wholly inexcusable, namely, the "laying of the corner-stone with Masonic ceremonies" instead of the ritual of the church. This latter fact proved so exceedingly offensive to some that they positively refused to support the movement any farther. Thus the church sustained a serious loss, and this too at a period in her history when she was least able to bear it.

Nevertheless, the work proceeded for a little while, but the decreasing resources together with the increasing liabilities, soon yielded their legitimate fruit. And the society found itself in the greatest financial embarrassment from which it seemed impossible to extricate itself; and hence operations on the building were necessarily indefinitely suspended, and this, too, at the most critical point in its construction; for the walls were erected to the full height designed, but were left without doors, windows or roof, while winter was at hand threatening their destruction before operations could be resumed in the spring, while even such a resumption seemed exceedingly improbable.

This was certainly a dark period in the history of this church; indeed, it is difficult to conceive a darker; disaffection and dissension in the ranks; a depleted treasury, an overwhelming debt; confidence destroyed; creditors clamoring for their money and indignantly denouncing the whole scheme a swindle; while other churches even withheld their sympathy. Indeed, so thoroughly discouraging was the outlook, that even Pastor Atmore abandoned the charge in the midst of the year for another and more hopeful field of labor. Very naturally, then, the embarrassed and deserted congregation became demoralized and scattered, some joining other churches, some drifting hither and thither, some backsliding entirely, while a small remnant held on, "standing still to see the salvation of the Lord." But to all except to the most extraordinarily sanguine, this seemed to be the end of this mission, which began so auspiciously, and promised so much. Accordingly we are not surprised to find in the minutes of the ensuing Conference, March, 1850, "*No Report*," the only report made concerning it.

But it has been said, "The darkest hour is just before the dawn;" so it proved in this case. As the disheartened Israelites were rallied and delivered from the oppressive yoke of Jabin, King of Canaan, through the heroic efforts of the prophetess Deborah, so this desponding society was rescued from the destroyer through the heroic efforts of a woman. That woman was Miss Margaret Rumford, then a member of the Asbury M. E. Church. At the critical period, in the fall of 1849, she, "touched by the mute appeals of the forsaken walls," personally contributed and solicited funds sufficient to put a roof on the building and otherwise protect it from the ravages of the winter. But for her efforts, seconded by a few others of like spirit, it is almost certain that Union Church would never have been completed.

At the Philadelphia Conference in March, 1850, the Rev. Andrew Manship was appointed to this charge which was now called "Union Mission," and henceforth "Orange street" appears no more in the Conference minutes. Why the name should have been changed is apparent, for it could no longer properly be called "Orange street" after its removal from that street. But why it was called "Union" does not appear on the records, so far as I know. But it is more than probable that the name was inspired by the hope that members of Asbury and St. Paul's would unite with the "Orange street" remnant and so resuscitate the mission.

Mr. Manship arrived soon after Conference, but alas! he found no Union, and indeed very little out of which to construct one. He found indeed a dismembered society, and also an unfinished edifice hopelessly encumbered by a debt of nearly $3,000. A Quarterly Conference minute book of those times says: "When he came he found no congregation nor church in which to preach, the former congregation that had commenced to build at Second and Washington streets, having been left without a pastor and consequently were scattered."

But it may be inquired "Why could he not have preached in the former place of worship at Third and Orange streets?" Because that was the private property of the Rev. E. Kennard; and it appears that after the departure of the Rev. H. S. Atmore in the previous year, Mr. Kennard resumed control of this place, preaching there for a short time himself, when, owing to the fact that the lease by which the ground was held was about to expire, he removed the house to Seventh and Walnut streets. Here it became known as Kennard's Church; here he preached; and here was organized the Sabbath-school which developed into the Scott M. E. Church. And after having been used for a variety of purposes, it at length became again what it was originally, "the first Methodist Protestant Church of Wilmington, Delaware," and since then it has been rebuilt and remodeled and very much improved.

But notwithstanding the discouragements, Brother Manship heroically faced the situation; and, with Mr. Edward Moore of St. Paul's as his surety, he rented the Odd Fellows Hall at Third and King streets for five dollars a Sabbath. This he used as a rallying point and here he re-organized the scattered members of Orange street together with others into the church thenceforth to be called "Union." On the first Sabbath in this hall he received two persons into the church, both ladies; and the first was the aforesaid Miss Margaret Rumford. It is only just to add that she still remains an honored and efficient member of this church; and though she may not be so strong in body now as she was then, yet she retains all of the spirit and zeal which made her the deliverer of "old Union" in the fall of 1840. She is still a regular and cheerful as well as liberal contributor to the support of the church of her choice; and though she resides about eight squares from the church, she is yet a regular attendant upon class and prayer-meeting, as well as upon the public services.

The Odd Fellows Hall was at that time the only theatre in Wilmington, and during the week it was used for theatrical purposes, which, of course, were in striking contrast to the Sabbath services. This fact was not only the occasion of many pleasantries, but also of much unfriendly criticism on this new society; and thus doubtless some were restrained from enlisting with them, who otherwise would have done so.

But nevertheless the society grew rapidly, several things contributing to this end. The earnestness of the preacher, and the novelty of the place, attracted large congregations. And besides this, there had for sometime been considerable friction at Asbury, which was now greatly intensified by the return of the pastor in the face of a decided opposition, and still further aggravated by some indiscreet utterances on his part regarding the opposition. And as Asbury was already full to overflowing, and a new church was a necessity and only a question of time, accordingly a large number seized this opportunity of withdrawing from the "old church" and uniting with the "new." An "old record" of Union Church, though imperfect, shows that about thirty persons were received by Mr. Manship by letter during the first month (April,) and about seventy-five more in the same way during the rest of the year. The record does not show whence these came, but under the circumstances it is more than likely that nearly all of them came from Asbury.

As the hall could not be obtained for religious services during the the week, the prayer and class meetings were held in private houses in different parts of the city, and, of course, the new church thus labored under some disadvantage. But again help came very unexpectedly. The trustees of St. Paul's Church, "endorsed by the entire congregation," generously granted Mr. Manship the use of their lecture room, without expense, two evenings of each week as long as it was needed.

In order to produce a more general interest in this new church enterprise, a meeting was called very early in the year in St. Paul's Church, which was attended by the ministers and leading Methodists of the city as well as by others. Bishop Waugh delivered an appropriate and soul stirring address to this congregation, which doubtless contributed greatly to Brother Manship's success.

The enthusiasm of the preacher, the number and character of the accessions, and the encouragement received from other sources, speedily inspired hope for the abandoned enterprise at Second and Washington streets. Accordingly at an early day a new board of trustees was appointed, consisting of Asa Poinsett, Geo. McGee,

John Rudolph, Grubb Talley, Albert Thatcher, Thomas K. Baynard and Edward Moore.

This board assumed all the obligations of the former, made satisfactory arrangements with the creditors, and then vigorously pushed forward the work to completion, at a cost of about $7,000. The church was dedicated by Bishop E. S. Janes, on Thursday, November 28, 1850. The Bishop preached at 10 A. M., and the Rev. Henry Slicer, of the Baltimore Conference, at 3 and 7 P. M. During the day the debt was reduced to $2,400, which balance was also paid off after a brief interval.

It is due to Brother Manship to say that he collected a considerable part of this money in Philadelphia, "down the Peninsula," and elsewhere, whither he went "on begging tours."

At the close of the first conference year Mr. Manship had the pleasure of reporting the church completed and nearly paid for; a society of one hundred and fifty-four members and one hundred and forty probationers; a flourishing Sabbath-school, which had been organized in the Odd Fellows Hall, of two hundred scholars; a Sunday-school library containing three hundred volumes; and collections as follows: For Missions, $51.00; for Bible Cause, $8.25, for Conference Claimants, $25.50. This is a record which few pastors have excelled, if any; and of which any might justly feel proud.

The following named persons, in connection with the trustees already named, constituted the first officiary of the church after its re-organization in the spring of 1850. *Class Leaders:* Barney C. Harris, John Boyce, Isaac McConnell, Wm. Edmundson, and Albert Thatcher. *Stewards:* Asa Poinsett, John Rudolph, George McGee, and John Guire. *Exhorters:* Wm. Edmundson, Frank Supplee and Cyrus Stern. Cyrus Stern was also the first Sunday-school superintendent, and Miss Margaret Rumford was the first female superintendent; both served in their respective offices for several years with great success and with eminent satisfaction to the school.

The society, now thoroughly established, grew so rapidly that within fifteen years a larger edifice was absolutely demanded. Accordingly, in 1865, it was decided to build a larger church and in a more desirable locality. The Quarterly Conference appointed the pastor, J. D. Curtis, Stephen Postles, Cyrus Stern, J. C. Pickels, Asa Poinsett, Wm. Edmundson, and Wesley Talley, a committee to secure the site for the new church. This committee selected the lot on which the present edifice now stands. The Quarterly Conference approved their action and referred the matter of building to the board of trustees; and this board appointed Stephen Postles, Cyrus Stern and Jethro

McCullough, three of their number, "a building committee, with full power to erect and complete the church." These men at once proceeded with the work and vigorously pushed it to completion, and the edifice is a standing testimonial to their efficiency and fidelity in this responsible position.

While, however, great credit is due to each of the three named, it is only just to mention the chairman, Stephen Postles, as deserving special credit; for he not only gave the work his constant personal supervision, but also cheerfully contributed considerably more than one-tenth of the entire cost of the church.

The lecture-room was dedicated December 23, 1866, and the auditorium November 17, 1868, by Bishops E. R. Ames and Levi Scott.

The entire cost of the church and lot was $30,000, which was all provided for and paid within a few years, making the church entirely free from debt. The edifice is most admirably located; is well planned and built, of first-class material, well adapted to its purposes, and is one of the handsomest and largest in the Wilmington Conference, a credit to the building committee and an honor to our Methodism.

The church, though once entirely free from debt, is unfortunately not so now. About the year 1876, the church was mortgaged for $1,000, which encumbrance still remains.

During the year 1882 the trustees purchased the house 513 Jefferson street, for $4,000, as a church parsonage. Of this amount about $1,000 remains unpaid, but is in a fair way of liquidation. The house is commodious and conveniently located, and every way suited for the purpose for which it was purchased.

Union Church has had only a brief, yet a very eventful history. Time and space, however, will not permit us to indulge the desire to recall the many interesting and thrilling events of her forty-two years' existence. Like nearly all churches having a large membership, she has had sunshine and storms. While in 1876 the roof was blown from the building by a terrific storm which swept over our city, the church has also been racked and torn by storms within, which carried away many of her members.

During the late war her intense loyalty to the government was well known. Frequently the walls of "Old Union" echoed the eloquence of patriotism, as it issued from the pulpit and the pew; in stirring appeals to men to rally around the "Star Spangled Banner," and in earnest pleading with God for the overthrow of the rebellion, the abolition of slavery and the triumph of truth. Those appeals were not in vain. Those prayers have been answered.

But the "Old Union" is no more. The building was sold and the proceeds were applied to the "New Union." The "Old Union" passed through many hands and was used for a variety of purposes, some of which I am informed were exceedingly disreputable. But the Reformed Episcopal Church of the Covenant finally bought the property and redeemed it from such base purposes, and occupied it as a place of worship for several years. But that church having also sold it, the present owner has demolished it and erected upon the site thereof several stores and dwellings, so that nothing remains to remind the passer-by of the former things.

It would be exceedingly interesting to know how many souls have been gathered into the heavenly garner through the instrumentality of Union Church; but this knowledge is denied us for the present. It has been in some measure a revival church, aflame with primitive Methodist fire, and hundreds of souls have been born to God at her altars.

At present the church is enjoying a season of quiet prosperity. She numbers six hundred and forty members who are divided into twelve classes. She has a flourishing Sabbath-school of about eight hundred scholars and about seventy officers and teachers, and a Sunday-school library of more than a thousand volumes.

The church has had twenty-one pastors, of which the following is a complete list, from its origin in Orange street in 1847 to the present year 1889.

"Orange street" from 1847 to 1850.—1847, Edward Kennard, supernumerary preacher of the Philadelphia Conference; 1848, J. Castle and E. Kennard, in connection with St. Paul's; 1849, H. S. Atmore.

"Union" from 1850 to the present.—1850-1, Andrew Manship; 1852-3, Joshua Humphries; 1854-5, James B. Maddux; 1856, L. T. Cooper; 1857-8, John Ruth; 1859-60, Wm. Barnes; 1861-2, John W. Arthur; 1863-4, James A. Brindle; 1865-6, J. D. Curtis; 1867-8, W. E. England; 1869-70, Samuel L. Gracy; 1871, J. H. Lightbourne; 1872-3, Charles Hill; 1874-6, T. E. Martindale; 1877-9, J. B. Mann; 1880-2, Adam Stengle; 1883-5, C. W. Prettyman; 1886-9, Adam Stengle.

While the vast majority of the members who came to the Union from Asbury in 1850, have joined the Church Triumphant and have entered into the heavenly rest, yet a considerable number remain lingering on this shore, amid the halo of a glorious sunsetting, awaiting the summons from the Father to enter the blissful abode of His saints beyond the bounds of time and sense. Among these are Miss Margaret Rumford, Cyrus Stern, Caroline Stern, Eliza Harris, Susan Sinex, Susan Foord, Catharine Kelley, Mary A. Flagler, Joanna Gordon, Hannah McDonnel, Mary Robinson, James Dawson, Mary Dawson, and perhaps others.

The Lord hath done great things for us, whereof we are glad and for which we ascribe to Him all the glory.

REV. WALTER E. AVERY,
Pastor of Mt. Salem Methodist Episcopal Church.

History of Mt. Salem Methodist Episcopal Church.

By the Rev. Walter Avery, Pastor.

The word Salem means "peaceful," and if the founders of the church had searched the Bible from Genesis to Revelation they could not have found a more appropriate name. It is in harmony with the quiet and peaceful surroundings of the church. A man of learning once remarked that he thought it was the duty of a historian to draw conclusions. Bishop Ames said on one occasion that he believed historians ought to state facts. It occurred to me, as soon as the sentence fell from his lips, that the bishop was right, and I have found no reason to change my mind since. Mt. Salem, like many of her sister churches, has suffered so far as her historical record is concerned, and it is very difficult, under the circumstances, to write a correct history. The Centennial of Asbury has not only kindled the fires of enthusiasm in our hearts and caused us to rejoice, as the children and grandchildren have paid their tributes of respect to their mother and grandmother, but it has incited us to search for facts in local church history which will make us better acquainted with the good men who have preceded us. Ancient church records, gray with dust and age, have been taken from their hiding places and carefully examined. The fathers and mothers in Israel have been interviewed and questioned as to their knowlege of the growth and development of their respective churches, and fragments of historic value have been gathered both from books and men. We have doubtless been impressed with one fact while listening to the many excellent papers which have been read during this Centennial week, and that is, that the fathers of Methodism not only made history rapidly, but they made exceedingly good history.

Mt. Salem Methodist Episcopal Church, according to the record, was commenced in the year of our Lord 1847, and finished in the spring of 1848. It was opened for divine worship on the 23rd of April, 1848, by the following ministers: Rev. Francis Hodgson preached the dedicatory sermon in the morning from Galations, vi: 14.—"But God forbid that I should glory, save in the cross of our Lord Jesus Christ, by whom the world is crucified unto me, and I unto the world."

Some who heard him preach are still living, and they say his sermon was powerful. It moved the hearts of the people wonderfully. Rev. I. T. Cooper preached eloquently in the afternoon from the eighth chapter and ninth verse of the II Epistle of Corinthians: "For ye know the grace of our Lord Jesus Christ, that, though he was rich, yet for your sakes he became poor, that ye, through his poverty, might be rich." Rev. Joseph Castle preached at night, but his text was not recorded in the minutes. The collections and subscriptions during the day amounted to nearly $400.

Mt. Salem Church was added to St. Paul's station under the pastoral care of Rev. Joseph Castle, and the pulpit was supplied by the local preachers belonging to the Wilmington and Chester circuit, as follows: John Talley, Jesse Ford, Samuel Hanez, Solomon Prettyman, Marcellus A. Keene, Beverly Waugh, Richard Martin, James Riddle, Franklin Supplee, with other brethren in the ministry. On Sunday, the 10th of September, 1848, a protracted meeting began under the superintendence of Marcellus Keene, who was appointed by Joseph Castle, preacher in charge, to take charge of the work at Mt. Salem, Bro. Castle not being able to attend to the work in person.

In 1847 the first board of trustees was elected. Their names are as follows: Franklin Supplee, president; Richard Martin, secretary; James Riddle, treasurer; Thomas Smith, Samuel Montgomery, John Miller and Jesse Elliott. In 1848 Bro. Keene died and Rev. Wm. Kirkman, a local preacher of Asbury Church, took charge. Bro. Kirkman was a ship-carpenter in the employ of the Harlan & Hollingsworth Company. Toiling hard all the week, he preached with great acceptability to the people. On one occasion, when he was not as clear in his statements as usual, he remarked that his mind had been full of ships all the week and he did not seem to be able to get rid of them on Sunday. As we study the lives of these two unassuming, yet earnest men of God, we find, in response to their fervid appeals, that men and women presented themselves to the altar and were saved.

Rev. Wm. L. Boswell, a graduate of Dickinson College, was Mt. Salem's first stationed preacher. A few months ago Bro. Boswell preached for us. He was surprised to see so many houses standing where corn grew thirty-nine years ago. Mt. Salem has had her dark seasons. Her life has not been all sunshine. During the pastorate of Rev. I. R. Merrill, a panic occurred. The factories were closed and many of the church's best supporters were thrown out of employment. The officials met to pay their pastor's salary, the members being willing to make sacrifices in order that he should not go to Conference unpaid. But their preacher, possessing the true Wesleyan spirit, said to the congregation: "I can do without the money better than you can," and refused to take it. Thank God for men who are willing to share losses with their people: they are "the salt of the earth," and "the light of the world." In 1858 a Sunday-school was started on what is known as "Riddle's Banks ;" called the "Union" or "Woods" school. An infant class was also taught in a private home. This school was not far from the home of one of the most philanthropic spirits that ever graced this earth. Bro. James Riddle, whose memory is a benediction to all who knew him, felt that a commodious house ought to be built to accommodate those needing religious instructions in that vicinity, for the Sabbath-school met, at that time, in a small school-house. Bro. Riddle built on his own land, near his home, a beautiful chapel, which was dedicated December 25, 1871, by Rev. George Watson. It was called Riddle's Chapel in honor of the donor. It cost $9,000, and seats between three and four hundred scholars. Riddle's Chapel Sunday-school is in a flourishing condition, and gave last year, for missions, $125. This godly man who said to one of his friends that he never went into a community without "leaving a school-house and a church," left this chapel as a memorial of his generosity. In him the worn-out preachers had a friend, the missionary cause a warm supporter, and all the benevolences of the church a large place in his affections. Heaven alone will reveal the good he did and is doing to-day. Mt. Salem Church looked upon him as a father. He was her father and in her early struggles she leaned upon him for support. When the pulpit needed a supply he could always be relied on, and his widow, as generous as her large-hearted husband, is seen in her church every Sabbath unless prevented by sickness or stormy weather. If time permitted, I would like to speak of the heroic efforts of the many loyal spirits who gave their time, influence and money to build up Zion in this place. It would be interesting to note the zeal which characterized the members of the first quarterly conferences: their willingness to give of their little means, and their love for their preacher: but their records are on high and God has chronicled every good deed that characterized their lives. In 1878, during the pastorate of Rev. Charles F. Sheppard, it was deemed advisable, because of its insecurity and lack of room to tear down the old church and build a larger structure. While the new building was in process of erection, the congregation worshiped in a temporary tabernacle.

The new edifice was built at a cost of $15,000, and dedicated by Dr. R. L. Dashiell, November 3, 1878. Bishop Scott was present, but was very feeble. The worshipers were not permitted to enjoy their handsome church very long. At two o'clock in the morning of February 2, 1879, it was discovered to be on fire, and was burned to the great sorrow of pastor and people. The disheartened company rose above their discouragements and decided to rebuild. Great sacrifices were made by these devoted followers of God. While the present church was building, the congregation worshiped in the Young Men's Christian Association room, at Rising Sun, and in Riddle's Chapel. It was completed, and dedicated by Dr. John H. Dashiell of the Baltimore Conference, July 13, 1879. Brother Sheppard deserves great credit for his noble work. In two years he collected $22,000. When it is known that our people were not rich, but felt every dollar they gave, this is one of the finest specimens of liberality in the history of Methodism. Rev. John Weston, who served the church from 1875 till 1877, fell at his post of duty and was buried in Mt. Salem cemetery. Mt. Salem Church has given some noble sons to the ministry. Rev. John France was licensed to preach by the Mt. Salem Quarterly Conference, and is to-day a member of the Wilmington Conference, and the honored Presiding Elder of the Easton district. Rev. A. J. Crozier, whose dust rests in our cemetery, was a member of this church, and also of the Wilmington Conference. Rev. George Cummins, who worked in the Henry Clay Cotton Factory, labored to build up the cause of Christ here, and is, at present, a member of the Philadelphia Conference and is considered one of its best preachers and ablest debaters.

Bros. Gregg, Kirkpatrick, Webb and Anderson, left here for larger fields of usefulness.

The following pastors have served the church: 1850-1851, W. L. Boswell; 1851-1852, Newton Heston; 1852-1854, Wm. Mullen; 1854-1855, T. W. Simpers and Wm. M. Dalrymple; 1855-1856, T. W. Simpers and John Dyson; 1856-1857, James Hand; 1857-1858, Isaac R. Merrill; 1858-1859, G. D. Carrow, whose place was filled by A. T. Scott; 1859-1860, A. T. Scott; 1860-1861, N. B. Durell; 1861-1863, D. George; 1863-1866, W. S. Pugh; 1866-1867, W. C. Johnson; 1867-1868, O. W. Landreth; 1868-1871, John D. Rigg; 1871-1873, G. D. Watson; 1873-1875, John France; 1875-1877, John W. Weston; 1877-

1880, C. F. Sheppard; 1880-1883, T. L. Tomkinson; 1883-1885, J. E. Smith; 1885-1888, R. C. Jones; 1888-1890, W. E. Avery.

In consulting the records I find that nearly all the fathers and mothers who blessed the first church with their presence and prayers have received their crowns and robes, and "exceeding great reward." Only a few, like the scattered leaves on the trees in the last days of Autumn, are left, and they are patiently waiting for the boatman to guide them over the river. They never heard an angel from heaven say, "Thy prayers and thine alms have come up for a memorial before God;" but they have heard the better angels of their natures say it a thousand times. To-day we thank them for their magnificent work. Age has not marred it. They trod the thorny road of duty, but made it smooth and easy for us, their children. They cut down the forests, and to-day the flower gardens greet us. They worshiped gladly and uncomplainingly in dimly-lighted and inconvenient sanctuaries. Pure, unselfish souls, with a steady flame of heaven glowing in their hearts! No poem has been written to immortalize their deeds, but their lives are poems read and remembered by those whose souls were made musical by their upright living. Time, the great historian of us all, has leveled many of their graves, but their immortal deeds have reached the eternal throne, and we gladly, entwine these wreaths of affection around their memories. They seem to be with us to-day. It may be that they are near enough for us to see them, if from our eyes these mortal films were removed. I rejoice that the ardor of the fathers is not dead.

The class-meetings at Mt. Salem are still loved and honored; the songs of Zion are sung there every Sabbath morning by the old, middle-aged, and young; the Sabbath-school room is thronged and the audience room well filled with souls hungry for the truth.

> As Salem means "peaceful,"
> "Let peace within her walls be found;
> Let all her sons unite,
> To spread with holy zeal around
> Her clear and shining light."

As the church of our choice has more wealth and is in better circumstances than ever before, we may flatter ourselves with the thought that there is no danger to be feared. There is more danger now than there was fifty years ago.

The most dangerous period of a nation's life is not when it is struggling for existence, but when it is resting in the lap of wealth. Methodism was safe when fathers did without new overcoats, and mothers deprived themselves of the pleasures of new bonnets to forward God's cause; but when men have plenty of overcoats and women plenty of bonnets and feel very little need for exertion, then it is that we are to be most watchful. The father who works "from morn . . . to dewy eve," taking advantage of every opportunity, is in very little danger of becoming a spendthrift, but the boy who never earned a dollar in his life and is left $50,000 is in far greater peril than his father. A precious legacy has been handed down to us, a legacy that was achieved by toil and blood. We have read of the struggles of the men who gave us this moral wealth. May we keep untarnished the treasure which has been bequeathed to us.

> God of our fathers,
> "From out whose hand
> The centuries fall like grains of sand,"

help us to sing with all their earnestness the words they loved so well:

> "I love Thy church, O God!
> Her walls before Thee stand,
> Dear as the apple of Thine eye,
> And graven on Thy hand.
>
> "For her my tears shall fall,
> For her my prayers ascend;
> To her my cares and toils be given,
> Till toils and cares shall end."

As Elijah cast his mantle on the ploughman, Elisha, and communed with him till he went home to join the brotherhood around the throne, so may we drop worthy mantles on the Elishas who shall succeed us. I feel, to-day, like making the lines of a good poet mine, and saying, "Unto Him that hath loved us and washed us from our sins in His own blood and hath made us kings and priests unto God and His Father,"

> "We thank Thee for the era done,
> And trust Thee for the opening one."

REV. VAUGHN S. COLLINS.
Pastor of Scott Methodist Episcopal Church.

History of Scott Methodist Episcopal Church.

By the Rev. Vaughan S. Collins, Pastor.

It seems quite the thing during this centennial occasion for all the Methodist churches of the city to call old Asbury their "mother;" but I am not quite sure that Asbury can claim the honor of being the mother of that lively church called Scott. Its birth was on this wise:

On the 28th of September, 1851, a few members from Asbury and Union Methodist Episcopal Churches, and Hanover Presbyterian Church, met and organized a Union Sunday-school in the building known as "Kennard's Church," corner of Seventh and Walnut streets. Now whether Asbury is father or mother to the new organization I am unable to say; and what is the exact relation of the three churches which seem to be parents of the new church, I know not; but one thing I know:—from the date of her birth until now, Scott has had the fire of old Asbury, the perseverence of a Presbyterian, and the concord of "Union" among her members.

At that organization meeting Judge Willard Hall led in singing and prayer, and Rev. Andrew Manship led in a collection—which amounted to $23. Forty-five scholars were present, and twenty-four volunteered their services as teachers. Jacob S. Weldin was elected superintendent, Stewart Carlisle, librarian, and Thomas Orpwood, secretary. From this first meeting to the date of his death, Brother Weldin was the life and soul of the new enterprise; and it is agreed by those acquainted with the facts, that without his sympathetic help, of time and thought, as well as of money, it would have been difficult, if not impossible, for Scott to have survived some of the dark periods of her history.

The notes of that year show increasing interest. On November

30, the school is taken to Asbury Church to listen to addresses by Judge Hall, Rev. A. Atwood, and a stranger from Baltimore. Seven hundred are said to have been present at the service. February 1, 1852, a prayer-meeting was held, it being the first Sunday of the month. At the close of the school the constitution and by-laws were adopted. February 15, 1852, it is noted that "Rev. J. A. Roche is present, led in prayer, and gave us a good little lecture." March 7, "A large attendance and a refreshing time." March 28, "Rev. A. Atwood is present, related several interesting anecdotes, and gave us a good little lecture." April 11, "Rainy, chilly, and unpleasant weather; had no school exercises to-day except singing, on account of being turned out of our house, and having to consider how and where to get another." April 18 finds them in the basement of the Old Free School House, corner Sixth and French streets, and J. T. Van Burkalow leads in prayer. April 25, "Adjourning early to attend church to hear Rev. Mr. Lee, a converted friar." October 17, 1852, it is noted: "In consequence of our being dispossessed of a place to hold our school in, and getting ready to build our house, we have been thrown into confusion, and have not kept our account correct. We are still encouraged to persevere in the cause of Christ." Where they met from this date until their own house was finished in December, I can not find out.

The little society were now anxious to have a building of their own. Brother Samuel McCauley, a good Methodist, donated them a lot at the corner of Seventh and Spruce streets. He told them to stake off just as much as they wanted. They staked off all they supposed they would ever need; but long ago they wished they had taken twice as much. At that time Seventh and Spruce was in the country. All east of Poplar and north of Sixth street was farm lands and brick yards; so these early workers did not suppose they would ever need more than they staked off. Work was pushed rapidly, and on the last Sunday in December, 1852, the new building, a one-story brick, 40 by 45 feet, was dedicated as a Union School House by the Rev. Andrew Manship, assisted by Rev. Nicholas Patterson of the Presbyterian Church, Rev. John A. Roche of Asbury, and Judge Willard Hall. Col. McComb was secretary of the meeting. From that day the church was never free of debt until the first day of December, 1887, when the last dollar of indebtedness was paid, and the mortgage marked "satisfied" on the court house records.

At this first dedication the following incident occurred, vouched for by an eye witness: The Rev. Mr. Patterson subscribed $10. Brother Manship said, "Put me down $10. I won't let a Presbyterian beat me."

Mr Patterson said, "Put me down $10 more." Some one in the congregation gave Brother Manship a wink and he promptly cried out "Put me down $10 more." Brother Patterson just as quickly responded, "Put me down $10 more." Brother Manship looked all over the congregation for another friendly wink or nod, but none came. After waiting in vain for some one to come to his rescue the arch beggar plaintively said, "My friends have gone back on me, and I will have to back down."

The first session in the new building was held January 6, 1853. The Presbyterians and other denominations, who had been working with our people, now gradually dropped out, until only the members of the Methodist Episcopal Church remained as workers. The sister church said that the Methodist Church had stolen the school from them. The charge was unfounded; but if it had been true, I do not think they ought to have complained. It certainly could not have gone over *in toto* to the Methodists unless God had ordained it; and if He had ordained it from before the foundation of the world the Methodists could not help it. The good Presbyterians certainly ought not to grumble at the eternal decree of Jehovah.

As the school continued to grow, some of the faithful ones who labored there thought it wise to organize a church. Until this time it had been called the "Seventh Street Sabbath-school." When the Presbyterians all withdrew it was called the "Seventh Street M. E. Sunday-school." It had been the standing rule from the inception of the movement, to devote the first Sunday in every month to a prayer meeting; and after the building at Seventh and Spruce was completed a week-night prayer meeting was started, which became a power for good. By the spring of 1854 everything was ripe for a church organization. On Thursday night previous to the session of the Annual Conference held that year, Rev. Robert Geary, pastor at Asbury, was invited by those engaged in the work, to hold a meeting to see what ought to be done. Brother Geary explained the *modus operandi* of organization, and asked all who desired to join in with the church about to be organized to volunteer their names. Fifteen gave their consent to enlist in the new departure, among them being Jacob S. Weldin, John Lonsdale, Joseph Spurway, George Mortimer, William H. Riley, Thomas Orpwood, Gilbert Holmes, William Bicking, John Dick, William Heisler, William Griffenberg, John B. Kindall, William H. Foulk and Stewart Carlisle. Of these original members many have died, others removed; so that now Brother Kindall is the only one left at Scott of the faithful fifteen who pledged to stand by the infant enterprise.

Being now organized as a church, the Philadelphia Conference, at its session in 1854, appointed Rev. Henry A. Hobbs pastor of Seventh Street Church. Immediately on the adjournment of Conference he came to his charge. It was late Saturday evening when he reached Wilmington, and he proceeded at once to the church. There he found some of the leading members busily fixing up a plain wooden altar, in order to transform the school house into a church; and as he came limping in, (for he had the rheumatism,) the brethren all dropped their work, and gathered around their first pastor, "as proud as a lot of kittens with their first mouse," as a brother, who was one of them, told me. As Brother Hobbs was a married man, it was necessary to provide a parsonage. The brethren responded promptly to this new demand upon them, and rented a house on Lombard street above Sixth.

The minutes of the first Quarterly Conference shows the following record: "Wilmington, April 24, 1854.—First Quarterly Conference of the Seventh Street M. E. Church, held at Bro. Jacob S. Weldin's. Bro. Stewart Carlisle was appointed secretary. Meeting opened with prayer by Bro. Anthony Atwood, P. E. Members present: Bro. Atwood, P. E., Bro. H. A. Hobbs, preacher in charge, Bros. Jacob S. Weldin, Jos. Spurway, Wm. Bickings, Wm. Griffenberg, Stewart Carlisle. On motion of Brother Hobbs, Bros. Jacob S. Weldin, John Lonsdale, Moses B. Gist, Jos. Spurway and Stewart Carlisle were elected a board of stewards. On motion of Brother Griffenberg the board of stewards were appointed a committee to estimate preacher's salary and report at the next Quarterly Conference. The preacher verbally reported the Sabbath-school in a flourishing condition. On motion, adjourned. Minutes read and approved. Stewart Carlisle, secretary."

It would be interesting to know the first list of membership, but I find no record of it. Besides the fourteen mentioned above, Joseph D. Aldred was among the very first to unite with the new organization. He had previously been a member of the school, and as soon as the church was organized he drew his letter from Asbury and cast in his lot with the new enterprise. From that day to this he has been a live worker in the church and school, and has filled acceptably almost every office in the church. He is still with us, and still active and zealous. God grant that he may be spared us many years!

In 1855 the Rev. Charlton T. Lewis was appointed pastor. The church seems to have flourished under his pastorate. The building would not accommodate the crowds that came to hear him. During the summer the church was enlarged to nearly twice its former size, and two class-rooms built at the rear of the church. It was with April of this year, 1855, that regular minutes of the Sunday-school teachers' meeting were kept, and of which we have an unbroken line to date. The officers and teachers of that date were Thomas Orpwood, Jacob S. Weldin, Wm. H. Riley, Gilbert Holmes, Joseph Spurway, Charles H. Heald, George Carpenter, James Grieves, Thomas Rogerson, Joseph D. Aldred, John Fisher, James Mitchell, M. B. Gist, Wm. H. Rumford, John Lousdale, Abraham Schrader, Lewis Jackson, Lewis Orr, Ricard Ameli, Sarah Jane Hastings, Hannah B. Fisher, Eliza Mortimer, Mary A. Riley, Mary E. Stewart, Sarah E. Biddle, Margaret Grieves, Margaret Rumford, Ann E. Worrell, Deborah Ogden, Anna M. Caudrass, Cornelia Benson, Mary E. Genn, Mary J. Staggers, Lydia M. Aldred, Margaret M. Caudrass, Isabella Fletcher, Elizabeth Faunce, Anna L. Jackson, thirty-nine in all.

It was during this year that the name was changed from "Seventh Street" to "Scott M. E. Church." On inquiry as to why the change was made, I was told "it was to get $100 out of Bishop Scott, and we did it, too," the brother laughingly added. The change in name first appears in the minutes of the Sunday-school association, under date of October 12, 1855.

While their church was being enlarged the Sunday-school met in the old German Baptist Church, corner Fifth and Walnut streets.

It was also during this year that something got the matter with their "constitution." I find that on Sept. 28, 1855, a committee was appointed to revise their "constitution." The next week the revised "constitution" was adopted. On the following week, Oct. 12, a new article was added to their "constitution." On Nov. 4 a new committee on "constitution" was appointed, and in July, 1856, the committee on "constitution" reported progress. Thus five times in ten months their "constitution" gave them trouble. I do not know what the matter was with it, but it must have been pretty badly out of order to have needed so much repairing, and it must have been pretty tough or they would have doctored it to death.

It was during this year that Scott had its first Sunday-school excursion. The school also began to have what it called a "Missionary Committee," whose duty it was to go out and hunt up children and bring them to the school. This was kept up for years, and was undoubtedly one of the agencies that tended to build up the school so rapidly. The first committee of this kind consisted of Abraham Schrader, Wm. H. Rumford, Lewis Jackson, Margaret Grieves, Cornelia Benson, Ann E. Worrell, and Mary E. Stewart.

It is only just to say that Sister Stewart, who afterwards became the wife of Bro. Isaac H. McKaig, and is now so well known as "Auntie McKaig," has been one of the most untiring workers ever in

Scott Church. She was a member of the first class, led by Brother Grieves, which met in a frame house on Sixth street. From the beginning until this day no one could ever say she did not do her part. For months, when the little, struggling society was not able to pay a sexton, she would do her day's work in the factory, and then go up to the little church and sweep and dust it out and prepare it for the Sunday services; and He who has promised a reward to him who gives a "cup of cold water to one of the least of these," will not forget to reward her in the days to come.

In 1856 the Rev. Andrew Longacre was appointed pastor; but because of feeble health he never entered the pulpit. Rev. H. G. King, supernumerary of the Conference, filled the vacancy. He was much beloved, and was quite successful in the work, both spiritually and temporally. During the revival held by Father King Brother Joseph Locke was converted, who is still an honored member. Brother Locke is the first probationer received into the church at Scott who is at present a member there.

The following incident occured during the progress of this revival: Father King had a great habit of crawling all around the church on his knees during time of prayer, praying, and groaning, and mourning as he went. On one of the front seats was a well-grown youth of seventeen or eighteen, who sat up on his knees at prayer, looking all about the room. He would stretch his neck out to the greatest length possible, and peep and peer to see all that was to be seen. When the congregation knelt in prayer Father King was away off on the opposite side of the room, and the youth had no idea he was anywhere about. But Father King had seen his actions during prayer and without the youth's knowledge had crowled up to him; and before he knew he was anywhere near, Father King brought his open palm with a resounding *whack* down upon his head with a force that knocked him flat on the bench, saying, "You had better get to praying." Whether the lad prayed or not was not found out; but he certainly kept his head bowed during prayer the balance of that meeting.

In 1857 the Rev. E. I. D. Pepper was appointed to succeed Father King. He was a successful revivalist, and a good pastor. Among those who were converted during his pastorate who are still members at Scott, are Isaac H. McKaig, Lewis T. Grubb, Sarah E. O'Daniel, Harriet Wode and George McCall. Perhaps it was due to his zeal for God that we find the Sunday-school officers and teachers on motion resolving, "that no child shall be permitted to use the libraries of this school unless they learn the catechism." This was afterwards repealed.

During the meeting in 1858, when nineteen penitents were at the altar, Brother Pepper called on Brother Stewart Carlisle to lead in prayer; and heaven was so opened and God's power came down in such measure that seventeen were converted during that prayer.

In 1859 Rev. Wm. H. Ridway, at present a member of the Philadelphia Conference, was appointed pastor. Being a married man a parsonage was secured on Eighth street, near Poplar, and comfortably furnished. The Lord blessed his ministry to the edification of the church. The church was crowded, and many converted, among them Rev. I. N. Foreman, now a member of the Wilmington Conference, and Sister M. Josephine Mearns. Brother Ridway remained two years.

In 1861 Rev. H. Bodine was appointed pastor. This is recognized as about the darkest period in the history of the church. There were "wars and rumors of wars," and the political and civil strife affected the church. There was a falling off both in membership and benevolences.

In 1862 Rev. Andrew Cather was appointed. He found the church in a very deplorable condition. The volunteering of members to aid in the suppression of the rebellion, the numbers thrown out of employment by business panic, and the other circumstances of that critical period, conspired to crush out the church. But he set himself zealously to work, and each of his two year's administration show an increase in membership and in benevolences.

It was during this pastorate that instrumental music was introduced. In the minutes of the Sunday-school board I find under date of December, 1863: Bro. George McCall moved to introduce a "harmonium" into the school, but not to bring it in until paid for. After considerable debate the motion was adopted by a vote of twenty-four to three. On February 5, 1864, committee reported harmonium bought and paid for. May 6, 1864 motion prevailed to allow the church to use the "harmonium" in the morning and evening service. Thus was instrumental music formally introduced at Scott. There are rumors of strong opposition on the part of some; but that was only to be expected. Some few went so far as to leave the church.

It was in the year 1863 that it was permitted men and ladies to sit together. The motion to so order was made by L. T. Grubb, in hope that it would tend to preserve better order, and to prevent men from spitting tobacco juice on the floor.

In 1864 Rev. Horace A. Cleveland was sent to succeed Bro. Cather. Many are the live reminiscences of the brother, still extant among our people. He believed in preaching for the Union, and the cause of the Union. Crowds flocked to the church to hear his eloquent lips plead for God and a united country. It is said he took for his text one day, "As Herod feared Jesus Christ, so did Gov. Wise fear John Brown." His theme was, "As John the Baptist was the forerunner of Christ, so was John Brown the forerunner of the rebellion." With such a text and such a preacher we may easily guess what the sermon was like. A brother who heard it says: "That was the time he took the bark off of them." Some men and women got up and started to leave the church. The preacher paused, waved his long arm toward them and said: "Go ahead. Leave if you want to. The shot bird always flutters."

At another time, when the good brother had been worried by members of the church and congregation going to sleep during the service, he stopped suddenly in the midst of his sermon, threw himself down on the old sofa in the pulpit, and for a minute or more snored as loudly as he could. Then, opening his eyes, mischievously asked: "Now, how do I look asleep in church? Not very pretty, I reckon; and yet I guess about as pretty as you do." Then getting up he went on with his sermon. It is scarcely necessary to add that there was not much more sleep there that morning.

Before leaving the war period I ought to say that Scott was loyal to the Union. When the President issued his call for volunteers, Scott sent so many members to the field that there were hardly enough left at home to man the church. At one time only two official brethren were left at home. Many times did her walls ring with the burning plea for fidelity to the Union; and while the pulpit issued no uncertain sound there came hearty "Amens" from the brethren in the pews. One Sabbath morning a drum corps stopped at the church and left orders for all volunteers to report at headquarters immediately. There was not much service that morning. Again, on the Sabbath of the battle of Gettysburg, the congregation was dismissed and the church closed, that all might go home to scrape lint and prepare bandages for the wounded.

In 1865 Rev. J. O'Neil found the church very much depressed. Debt and hardship were sapping what little life remained. The good friends of Asbury very kindly offered to take Scott under their care as a mission; but the offer was declined.

A movement was now on foot for the erection of Grace Church. In order that it might be carried forward successfully, Scott was joined to Grace—at least in name. Rev. W. J. Stevenson had served St. Paul's the full legal term; and Grace was to be organized principally by members from St. Paul's; therefore Brother Stevenson could not be legally returned to Grace, as yet unbuilt, as its pastor; and the brethren at Grace thought Brother Stevenson was essential to the success of their enterprise. So they asked Scott to lend its aid to help them out of the difficulty. Scott agreed, and by joining the movement the majority of members now were not parshioners of Brother Stevenson, so the legal difficulty was removed. The Conference of 1866 agreed to the arrangement, and Brother Stevenson and Rev. J. J. Jones were appointed to Grace and Scott—the latter, of course, to be Scott's pastor. For a year the name "Scott" was dropped, and "Grace Chapel" substituted. The brethren of Grace helped Scott handsomely on their salary, and at the New Year the union was dissolved, and Grace and Scott were again two separate societies. The trustees were also relieved somewhat this year. By selling the old camp meeting tent and fixtures, and by having a big supper at which over $500 were cleared, the pressing need of the trustees were tided over for the time.

In 1867, Grace having been built, and there being no need of continued union, Scott again appears, with Rev. L. Dobson as pastor.

In 1868 Rev. A. Cather was returned to Scott for the second time. At once he began to agitate rebuilding. Plans were made to extend the room to eighty-three feet in length, and to make the main audience room twenty-four feet high. Work was at once commenced. The congregation met in Institute Hall, and part of the time in City Hall; and the Sunday-school met in the public school on Spruce street just opposite the church. When the work was well under way, the roof off, and the front wall down, Brother Cather suddenly announced his appointment to a mission in the Far West. Scott was now in a predicament—without a pastor, and without a church. Rev. J. D. Curtis, pastor of Asbury, now came to the relief of the brethren, and told them he was at their service. Never will the old members at Scott forget how that faithful brother stood by them—preaching for them whenever he could supply his own pulpit, and paying them a regular sum in cash every month to help them on their current expense. Brother Moody, of precious memory, was by common consent put in charge of the religious affairs of the church; and by standing together the members were able to run a successful revival meeting for several weeks. At last, after many difficulties, they succeeded in enclosing the building, and in furnishing the lecture room. This was opened for service. Bishop Scott officiated, assisted by Brother Curtis. While this rebuilding was going on a portion of the front wall fell out into the street, instantly killing a hod carrier, who had been at work, but had now stopped, it being to a quarter to six o'clock. If he had not been in such haste to shorten his day's work, he might have been alive to-day.

On March 17, 1869, the first session of the Wilmington Annual Conference met in Asbury Church, Wilmington. At this Conference Rev. F. M. Chatham was appointed pastor. For three years he labored faithfully in this field. The records show his guiding hand in every department of work. There was an almost continual spirit of revival during his entire pastorate. He is still remembered in love by many of the people. One of the first duties he was compelled to perform after coming to the charge, was to bury the much beloved Brother Moody. A large concourse of friends and brethren attended the funeral and followed him to his last resting place. Brother Moody was noted for the wonderful power he possessed in exhortation. While he spoke God owned his words; and often sinners were overwhelmed, and saints were made to shout aloud, or fall prostrate under the power of God. Brother Chatham labored hard to fit up the main audience room of the church, and to pay off the debt. His success was remarkable; but the task was too heavy for him to fully accomplish his desire. After three years of hard labor on the charge he was obliged to leave with the audience room not quite finished, and the debt not quite paid. Some think that overwork at this time was the beginning of that nervous prostration which finally wrecked the mind, happiness, and life of our good brother.

In 1872 Rev. T. L. Tompkinson was appointed to succeed Brother Chatham. The work begun by Brother Chatham was completed in May of this year, 1872. It seemed almost a miracle that the little church that had struggled so many years for its life should at last have a large, commodious building it could call its own. It was dedicated in May. As the General Conference was in session in New York, Brother Tompkinson wrote up to secure the services of a good preacher and beggar to take charge of the dedication; but on Saturday afternoon a telegram was received saying that Brother Ives, who had promised, could not come. Brother Tompkinson at once went to Philadelphia and secured Rev. J. Neil to come help him. It was dedicated next day, and was supposed to be free from debt; but it was found, when the subscriptions were collected, that there was a deficit of over $2,000.

It was during this pastorate, the last Sunday in March, 1873, that the morning Sunday-school was organized, with L. T. Grubb, superintendent, and Levi Coverdale, assistant. In order that this movement should not be a financial burden, these two brethren provided the money to run the school for the first year of its existence.

In 1874 Rev. J. O. Sypherd was appointed pastor. During his pastorate the church was greatly strengthened by a most wonderful revival. It is still called the "big" revival. Brother Sypherd was greatly beloved.

In 1877 Rev. C. M. Pegg was pastor, and in 1880 was succeeded by Rev. P. H. Rawlins. Brother Rawlins made an effort to rid the church of debt, but failing to receive the proper support was obliged to abandon the attempt.

In 1882 Rev. T. R. Creamer was appointed pastor. During his three years' term of service the church was blessed with revivals; and the lecture room was repainted and reseated at a cost of $1,700, which was paid.

In 1885 Rev. N. M. Browne was sent to Scott. One thing, at least, he determined to do: to pay off the indebtedness. He set himself systematically about it; and to say he succeeded hardly does justice to the labors of the pastor and the self-denying brethren and sisters who stood by him.

As a history of Scott Church cannot be written without writing a history of the debts, here will be the place to introduce it. Scott from its inception seems to have had a facility in getting into debt, but a wonderful tardiness in paying them. When it was first dedicated in 1852 there was a balance unpaid. When it was enlarged in 1855 this debt was increased. It finally was placed with Bro. Samuel McCauley; and on September 5, 1856, a bond and mortgage was executed to him for $600. That bond ran on for thirty-one years and three months, less one week, before it was paid. Delay in payment of bills seems to have been the rule. This bond was given in September, 1856; paid for recording same, July, 1858. The corporate seal bought in 1855 for $9.00, paid for ten years after. In 1864 W. H. Foulk was ordered to cut a door between the two back class rooms for an infant school room, *provided he would wait two years for his pay*. If these small bills were thus neglected, it is surprising that the larger ones were not paid? In 1861, July 11, the bond was transferred to Brother Jacob S. Weidin, who held it for fifteen years. He then proposed to the church that if they would pay the principal he would donate the interest due. The money to pay this was borrowed from Sister Josephine Mearns, and Brother Weldin's claim satisfied. The debt was not paid, only changed hands, with the advantage of the donation of interest.

After the rebuilding and repairing which was completed under Brother Tomkinson, there was found to be a large deficiency. Many were not able to pay what they had pledged, and others would not pay; while others who would have paid were not called on for the money until they had lost all interest in the matter. The consequence was that there was a deficiency of $2,000; and what to do the trustees did not know. In the extremity Sister Mearns again came to the rescue, and furnished the $2,000; in return for which a new bond was executed June 1, 1876. Sister Mearns kindly carried that $2,600 for over eight years, before transferring the obligation to George D. Armstrong, which she did August 7, 1884. And besides these bonds there was a whole batch of old bills for gas, and floating debts, and current expense that had been allowed to run behind. All these were before our brother when he took charge of the church; and they were enough to make even his two-hundred-and-fifty-pound soul tremble within him. But he set about the work.

Brother Browne reported to the Conference of 1886 that he had raised $375 on old indebtedness. In 1887 he reports $1,100 paid on the debt, as the result of his second year's effort. Pastor and people determined to cancel the debt during his third year. May 29, 1887, was set apart as the day for that great effort. In the morning at 10.30 Rev. Vaughan S. Collins preached ; and at the close of the sermon $1,300 were pledged. In the afternoon the Sunday-school pledged $150 more. At night Rev. S. H. Morgan preached, and Rev. W. L. S. Murray, Presiding Elder, assisted in the finance, when $800 were pledged—making a total sufficient to pay off all the debt. By the first of December the subscriptions had been paid, and Brother J. T. Bartlett had paid the bills, and had the mortgage marked "satisfied" on the records of the court. When on the 11th of December, 1887, pastor and people gathered around the altar, which was now the funeral pyre of those old bills and mortgages, and watched them slowly turn to ashes, I am not surprised that they sang "Praise God from whom all blessing flow" as they never sung it before. Brother Browne will long be remembered as the Moses who led Scott from the bondage of debt.

It was during this year, 1887, that Sister Ann Perkins, a member of Asbury, made a very valuable and timely gift to Scott—a house and lot at 800 Poplar street, on condition that the trustees pay her $13 per month as long as she lives. The trustees accepted the proposition most gladly. Brother Murray, our active Presiding Elder, was largely instrumental in bringing about this glad consummation.

In 1888 the writer was appointed pastor. During the first year the benevolences went up to $461—the highest in the history of the church. The membership was increased by receiving twenty-one by letter, fifteen into full membership, and one hundred and thirty-seven on probation. Toward the close of the year the brethren set about fixing up their own property, so that it could be used as a parsonage for their pastor.

On returning from Conference of 1880, the writer and his wife were cordially greeted by a company of the members in the new parsonage. An addition had been built to the rear of the old building, for a kitchen and bath room, the entire house renovated and papered, and painted, while the "Ladies' Aid" had put in new carpets for the parlor, one bed-room carpet, a new bed-room suit, and some other improvements. The total cost was about $1,000.

At this writing it is not quite paid for; but will be before the session of the Conference. To date eighty-four of those received on probation last year have been received into full membership, and others are to follow.

The present official board consists of:

Local preachers.—Revs. D. Dodd and F. A. Roop, M. D.

Exhorters—A. S. Feaster, L. T. Grubb, E. L. McKeag, and George Davis.

Stewards. L. T. Grubb, E. L. McKeag, A. S. Feaster, Mark H. Pierce, W. H. Valentine, Harry S. Valentine, Charles Seyfried, W. H. Updike, Owen Hughes, F. O. Bennett, T. J. O'Daniel, Enos W. Clair and J. C. F. Carver.

Trustees.—Thos. Wilson, J. T. Bartlett, George Davis, Jos. H. Davis, John B. Kindall, W. H. Valentine, A. J. Harvey, I. H. McKaig and James F. Lank.

Sunday-school Superintendents.—Enos W. Clair and Mark H. Pierce

The following are the dates on admission on probation of some of the oldest members of Scott:

1857.—January, Jos. Locke; February 18, Margaretta Phillips; September, Mary Guthrie.

1858.—February 21, I. H. McKaig; February 28, L. T. Grubb, Henry Biddle; March 7, Catharine Wilkinson; March 14, Harriet Wode; April 25, George McCall; September 26, Mary E. Grantland; December 26, Sarah E. O'Daniel.

1859.—July 17, Elizabeth J. Davis; October 16, Isaac N. Foreman, now of the Wilmington Conference.

1860.—September 23, Sarah E. Brown.

1861.—February 24, M. Josephine Mears.

1863.—January 18, David W. Hall, Martha T. Hall and W. H. Valentine; December 13, Elizabeth Scout. Among those who were converted and joined during the "big revival" under Brother Sypherd are: Isaac T. Parker, W. H. Grantland, Josephine Locke (now Campbell), Emma R. Feaster, Margaretta G. Wiley, Hannah Talley, Lottie P. Cummins, Maggie J. Kelly, Fannie E. Litzenberg, Maggie D. Updike, William H. Updike, John B. Lloyd, Alice E. Lloyd, Emma I. Brown, Wm. T. Gallagher, Anna M. Applin, John T. Bartlett, Virlenia Bartlett, Emily L. Wiley, Henry W. Perkins, Thos. H. Wilson, Margaret Wilson, Fannie L. Thomas and Anna M. Underwood.

There are many of our brethren and sisters at Scott whose names are worthy to be recorded among those who have built up that sanctuary. I can not name them here, however; nor is there need that I should. Their names are written in the Lamb's book of life. And when the faithful of the Lord are crowned and blessed in that last great day, I feel sure that among them will be many who have lived, and loved, and labored for God in the humble church at Seventh and Spruce.

REV. C. A. GRISE, PH. D.,
Pastor of Brandywine Methodist Episcopal Church.

History of Brandywine Methodist Episcopal Church.

By the Rev. C. A. Grise, Ph. D., Pastor.

About the year 1839 Sarah Haislette and Sarah Morrow, both of Asbury M. E. Church, went into Brandywine village and gathered what children they could into a Sunday-school class, which held its meetings in the Old Academy. This old stone building is yet standing on Vandiver avenue, near Market street. At this time the village was not a part of the city proper, and had less than 400 inhabitants. This Sunday-school class teaching continued and grew in interest other faithful workers helping, until about 1853, when the work was somehow transferred to a band of workers from Union M. E. Church. They held the field until 1856 or 1857, when the work again passed into the care of Asbury. Who were leaders in these transfers I have not been able to learn, but it seems that one Wm. Calvert and Elizabeth Stevenson were the male and female superintendents after the last transfer. They were assisted in the work by Rev. S. Thomas. Dennis Orpwood, Thomas Orpwood, Isaac Preston, Rev. Joseph Smith, Jacob M. Garretson, and a Miss Stevenson, sister of the female superintendent.

About this time prayer-meetings were held in the academy by Rev. Isaac Stratton, whose faithful labors were crowned with a gracious revival, which began early in 1856. They well remember the dimly-lighted room and the smoky tallow candle of those revival times, as to-day they worship under an electric blaze which pales the stars and transforms night into day. But the spirit of the Lord was there, and among those who worked and worshiped in this dingy place, at the time of which I write, may be found the names of men who have since graced the pulpits of our churches, as Joseph Smith, S. W. Thomas. John France, Mr. Kellem and Matthew Barnhill, the last three having been among the boys who were gathered into the school. In the fall of 1856 the first Methodist Episcopal society was formally organized in the Old Academy, and Rev. Wm. J. Kennard, of Asbury, was placed in charge. As far as I have been able to ascertain, the following are the names of those who deposited their certificates to form this nucleus: Sarah Rigby, Mary A. Hill, Catharine Labele, Sarah Morrow, Elizabeth Hill, Emeline Bullock, Mary Hill, Edgar Pierce, Rebecca Burton, Franklin Lloyd, Elizabeth Lloyd, James H. Spencer, Sarah E. Spencer, all from Asbury, and James Dangle and wife, Joseph Bratton, Elizabeth Bratton, Annie E. Pierce, David Lurten, Elizabeth Lurten, William A. Brian and William H. McKenny, from other charges.

On November 10, 1857, the society met in their place of worship and elected the following board of trustees: Rev. Charles Moore, Geo. W. Sparks, Geo. Tally, Lewis Weldon, Wm. Todd, Garrett Morgan, John T. Gause, John S. Kennard and John S. Crossley. It became an incorporated board of trustees of the M. E. Church on May 3, 1858. Meanwhile active preparations for building a church were made. A lot well out of the center of population, at Twenty-second and Market streets, was obtained of Joseph Tatnall, for which the deed was not obtained until February 10, 1860. A two-story brick building, 40 x 65, was begun, the corner stone being laid on September 28, 1857, Revs. Alfred Cookman and Newton Heston officiating.

In the spring of 1858 Wm. J. Kennard was re-appointed, but left the work in the middle of the year, and Rev. John France was transferred from Oxford to Brandwine by Presiding Elder Wm. Urie. He found the building nearly finished and a small, struggling society, whose finances had been badly managed, and a burdening debt of $6,000. The church cost a little more than this amount. The society was small and poor, as well as wronged and discouraged. Just when they transferred worship from the academy to the church, or who dedicated the church, I have not been able to learn.

Rev. A. Manship did the financiering on the day of dedication. Our worthy chairman, Bro. Grubb, distinctly remembers that, because some one sat upon and mashed his silk hat during the excitement caused by Bro. Manship's appeals for money. Now began a struggle with dark times—poverty, distrust, festivals, fairs, entertainments, excursions, creditors, and the sheriff, the history of which I dare not take time to relate in full. I will only give the outline. During this struggle the pastor's time was taken up by planning and begging to liquidate debts, while the church was left by necessity to do the best it could for its own spiritual life. The salary was $400, $150 of which was missionary donation. Bro. France remained in charge until 1860, when Thomas Montgomery was sent to serve as pastor. He found a mortgage for $2,000 and a floating debt of $2,800 against the church, and could do but little because of the discouraged state in which he found the people. In the spring of 1861 Wm. H. Fries was appointed preacher in charge, and served until January 1, 1862, when he left to go into the army. This man is remembered as one of striking peculiarities, one of which was the swinging of his hand to his back and excitingly rubbing the back of his coat while preaching. When asked why he did it, he replied that he was scratching for ideas. It may be noted that during his pastorate the first marriage in the church took place, Edward Morrow and Miss Rebecca L. Burton, two active workers in the church, being the contracting parties.

Creditors now began to get restless, so much so that the trustees had been afraid to secure the deed for the property lest litigation should result. Hence it is recorded that a committee was appointed to wait on the creditors and ask them if they would be patient, provided the deed was secured, and give the church time to make strenuous efforts to raise funds with which to pay off their claims. Eli Mendinhall, and Wm. H. Fries were appointed a committee to canvass the city and solicit aid. One creditor was going to push for his claim of $700. Lectures and stereoptican entertainments were given, but the lecturer and managers usually took all the proceeds. Brother Mendinhall and Fries made the canvass and received but little encouragement and no help. It seemed that the church must go. At night, after a fruitless days effort to get money, Brother Fries said to Mendinhall, "What shall we do?" "I will go home," said Mendinhall, "and tell the Lord about it." The next day the burden was made lighter and hope again infused, when Fries received a check for $100 from Sabilla Stone. This check was the means of tiding over the first crisis.

Rev. Benjamin Crist, whose wife and child had been killed by the Indians in a massacre at a place in Minnesota, where he had been stationed, and who had came East for rest and change, was appointed to fill out the unexpired term of Wm. Fries, from January 1 to March, 1862.

The Conference of 1862 thought perhaps a good singer would make the church more prosperous, hence Thos. McClary was appointed preacher in charge. Soon another crisis was apparent. On January 30, 1864, the trustees made this minute.

Resolved, That in view of the failure to secure help it is our deliberate judgment that the sheriff should be allowed to sell the church for the benefit of the creditors.

Some of the members refused to vote and the motion did not prevail. A committee was then appointed to wait on the trustees of Asbury, Union and St. Paul's, and ask them to make Brandywine a city mission under their joint care. The committee reported having waited upon the aforesaid boards who refused to take any official action, but who consented to allow Brandywine's claims to come before their several congregations.

The distressed society made its next appeal to the annual Conference in 1864, to which it stated that it was not able to support a preacher, and if one was sent it would be at his own risk. The church was then put under the care of W. C. Robinson, pastor of Asbury, who supplied the pulpit by local preachers until the midde of the year, when the Presiding Elder appointed Eli Wilson preacher in charge. About this time all the trustees except Chas. Moore are said to have resigned. This faithful man stood by the church with noble sacrifice.

He, Capt. Alex. Kelly, Jos. Pyle and H. F. Pickels took plates of ice cream at an ice cream saloon and became so impressed with Brandywine's financial embarrassment, as they ate and talked, that they each gave $50 ere they left the saloon.

The sheriff had now advertised the church for sale, and just before the sale was to have taken place, in the fall of 1864, Harry Pickels, Capt. Alexander Kelly, and Joseph Pyle, three noble-hearted Christian gentlemen, whose names perfume the records of the church they saved, came to the rescue and stopped the sale by assuming the responsibility for the debt. Soon a change in the board of trustees was made, and Bros. Pickels, Kelly and Pyle, of St. Paul's, having consented to serve on the board, were elected. These three, together with Rev. Chas. Moore, the chairman of the board, and one who had worked and struggled and sacrificed all along, said to Eli Mendinhall, we think it essential to have a young, active preacher. We will take care of him and leave the church, lead by your financiering, to look after the debt. The church was paying $250 salary. These brethren went to Conference in 1865, and asked that John France be appointed to Brandywine, promising to pay him $1,000 and house rent.

Joseph Pyle and Harry F. Pickels each pledged himself for $300 of this salary, leaving the trustees and the church to raise the remaining $400. Besides paying $300 each, annually, these brethren furnished the parsonage at an expense of about $175. The help of these faithful men and that of Capt. Alexander Kelly, in this time of struggle, was a lasting blessing to the church. Mr. Pyle was for some time superintendent of the Sunday-school. During this time he would drive over on Sunday and put his horse under the shed at the hotel during school hours, always paying the hotel keeper for the privilege. One day the hotel keeper objected to receiving the money, saying that Mr. Pyle was coming over to attend the Sunday-school at a sacrifice, and that it was a good work and he would like to donate the use of horse shelter to the work. Mr. Pyle told him that he had no sympathy with the business of selling liquor, and if not allowed to pay for horse shelter he would not take his horse there any more. The hotel keeper then accepted $5 for a year's rent.

The first organ was put in the school during Mr. Pyle's superintendency, and donated by him. There was some objection to an organ in church. One old lady made special objection. The organ was placed in the class-room so that no one who went into the church could see it. The superintendent opened the school by reading the 150th Psalm. At the conclusion of reading the psalm, four young men, who were in readiness, brought the organ in and placed it behind the chancel. Mr. Pyle's daughter played the opening hymn, after which the old lady seemed entirely satisfied.

During the pastorate of Bro. France, 1865-68, the church overed her greatest struggle. Early in the summer of 1865 John Gouley, a former member of Brandywine but then of St. Paul's, arranged to run an excursion to Cape May for the benefit of Brandywine. Bro. Gouley had toiled and done much all through her struggles, but this effort was the climax and practically settled the struggle with the debt. The steamer Manhattan was chartered, the excursion went, and $1,000 was netted. This gave a new impetus, and efforts were vigorously pushed to raise the other $1,000. So happy was the result that by the close of 1867, just ten years from the beginning, the church was for the first time in her history free from debt. The last collection to pay off the final portion of this debt was taken up in the parlors of Joseph Pyle's private residence.

Much has been said about sacrifice for the church, but to enumerate the struggles, denials and sacrifices made by this Spartan band of Christian heroes through this whole struggle of ten years' duration, would make a volume of pathos. You may hear of men taking turn at keeping the church, of women scrubbing the walls and floors, of many wearing rusty-looking clothes, of men wearing the same hat for three years and going without an overcoat, of men and women not having shoes sufficient to attend church, all in order to help pay the debt and have something with which to help support the gospel. The burden fell on about eighty members, for the names of whom I refer to the church records. Debts all paid and the struggle over, a reaction and rest ensued, in which the salary dropped to $700, and very little of importance took place.

Pastors during this period were: Joshua Humphries, 1868-69; John Shilling, 1869-72; T. B. Hunter, 1872-74; Wm. M. Warner, 1874-75. During Bro. Shilling's pastorate $1,000 were expended on improvements, $500 of which was borrowed and a mortgage given. In the spring of 1875 A. W. Milby was appointed preacher in charge. Another dark period was approaching. Money was scarce, the panic was on, and spirituality was at low ebb. Conference was approaching and Bro. Milby's salary was over $300 behind. A dear brother, now present, told me that he stood on the pavement talking with Bro. Milby one night after a very dull prayer-meeting. He said, "I told Bro. Milby that something must be done. I was so depressed that I came near sinking upon the curbstone. Oh, how gloomy the prospect seemed. In a few weeks the first of the two greatest revivals that Brandywine ever had broke out. Many joined church on probation. This made the people forget hard times, and the $300 deficiency was all raised on one Sunday.

J. W. Pierson was pastor from 1876-78; E. E. White, 1878-81, and John Shilling, 1881-84. Slight improvements were made during Bro. Pierson's pastorate, amounting to about $150. In the fall of 1876 Eli Mendinhall presented the trustees with $500 to pay off the mortgage which had been placed on the church six years previous. Improvements amounting to about $600 were made during Bro. White's pastorate, when the church was again mortgaged for $500.

The church deserves special mention for the way it helped Brother Shilling during his late illness. Early in 1883 Brother Shilling's health failed. Many thought it wise to secure another pastor, but his flock said no, we will care for him, though he be not able to preach to us. Rev. Eli Mendinhall looked after the pulpit supply, while Richard McClure, M. B. Bullock, and others of the church, assisted in looking after the salary. Another discouraging struggle for existence seemed manifest at the end of this year.

The appointment of E. L. Hubbard to the pastorate in 1884 marks the beginning of a new epoch in Brandywine Church history. Up to this time the membership vacillated between seventy-five and one hundred and fifty, averaging about eighty members, which was about the number Brother Hubbard found. Early in the year improvements and enlarging the church were begun. Fifteen feet and a recess pulpit were added to the length of the building, with the other improvements costing about $4,800, all of which was raised on or before the re-opening, at which Drs. Jacob Todd and J. R. Boyle assisted the pastor. While the improvements were in progress a tent was pitched on a lot at the corner of Twenty-fourth and Market streets, in which revival services were held. Here the second great revival, during which a great many joined the church, broke out. A singular fact is that these two most sweeping revivals succeeded the two darkest periods of the church. When the church went into the improved building, it took a new life, of which the present flourishing condition is the result. Brother Hubbard served until 1887, when the writer was appointed to the charge. During 1887 $900 were raised to liquidate the old mortgage of $500 and a floating debt of about $400.

The change was also blessed with a gracious revival during the year. In the early part of this year ('89) cathedral glass windows were put into the audience-room at a cost of $400. A few days ago the Sunday-school, under the leadership of A. M. Pierce and Jas. T. Mullin, purchased a lot 31x70, for $690, in the immediate rear of the church, on which a neat chapel will be built in the near future. Work has already begun.

This brings me to the close of the history of one of the most noble struggles of a loyal Methodist Episcopal society. Time will not allow me to mention the names of all who took part in the struggles. In addition to those whose names form the first record of membership, the trustees and stewards whose names run through the period, I must take space to make special mention of Elizabeth Lloyd, Mary A. Tally, Mrs. Wesley Hawkins, Mrs. Daniel Urmy and Sarah Warden. But there is the name of one man woven all through the records from the beginning until now. That man might be seen roving the city with the pastor to solicit and collect funds; in the class-room encouraging the despondent; in secret on his knees before God pleading for Brandywine; in her pulpit supplying the place of a regular pastor; handing the trustees of his consecrated means to save them from embarrassment; at Conference looking after the interests of Brandywine; helping the stewards in their struggles; always interested. That man is Rev. Eli Mendinhall, licensed to preach while a member of Brandywine, during the pastorate of Wm. Fries. His patience, faith and hope have been ingratiated into the hearts of a grateful membership.

Would the mother know what the third daughter has done? She has taken a noble part in transforming the moral condition of the

Ninth ward. When she went there rum and ruin were rampant. Saloons were numerous. Now she dwells amid a population of nearly 4,000, with but one hotel where liquor is sold. She has graced your age with one worthy grandchild—a neat chapel at Edgemoor, 35x70, erected during Hubbard's pastorate and largely through his efforts.

Over 1330 souls have been converted at her altars. Her membership is 319 with a Sunday-school of 750 scholars. This is her record at the age of thirty-two.

REV. D. H. CORKRAN,

Pastor of Epworth Methodist Episcopal Church.

The History of Epworth Methodist Episcopal Church.

By the Rev. D. H. Corkran, Pastor.

Epworth Church had its origin in a revival and missionary spirit in St. Paul's Church.

Whether or not this spirit was wide-spread in the church I am unable to say, suffice to know, that the burden of souls was laid so heavily upon the hearts of a few godly men and women of that church in the autumn of 1863, that they went out into the highways to seek and save the lost.

At this time there was a section of the city east of Church street without either fold or shepherd. It was not an inviting field of labor to the ease-seeker or the searcher after mere worldly fame. Only those who were possessed of the Christ Spirit, and with an intense longing to save the perishing, would have chosen it as a place in which to begin the work of evangelization. *The people were poor, illiterate, and desperately wicked.* The name given to this section by the up-town folk was synonomous of everything that is bad in human nature. But as Christ while on earth sought the wicked and most neglected classes that he might win them to himself, so these persons in casting about for a wider field of labor than the circumscribed limits of their own church parish were soon attracted by the pitiable condition of this section, which condition was to them a Macedonian cry. They were not heedless of this voice. One bright October afternoon in the year 1863, might have been seen a small company of five or six persons, with Bible and hymn book in hand, wending their way toward this neglected part of the Master's vineyard. Whither bound or on what mission bent was known to but few, if any, except themselves.

Their object, however, was not long a matter of conjecture to those who observed them. At the southeast corner of Seventh and Church streets is a private entrance to Old Swedes Cemetery, on either side of which stands an old stone building of unique design, connected the one with the other by a gothic archway. One has recently been remodeled, and is now the parish rectory, but the other stands to-day as on this October afternoon. At the entrance of this cemetery the company paused. One of the buildings was untenanted at the time. Permission was given to hold religious services in one of the rooms. The company entered, sang a hymn, and prayed in good Methodist fashion. Down the street apiece were seen some boys playing in the gutter. A delegation was sent out to induce them, and as many more as could be found and persuaded, to come to this little room, and hear singing and talking, and help make up a Sunday-school. The delegation, after diligent search, in due time returned, bringing with them three ragged and dirty urchins. Work began in earnest. A part of the company kept order, while the remainder endeavored to entertain and instruct, by singing and Bible stories, these first fruits of their labors. Here, and in this manner, was planted the mustard seed which has since sprung up, grown to be a church, under whose care and influence hundreds have found rest to their weary souls.

The names of all this company are unknown to me. But at its head was Job H. Jackson, Bro. Crouch, Wm. H. Billany, and Miss Lizzie Spearman. Much encouraged in their enterprise, and perceiving that God had opened to them an effectual door, which no man could shut, they soon took steps toward organizing a Sunday-school according to the laws of the church. Early in November the organization was effected, with the following officers: Superintendent, Bro. Crouch; assistant, Job H. Jackson; secretary, Miss Lizzie Spearman; musical director, Wm. H. Billany. In connection with the mission Sunday-school, Miss Mary Belt formed also a day school in the same section about the same time. In this school several business men of this city received the first rudiments of an education. Both schools grew rapidly. Soon the room at Seventh and Church was inadequate to the demands made upon it by the increased attendance. More room was needed; what should be done? In this hour of need, J. Taylor Gause, a man of God, whose wealth was consecrated to his Lord and Master, erected at his own expense a frame structure, 30x50 feet, at the corner of Seventh and Buttonwood streets, for the use of the Sunday-school.

About the same time Rev. Alfred T. Scott began preaching and pastoral work in connection with the Sunday-school. His labors were abundantly blessed, souls were converted. Some are still members of the church militant, others of the church triumphant. A class was formed with William Jackson as leader. The class grew apace with the Sunday-school.

In the meantime the society of Grace Church was formed, including among its members the founders of this mission work, hence the child of St. Paul's became the adopted child of Grace. About the same time also the superintendency of the school, by the removal to another field of labor of Mr. Cronch, fell upon Mr. Jackson. The pastoral care also passed from Bro. Scott to Rev. Bro. Criss. Under the leadership of these two men the work entered upon a period of renewed activity. The keen insight and foresight, as well as the unsurpassed business tact of Bro. Jackson, combined with, or rather supplemented by the intrepid zeal of Bro. Criss, formed a force which no ordinary obstacle could withstand.

The time had now apparently come for some permanent form of church organization. But the present location, being but two squares from Scott, was not to be thought of as a place of location. On the east side of the Brandywine Creek, opposite Eleventh street ferry, the population was increasing. At this time the creek was being bridged, and there being no church organization in that part of the city, it was deemed wise, by Mr. Jackson and those associated with him in the work, to remove as far away from Scott as possible, and yet be within easy reach of that section of the city so much needing care, also to be within easy reach of the settlers on the east side of the creek. Accordingly a lot 100 x 150 feet, running from Church to Bennett, on Tenth street, was purchased by the Sunday-school Union of Grace Church, from Mr. Hillis, for the sum of $2,000, for which amount a mortgage was given to Chas. Howland.

The erection of a building 36 x 56, gothic in architecture, was soon begun. In the erection of this building Mr. Jackson was deeply interested. By his personal solicitation most of the material was contributed for the building. In April, 1869, the building was completed and dedicated to the service of Almighty God. Dr. Stevenson preached the dedicatory sermon. The march from the Seventh Street Mission to the new church on the day of dedication is an event in the history of Methodism in east Wilmington, referred to with happy memory by many who were then little children and are now pillars in the church. Brother Criss continued to be pastor until the following spring, when he was succeeded by Rev. H. H. Davis, a local preacher of the Philadelphia Conference. Brother Davis was not a great preacher, but a man of deep piety and indefatigable energy. He soon won the affection of all who knew him. During his ministry many were won to

Christ. He served the church six years. Father Davis, as he was called, left the imprint of his character upon the lives and character of his people so indelibly that eternity will never efface it. He was succeeded by Rev. A. D. Davis.

Brother Davis' appointment marks an advance step in the church's history, it being by Conference arrangement. Epworth now began to take the form of a regular Conference appointment. His brief pastorate was one of great prosperity in revival work. At every public meeting held during the one year of his pastorate, there were penitents at the altar of prayer, with one exception. At the expiration of Rev. A. D. Davis' term, Rev. L. E. Barrett was appointed and served two years, 1876 and 1877. The church grew apace during these two years. The records show it to have been a period of financial prosperity, as well as of vigorous spiritual vitality.

From 1877 to the present period, the following named brethren served as pastors in the order mentioned: Revs. E. C. MacNichol, W. S. Robinson, E. Davis, J. W. White (local,) C. A. Hill, W. B. Gregg, and the writer. Revs. MacNichol, Robinson, White, and Hill, served one year each; Revs. Davis and Gregg two each. The present pastor is now serving his fourth year. The Sunday-school work has always been very closely identified with the growth of the church; Job H. Jackson, and W. H. Billany, continued their connection with the school until 1873. In 1872 Mr. Jackson resigned the superintendency, and Mr. Billany became its chief head for one year. These two brethren who so faithfully labored in this school, and whose lives and labors were the means of saving so many souls, will be remembered through eternity by those to whom they were benedictions. Although not now connected in any official relation with the church work, which they founded and prosecuted so well, nevertheless the bond of sympathy with, and love for this their God child, causes them still to watch with anxious care and solicitude over its welfare.

In 1873 Rev. J. White, a local preacher of the church, was elected superintendent of the school. For sixteen consecutive years he has been elected to this responsible position. Brother White has proven himself to be a workman that needeth not to be ashamed. He has won the affections of both the church and school. He has sown good seed; already the harvest is being gathered. The history of Epworth has not always been bright. It had a long and dark night, so dark that the last beam of hope at one time was well nigh extinguished.

In the year 1878 the church seemed to meet with reverses; one after another followed. The revival spirit which characterized the place and people in former years seemed to die out; congregations diminished. The iron works, upon which most of the membership of the church depended for a livelihood, suspended operations; many members were under the necessity of moving to other parts of the country. An unmethodistic element settled in the community. The church building became old and uninviting in its appearance. Effort after effort was made to regain the lost ground, but without avail. The membership decreased from two hundred to about seventy-five. These were dark hours, but for a few families the church must have been a failure. Those who bore the burden in this dark hour, and constituted the principle part of the congregation from Sabbath to Sabbath, were the following:

Revs. John and Wm. White (local preachers,) Wm. P. Booker and wife, with their two devoted sons, George and John; Joseph Graham and wife, G. V. Anderson, wife and mother, Wm. Robinson, Mrs. Mary J. Brice, Thos Corson and wife, Geo. King, Mrs. Emmons, Mrs. Spring, and a few others which time will not allow me to name. These seemed to love the place more than others, and were always in their places whatever the discouragements. So desperate had the condition of affairs become, and so hopeless the outlook, that in the winter of 1888, preparations were being made to abandon the place, and divide its membership between the other churches. The matter was thoroughly discussed by the Sunday-school Union of Grace Church. Many of the members advocated blotting out Epworth forever, and this would inevitably have been the sequel of the deliberation, had not such men of keen insight and foresight as J. G. Baker, the honorable chairman of this meeting, Job H. Jackson, and W. H. Billany, the church's God fathers, Washington Hastings and J. T. Gause, friends of the struggling society, interposed their objections, and in every possible way opposed it. They believed that to be the proper place for a church: financial aid was promised.

The faithful few encouraged, resolved to make one more effort before writing Ichabod over the portals of the place, where, in former years, had dwelt in power the majesty of the Most High. They sought the throne of grace. Their prayer, like those of Cornelius, seemed to have come up as a memorial before the Lord. They were answered. In September, 1888, a protracted meeting was begun with but little prospect of much success, but the people tarried and prayed. The spirit came. It was noised about the city. The people came flocking to see what it all meant. Night after night from September, 1888, to May, 1889, a period of nearly nine months, the church was taxed to its utmost capacity to accommodate the people. During that time four hundred souls were converted; two hundred and eighty of which joined the church, one hundred and twenty joining other churches in the city and outlying charges. The old-time fires were kindled. The people got happy and shouted and leaped for joy, and are at it still.

The pastor and people were aided in this great work by Andrew Dalbow, an exhorter of Asbury Church. For nearly six months, night after night, this devout man of God, after working hard all day, would come and sing his soul-inspiring hymns, and exhort and preach with the power of an Abbott. He never failed to hold and enthuse his audience. The result of his labors will last throughout eternity.

Early in the meeting very efficient aid was given by Rev. J. Thorp, a local preacher from Mt. Lebanon charge. Both these brethren are now engaged in evangelistic work and are meeting with abundant success.

The church was now too small. Plans were drawn up, and early in May the work of rebuilding and remodeling the church was commenced. July 28 the building was re-opened. The work of repairs cost $3,300. In the meantime the church property was conveyed by the Sunday-school Union of Grace Church to trustees of Epworth in consideration donation of the sum of $2,000. Epworth is now a beautiful church with a seating capacity between 600 and 700 persons, with prayer class, infant school and library room. The full members with the probationers in good standing make a membership of a little over 300, and a congregation larger than the church will accommodate.

In the early summer of this year the Lord put it into the heart of Sister Ann Perkins of Asbury to deed to the trustees of Epworth, to be used as a parsonage, a three-story brick house on Third street, between Poplar and Lombard, on the most favorable conditions. The property was accepted by the trustees. With a parsonage, a large and beautiful church, and a large and active membership, this church which had such an humble origin, bids fair to be the peer of most of her sister churches in the city. Epworth congratulates great-grandmother Asbury on this, her Centennial anniversary, and prays that age nor sin may never abate her wonted power. She also assures her that her great-granddaughter will keep the revival fire upon her altar and be loyal to the faith of our fathers.

History of Grace Methodist Episcopal Church.

By Wm. H. Billany, Esq.

"Grace" is the grandchild of "Asbury," and she comes to day, at the age of twenty-five years, to greet and congratulate you upon attaining the age of one hundred years, and to give due praise and honor to the faithful and earnest Christian men and women, who for a century have maintained the cause of Christ in this community.

You are justly called the mother of Methodist churches in this city, for from you have gone out directly and indirectly twelve churches, of which you have no reason to be ashamed, to own them as your children. For they all are doing a good work for God and humanity.

It was during the successful pastorate of Rev. Wm. J. Stevenson at St. Paul's in 1863-4, that there was a felt need for further and enlarged Sunday-school and church accommodation, as the attendance in church and Sunday-school had increased beyond the capacity of the building to accommodate, comfortably, the membership and friends.

During the fall of 1863 and the early part of 1864, the congregation and Sunday-school had so largely increased that more room seemed absolutely necessary. It was at first concluded to erect a building somewhere in the vicinity of the church for the accommodation of the schools.

With this object in view, a few friends, members of the Sunday-school, purchased the lot at the southwest corner of Seventh and Market streets, running through to Shipley street, known as the "Milligan" property, with the intention of erecting thereon a chapel and Sunday-school room. But there was objection on the part of some members to demolish or sell the old church, and it was determined that the property purchased was not large enough for a church and chapel for Sunday-school purposes.

The idea of an entirely distinct church in a different section of the city became fixed in the minds of many; and it was not long before this culminated in a design to erect a costly and handsome edifice, as a thank offering in the centenary year of American Methodism.

"The first meeting of the friends of the enterprise was held in one of the class rooms of St. Paul's Church, on Thursday evening, November 17, 1864, eleven persons being present, namely: Rev. W. J. Stevenson, J. Taylor Gause, Geo. W. Sparks, Delaplain McDaniel, Henry F. Pickels, Dr. Geo. Pepper Norris, Edwin Albilmer, Job H. Jackson, C. F. Rudolph, S. M. Harrington and W. H. Billany. After an earnest invocation for the blessing and favor of God, the subject of building a new house of worship was fully discussed. It was unanimously

"*Resolved*, That we pledge to each other our most zealous efforts and constant labors in the work of constructing a new and handsome Methodist church in this city; and that with the blessing and help of God our labors shall not be relaxed until this great and good work shall have been accomplished."

A committee was immediately appointed to procure plans.

The movement thus started met with favor from the people. When a second call was made for a meeting, which was public, and held in the lecture room of St. Paul's Church, on Friday evening, January 6, 1865, George W. Sparks presided, and Bishop Simpson eloquently addressed the meeting, which gave great encouragement to the friends of the enterprise.

The following resolution was unanimously adopted:

"*Resolved*, That it is the unanimous sense of this meeting that the interests of Methodism, church enterprise and city improvement, unite to encourage the erection of a new church somewhere in the improving western section of the city; and that the congregation of St. Paul's M. E. Church, and the friends of the enterprise, will build a new church on some eligible site in the western part of the city."

The enterprise was now fairly started, and its friends were fully committed before the church and public to perform the "great and good work." It became now necessary to form a legal organization. For this purpose, pursuant to a call signed by J. T. Gause and others, a meeting of the friends of the enterprise was held in the lecture room of St. Paul's Church, on Friday evening, January 27, 1865, for organization.

The following named were elected trustees for the new church: Daniel M. Bates, Delaplain McDaniel, C. F. Rudolph, Job H. Jackson, John Merrick, Dr. Geo. Pepper Norris, Jarratt Megaw, Geo. W. Sparks and J. T. Gause. Of the nine members composing the first board of trustees, but three are living, the others have gone to their reward, and their works do follow them. At this meeting "Grace" was chosen as the name for the new church. An address was issued to the public, and a soliciting committee appointed to procure subscriptions.

The first meeting of the board of trustees was held at the house of Daniel M. Bates, on the evening of March 24, 1865. The board organized by electing Geo. W. Sparks, chairman, S. M. Harrington, secretary, and Wm. H. Billany, treasurer. The board was soon called upon to lament the death of one of its members, Dr. Geo. Pepper Norris, occurring at a time when his career promised so much usefulness to the church and to society. But recognizing the wisdom of God and faithfully trusting Him, the board firmly resolved that "though the workmen die, the work *must* go on." H. F. Pickels was elected to fill the vacancy caused by the death of Dr. Norris, on March 28th. The trustees elected Geo. W. Sparks, J. T. Gause and Job H. Jackson a building committee, and adopted plans for the new building, furnished by Thomas Dixon of Baltimore, formerly of Wilmington.

On April 6, 1865, the lot at the corner of Ninth and West streets was purchased for the sum of $10,000, and on the evening of April 13th the trustees instructed the building committee to commence operations immediately, and to build the chapel this year.

The ground for church and chapel was broken in the early morning of a day not long after, the building committee and a few friends being present. Geo. W. Sparks dug the first spadeful of earth.

And now commenced the hard work of the enterprise. It was a comparatively easy thing to say, let us go up and build; yet this required faith in God and His people. "Work must now be linked with faith," and thus united, with big hearts and willing hands, and the blessing of Almighty God, success is assured.

The struggle which continued for several years, had now commenced. Could we have seen the end from the beginning possibly some would have fallen at the outset.

Plans for the building had been procured, contracts entered into, ground had been broken, and the work was progressing. Money must be raised, as the workmen must be paid promptly, bills for material were maturing. True, liberal subscriptions had been made, and the soliciting committee was working nobly; but the full amounts were not collectable, as the subscriptions had been made payable in installments. Whilst the subscribers responded promptly, yet there were times this year and the years following, when the building committee was sorely perplexed for want of ready money; but the way was, in the Providence of God, opened, and the means provided as needed.

The corner-stone of the church was laid by Bishop Simpson, on the afternoon of October 7, 1865, who, with others, made addresses. The exercises were appropriate and impressive, a large concourse of people being present.

The ladies of the church had not been idle in the meantime. During the summer and autumn of this year, they had been working and making preparations, with an enthusiasm which was unbounded, to hold a fair for the purpose of raising money to furnish the chapel and Sunday-school hall. The fair was held in the Institute Hall, in the month of December, 1865, and was a social and financial success, some $3,000.00 being realized as the result of their effort.

I have said that it was a social success, for many persons not connected with any church, were attracted to the fair, became interested in the church enterprise, and came under Christian influences which bore fruit in the revival meetings which followed in January, 1866, for the church. "St. Paul's" was in a good spiritual condition. Many of the persons referred to were converted, and became active and useful members of the church. A number identified themselves with the new movement, and some have held and others are at this time holding responsible positions in Grace Church. Work on the chapel progressed steadily during the autumn and winter, to have it ready for occupancy by March at the commencement of the next Conference year.

The first service was held in the lecture-room, on Sunday morning, March 25, 1866. There was preaching by the pastor, the Rev. W. J. Stevenson, who had been assigned to the new congregation, at the late session of the Philadelphia Conference. The congregation was large, every available seat being occupied, and the deepest interest manifested.

The Sunday-school held its first session on the afternoon of the same day, in the lecture-room. The hall not yet being finished, the organization of the afternoon session of the school was effected on the evening of March 16, 1866, at the residence of C. F. Rudolph. J. T. Gause was elected superintendent, and C. F. Rudolph, assistant. The morning session was organized March 11, 1866; Wm. H. Billany, superintendent.

Friday evening, March 30th, the first prayer meeting service was held. After the meeting the public rental of the pews in the chapel took place, the rental being $2,360.00; the premiums, $1,250.00; total, $3,610.00; almost every pew was rented.

Out of this money, the first received by the new church, $550 were appropriated to the Sunday-school, in recognition of the fact that the church had its origin in the wants of the Sunday-school, and that this was expected to be the main source of her success, influence and membership.

The chapel was dedicated to the worship of God on Sunday, June 10, 1866, at 10.30 o'clock, A. M. After a most able and eloquent sermon by Bishop Ames, on the subject of "Faith," the chapel was presented on behalf of the trustees, by the Rev. W. J. Stevenson, pastor, in an address of grateful acknowledgement to God, as a centenary offering, thus giving to Him glory for the one hundred years of His favor and goodness to the Methodist church in America.

"And now, in grateful recognition of the mercy and love of God, the trustees of Grace church have

"*Resolved*, That we present this church, through the formal act of dedication by our honored Bishop Ames, as a centenary offering, with fervent prayers that God will accept it and make it instrumental in the salvation of souls; and that we invoke His blessing upon all its members, and upon those who may join them in Christian fellowship; to increase their faith and love, and to sanctify to eternal life; that pure religion may abound; that peace and harmony may prevail; that His cause may be advanced, and that the coming hundred years may witness the victories of truth and righteousness, giving glory to God in the highest, and on earth peace and good will to men.

"*Resolved*, That a suitable stone bearing the inscription, 'Our Centenary Offering' be placed in a prominent position in the main church edifice, as an abiding witness, of the motives that have inspired us and our fellow members, in the erection of this Temple."

The stone was placed as resolved upon.

The Bishop then received the offering, and consecrated it with prayer to the service and worship of God. In the evening the pastor, Rev. W. J. Stevenson, preached a most excellent and appropriate sermon. On Sunday, June 17, 1866, the Sunday-school was dedicated with appropriate ceremonies.

At a trustees' meeting held on May 9, 1866, the building committee was instructed to proceed with the work on the church. Thus far only the excavations had been made and the foundation walls built, and the first floor joists laid. So the work went on, amid trials, and vexations of many and various kinds: difficulty in getting stone, trouble with workmen, and above and beyond all, trouble and worry to raise money. Many months the pay roll amounted to five hundred dollars per week. Brother Sparks, chairman of the building committee, nobly maintained the credit of the church, aided by Brothers Gause and Jackson. It took hard work and good financiering to raise the large amounts needed. It will be well to state just here, that we started out to build a church to cost $75,000. With the commencement of the year 1867, we had received subscriptions amounting to $52,276. Of this amount $9,729 was unpaid. In addition to these unpaid subscriptions we needed $20,000 to pay bills and loans, and the work was not half done.

Labor and sacrifice were required, and these were not withheld; for had we not consecrated our all to the service of our Master and His cause? I could relate many instances where our members made sacrifices, which they felt keenly, for the good of the cause; where a careful housekeeper would postpone the purchase of a needed carpet, and a good brother would relinquish the need of a new overcoat and wear the old one a year longer. It was really wonderful how the people lived to give. As an instance, the trustees resolved to ask the people for $10,000. Sunday, April 7, 1867, was the day selected.

A numerous audience collected to hear Bishop Simpson. After an eloquent and powerful appeal the sum of $15,300 was subscribed in less than one hour. The subscriptions came in more rapidly during the last ten minutes than at any previous time. For fear that I weary you with these recitals, I pass on to the day of the dedication of the church, which occurred on the morning of Thursday, January 23, 1868. The weather was unpropitious, rain and sleet, and the pavements were covered with ice; but this did not deter the crowd from assembling, for the church was packed with an interested audience. Many strangers from different sections of the country were present. Rev. Dr. Stevenson read the preliminary portion of the dedication service. After singing, and prayer by the Rev. Anthony Atwood, Bishop Simpson preached the dedicatory sermon from the text: "For unto us a Child is born; unto us a Son is given, and the government shall be upon His shoulder, and His name shall be called Wonderful, Counsellor, the Mighty God, the Everclaasting Father, the Prince of Peace."

After the eloquent and powerful sermon, Psalms cxxii was read responsively by Bishop Scott and the congregation. Bishop Ames read the consecration service. Geo. W. Sparks, president of the board of trustees, presented the building for consecration. The prayer of consecration was also made by Bishop Ames.

It is unnecessary for me to give any description of the building. The press of the day pronounced it the finest Methodist Church in America, and, as was remarked by Dr. Stevenson, it would build many more; which it has done, notably, the Metropolitan, Washington; Mt. Vernon, Baltimore; Arch Street, Philadelphia; St. John's, Brooklyn; Grace, Harrisburg; Union, in our own city. Many others could be named did time permit. The cost of the structure, including the organ and furniture, was $210,000. A debt remained of about $100,000, which was left for a future generation to take care of.

During the pastorate of Dr. Todd, in the year 1871, an effort was made to provide for a portion of the debt. A meeting for this purpose was held in the Sunday-school room in May, 1871, and all that was asked for was freely given, $43,000.

And later, just ten years since, Dr. Stevenson, then pastor for the second time, was impressed with the idea that the time had come when an effort should be made to extinguish the whole debt, and under the influence of the Holy Spirit, and with the blessing and help of God, he was successful in enlisting the interest and sympathies of the congregation. In a short time he had $68,007.58 subscribed.

A congratulatory meeting of the members and friends of Grace Church was held in the Sunday-school hall on Friday evening, November 7, 1879. After an hour pleasantly spent in tea drinking, H. F. Pickels, chairman of the board of trustees, announced that Geo. W. Sparks would preside at the meeting to follow. Addresses were made by Bishop Simpson, and Drs. Todd and Stevenson.

This ended the efforts of the friends at debt-paying. The church was now in a good financial condition. We felt that a great burden had been removed. Is it any wonder that we sung rapturous praises unto our God, who, during all these fifteen years, had so wondrously blessed and prospered us, and we are led to exclaim in the language of one of our beautiful hymns:

> "When all Thy mercies, O my God,
> My rising soul surveys,
> Transported with the view, I'm lost
> In wonder, love and praise."

Notwithstanding the burden of debt which rested upon us for so many years, our people measured up to their responsibilities in other directions. The benevolences of the church were not neglected, as will be seen from the following exhibit, which are the contributions to the commencement of this year. For ministerial support we have paid

To the pastor of Grace church	$53,700 00
Epworth and Madeley	13,750 00
Epworth and Madeley Building	8,000 00
Expenses of Sunday-schools	11,400 00
Presiding Elders	4,832 00
	$91,682 00
Foreign Missionary, Church	10,250 80
" " Sunday-school	42,978 48
Woman's Foreign Missionary Society	4,141 31
Home Missionary Society, four years	914 00
Domestic Missions, three years	158 00
	$58,442 59
Other Conference collections	$19,280 54
Recapitulation:	
For salaries, etc	$91,682 00
Missions	58,442 59
Conference collection	19,280 54
	$169,405 13

These figures do not include collections made for the sufferers of the Chicago fire, yellow fever sufferers, Charleston earthquake, and Johnstown disaster. Nor do they include church expenses, such as sexton's salary, light, fuel, etc., rent of parsonage (some $15,000), interest on bond and mortgage.

This sketch, imperfect as it is, would not be complete without mention being made of "Epworth" and "Madeley" churches.

Epworth had its origin in St. Paul's, in 1863, was adopted by Grace upon the separation, and has had the care and responsibility of the church, from that time until early in the present year, when the Sunday-school Union made a deed for the property to the trustees of Epworth, and they assumed full control. We bid them God speed.

Being imbued with the missionary spirit and zeal in the Sunday-school cause, some of our members felt called of God to go out and established a mission on the South Side, which resulted in the organization of Madeley Sunday-school, April 20, 1871, with C. F. Rudolph as superintendent.

The following named, who were identified with the new church enterprise in the beginning and held official positions, have since died: Dr. Geo. Pepper Norris, R. Emmett Robinson, S. M. Harrington, Delaplain McDaniel, George W. Sparks, Daniel M. Bates, Edward Moore, Jarrett Megaw, L. F. Riddle, John Merrick. And we may also add the names of Bishops Simpson and Ames.

The pastors of Grace have been:

1866-67, Rev. W. J. Stevenson; 1868-69-70, Rev. Alfred Cookman; 1871-72, Rev. Jacob Todd; 1873, Rev. L. C. Matlack, D. D.; 1874-75-76, Rev. Joseph E. Smith; 1877-78-79, Rev. W. J. Stevenson, D. D.; 1880-81-82, Rev. G. W. Miller; 1883-84-85, Rev. J. R. Boyle, D. D.; 1886-87-88-89, Rev. Jacob Todd, D. D., the present acceptable incumbent.

The membership of the church at present is 510; officers and teachers of Sunday-school, 78; scholars, 730. All the services of the church are well attended, and the Sunday-school, under the superintendency of Wm. H. Curry, is in a flourishing condition.

It is impossible, in the time allotted me, to make mention of the good work done in these years by the faithful ministers of God who have served the church, and who have labored so assiduously for the building up of God's kingdom, and of the members who so faithfully held up their hands.

God has graciously blessed our efforts as put forth in every direction of church work.

History of Madeley Methodist Episcopal Church.

By the Rev. H. W. Ewing, Pastor.

This historical sketch will be brief, for two reasons. First, the time given for its delivery is limited. Second, and chief, the available facts are few. Records of this organization were no doubt made, but unfortunately very few have been preserved. It has a history, indeed, but most of it must remain unwritten. Had the keepers of the records known that the facts connected with this church would be in demand during such an important event as the "Asbury Centennial," they no doubt would have been more careful in preserving the records. But prescience is not given to mortals.

The part of the city lying east and south of the Christiana Creek, familiarly known as "South Wilmington," had been long neglected by the religious people of the more favored part of the city. The people, and especially the children, were rapidly approaching a state of semi-heathenism. The preacher who went over that way on a certain Sunday afternoon to preach or arrange for a Sunday-school service, finding his congregation not very large, thought to swell the numbers by hunting the by-ways and hedges, and thus fulfilling the command of scripture and compelling them to come in. On looking around for some additional recruits his eyes fell upon some boys hiding behind a hedge fence. The genial gentleman approached them with the laudable purpose of persuading them to attend the service, but scarcely was he in speaking distance of them, when they bounded away across the vacant lots like deer upon their native heath.

If we can place confidence in common report, no place in the State of Delaware needed the civilizing influences of a Sunday-school

REV. H. W. EWING,

Pastor of Madeley Methodist Episcopal Church.

more than this, and be it said to the praise of the faithful and zealous workers in their field, no place in the city has brought larger returns; for we have to-day as orderly and as intelligent a school as can be found in any of the suburban churches of the city. Perhaps no certain date can be given as to the beginning of the Sunday-school work in this part of the city. Asbury, ever fruitful in good works, claims to have been the first to establish a Sunday-school here. Accordingly the following persons, Caroline Jones, Ann G. Perkins, Levinia Tubbs, Thomas Houpt and Mary Pennell, commenced the work. But I have been unable to discover the date of its inception, how long continued, or how successful it proved. An entry is found upon the records of that church to the effort that a proposition had been made to them by certain members of Grace Church offering to take the Sunday-school work in the "South Side" off their hands. The proposition was accepted by them and the work transferred to the tender mercies of Grace Church. And here the record begins. The opening exercises of the school, as undertaken by these laborers from Grace, were held in a tent erected for that purpose on a vacant lot situated at the junction of Claymont and B streets, on Easter Sunday, April 9, 1871. Surely a fitting day for the inception of a work which has resulted in the resurrection of multitudes of precious souls from a life of sin into a life of righteousness. These services were under the directions of Rev. H. H. Davis, who was then acting as pastor of Epworth Chapel, the first offspring of Grace Sunday-school Union.

The tent erected for these services could not withstand the fury of the wind, and the young school was soon without a home and shelter. But the old saying is a true one, "It is an ill wind that blows nobody good," for it was the means of securing better quarters for the school. A force of workmen, under the efficient direction of the Jackson & Sharp Company, went to work vigorously, and a small chapel was erected on this same lot in the short space of three days. The first service in this chapel was held April 23, 1871, in charge of C. F. Rudolph. There were no sash in the windows, and Brother Rudolph reports that although the bitter cold wind was driving through the open windows, compelling him and the other teachers to button closely their heavy overcoats, the children, some of whom were very scantily clad, did not seem to mind the cold in the least, so eager were they to attend Sunday-school. Thus was the school in a fair way to succeed. At a meeting of the Grace Sunday-school Union, held in the chapel of Grace Church, Wednesday evening, April 5, 1871, a committee previously appointed to consider the "advisibility of building a chapel over Third street bridge, reported through its chairman, Mr. Job H.

Jackson, that land owners in that vicinity had donated a lot, and that another adjacent lot had been secured upon which to build the chapel." He also reported that residents of that community had agreed to raise $1,500 toward the enterprise, provided the Sunday-school Union would do the same. The lot secured cost $250, and the estimated cost of the building was $6,000; but before it was finished the advance in the price of building materials increased the cost to $8,000. Of this amount $5,000 was raised and paid chiefly through the efforts of the efficient superintendent of the Sunday-school, C. F. Rudolph.

At a special meeting of the Sunday-school Union, held some time between June 6, 1872, and September 5 of the same year, the plans submitted by the building committee of which Job H. Jackson was chairman, were adopted and the building ordered.

The first chapel which was erected in April, 1871, was sold to the colored people, and the corner-stone of the new one was laid with appropriate ceremonies in the month of August, 1872, and the building was dedicated December 29, 1872, by Dr. J. W. Stevenson. To Dr. J. W. Stevenson belongs the honor of suggesting that the name of the new church should be "Madeley," named, no doubt, for the parish in England where the great and saintly Fletcher labored in the Lord's vineyard.

The Rev. H. H. Davis acted as the first pastor of the new society before the present building was erected, and while they were yet worshiping in the tent and small chapel.

The Rev. Thos. F. Plummer succeeded him, but served only a short time. On May 30, 1872, before the corner-stone of the present building was laid, the Rev. I. N. Foreman, a local preacher, became the pastor, and continued to act in that capacity till March, 1875. Brother Foreman reports his first congregation as consisting of eight persons, two of whom were members of Grace Church, viz: Brother Stimmel and Dr. Shelp. The only full members of this church to greet their new pastor were Ephraim Start and his good wife, Mary A. Start. Thus Brother Foreman started. It appears that under the labors of the former pastor a class of thirty probationers had been received, but only nine of these could be found and only six of the nine were recommended for full membership. Thus with eight full members and three probationers—eleven in all—this young society started out on its checkered journey.

After a very successful pastorate of nearly three years, Brother Foreman was succeeded, in March, 1875, by Rev. A. D. Davis, now a veteran in the Lord's army, who also had charge of Epworth at the same time.

In the spring of 1876 Rev. J. E. Mowbray was appointed pastor, and it is reported that large congregations attended his ministry and many persons professed conversion.

From 1878-80 the Rev. David Dodd was the pastor. He was succeeded by Rev. T. A. H. O'Brien, under whose supervision the church building was frescoed and otherwise improved. There was also quite a large ingathering of souls during this pastorate.

From 1883-87 the charge was served by Rev. B. F. Price, under whose management the chapel was changed into a regular church organization with a quarterly conference of its own.

In March, 1887, the writer of this sketch became pastor, and so remains until this day.

I have thus briefly given the history of the founding of this church, and of the men who have served it as pastors; but its history would be very incomplete were I to neglect to mention the men who have been the superintendents of the Sunday-school, and the faithful teachers who here imparted instruction from the word of life. As already mentioned, Mr. C. F. Rudolph was the first superintendent, and held the position for a period of ten years. In that time he did a great work, sparing neither time nor money in making the school a success, therefore he had the joy of seeing the "pleasure of the Lord prospering in his hands." Resigning to take charge of the afternoon school of Grace Church, he was followed by H. C. Conrad, Esq., who labored faithfully for a period of five years. He was in turn succeeded by John S. Mullin who still acts in that capacity, giving liberally of his time and money for the success of the school. Under these men, faithful teachers, members of the society, and from the other churches in the city, have labored earnestly, and the good seed thus sown has already produced an abundant harvest, the full extent of which can only be made known in the day when all things shall be revealed. During the entire history of this enterprise the Sunday-school Union of Grace Church has been its financial strength, having, during the entire period of the society's existence, paid the pastor's salary in full or in part, and at the same time contributed largely to the other running expenses of the church.

There have been dark times in the history of this organization. The hopes of its founders were not always fully met, and in the records of the Sunday-school Union, we find steps being taken at one time toward the refusal of any more money for the preacher's salary, but happily the resolution was not passed. So dark indeed was the outlook at one time, that one member of the Sunday-school Union suggested that "Madeley was not fit to be an independent charge, and that the

Sunday-school Union ought to be rid of it, and of the expense attached to it." But other opinions and feelings prevailed, and the Sunday-school Union still continues to give nobly to the help of this charge.

As has been justly remarked by one who has watched the growth and has been familiar with the history of this church, Madeley does not get the credit for the real work that has been done by her. Perhaps more than any other church in the city, because of her location, and because of the physicians, Madeley has been crippled time and again by the exodus of her membership. They have come and gone like the birds with the seasons. Under the most careful and earnest pastors the work has not grown, from the simple fact that the people who once belonged to her have not remained within reach of the church. We, therefore, cannot measure the success of the church in these past years by her numerical strength now. Many who have been converted there found a church-home in other places, and till the roll of the finally faithful is called, we will not be able to estimate the extent of her usefulness.

It may be proper to state here, in a few words, her present condition. There is a membership, including probationers, of two hundred and thirty persons.

One interesting fact connected with the present pastorate may not be overlooked. Being called one day, soon after my appointment, to visit an aged sick man, I was surprised to learn that he was a grandson of the famous Benjamin Abbott. He was seventy-six years of age, and had up till that time neglected to seek the God of his fathers. But he was an earnest inquirer, and in a short time was soundly and happily converted to God. He joined the church, and though too feeble to be present at that time, lived long enough to be admitted into the church as a full member before he was translated to the church above, which event occurred June 23, 1889. His widow, a granddaughter, and a grandson, are the only representatives of the name remaining in the church at this time.

The oldest member of this church is Mrs. Elizabeth Powell, now in her ninety-eighth year, who eighty years ago, in England, gave her heart to God, and her name to the Methodist Church. She is still remarkably active in all church work, visiting the sick, exhorting the ungodly, and attending almost every service of the church.

In conclusion, let us hope that while the history of the church has been a varied one, success and failure alternating often in quick succession, the future may be a glorious one for God and mankind. And when the Centennial of Madeley shall have been celebrated, may she be found to be the mother of as many, and as thrifty children as the grand old church whose Centennial we now celebrate.

History of Haven Chapel.

By the Rev. Jas. H. Scott, Pastor.

Haven Chapel is a granddaughter of Asbury by her eldest daughter, Ezion.

She was born in the year of 1869 in this wise:

In a part of Wilmington, lying along the P., W. & B. R. R., commonly known as Browntown, there was a settlement of colored people, most of whom hailed from the lower counties of Delaware and the Eastern Shore, Maryland. They were not the cream of the race.

This region was notorious for its gamblers, drunkards and low women. Like Nazareth, it was wicked to a proverb.

It might well have been asked "Can any good thing come out of Browntown?"

Rev. Charles Smith, then exhorter of Ezion, noticing the great number of children in Browntown, with no religious instruction, running the streets on the Sabbath day, began to urge the people to send their children to Sunday-school. Like those bidden to the marriage supper, they began to make excuses; the most striking of which were: Ezion school was too far off, and they were unable to dress their children suitably to send them.

He then inquired how they would like to have a Sunday-school in their midst. One very wicked old man said: "I know I am no meetin' man, but I appreciate meetin' people. I haven't many things in my house. You can have a room there to hold your school in if you mind to." His offer was accepted and the school was started with good results. Soon was needed and obtained an additional room. Several members of Ezion volunteered and came to the founder's assistance. So the school grew and prospered.

Brother Smith, true to his calling as an exhorter, began to sigh for a prayer meeting. He asked some of the brethren of Ezion to come over and help him pray for these people. They responded readily, and God began to pour out of His spirit upon them. Sinners were converted and great interest was manifested. Some who hardly knew what a church meant attended these meeting.

Brother Smith, jubilant over the success the effort was obtaining, commenced agitating the notion of building a chapel in Browntown. The advice of Bro. Abraham Murray, the then leading laymen of Ezion, was sought. As the result, Rev. J. D. Elbert, then pastor of Ezion, organized a mission of twenty members. Efforts were immediately put forth to erect a suitable building.

Dr. Brown, who owned considerable real estate in this section and in honor of whom the region took its name, was much pleased with the idea of estsblishing a chapel among these people. He remarked, if ever a church was needed anywhere, it was needed in Browntown. He, therefore, offered to sell them a piece of ground on favorable terms.

The trustees of Ezion accepted the offer and secured an old colored man named Peter Smith, a resident of that neighborhood, to build the chapel.

Soon there was a building in Browntown dedicated to the service of the Lord, bearing the name of Mt. Zion M. E. Chapel.

The mission immediately entered on a life of prosperity. Hard old sinners were brought to the feet of Jesus, some of whom have died in the triumph of faith ; others have proclaimed the glad tidings of redemption ; others are still among the rank and file of the militant hosts of God. It can be truly said of this chapel: "This and that man was born in her."

Rev. Elias Williams a local preacher connected with our church at Newport, Delaware, was first to have charge of the chapel under the appointment of the pastor of Ezion. Joseph Williams, still a member of Haven, was the first class leader and continued to fill that office till recently disabled by ill health. Absalom Caulk, now exhorter at Haven, was among the leading lights of the organization.

The chapel continued connected with Ezion as a mission until 1876, when it was organized into a circuit with Whittington Chapel. Rev. Wm. Holland was the first pastor appointed by the Delaware Conference. During his administration the church prospered spiritually and a few were added.

In 1877 Rev. I. H. White, now Presiding Elder of Salisbury District, of the Delaware Conference, was appointed. Simpson Church, Newport, had now been added to the circuit. Rev. White continued pastor two years, and was particularly successful in strengthening the organization financially. He was succeeded in 1879 by Rev. T. M. Hubbard. In this year the trustees of Ezion sold the church at Browntown to the P., W. & B. R. R., as the tracks of the company were being laid uncomfortably near the chapel. They purchased the present site on West Third street, between DuPont and Scott streets, and built under the supervision of the late Dr. Wm. F. Butler, pastor of Ezion, the present building.

The name was now changed to Haven, in honor of the late Bishop Gilbert Haven, and in appreciation of his noble efforts for the elevation of the people of color.

The chapel now being situated in a growing colored settlement began a new life of prosperity. In 1881 Rev. Hubbard, having completed a pastorate of two years, was succeeded by Rev. Harrison D. Webb, who served a term of two years. July 5, 1882, the chapel was turned over to a board of trustees selected from among the members of Haven by the trustees of Ezion in consideration of the payment of $200.

Rev. J. J. Campbell was appointed in 1883 and served a term of one year. In this year a front gallery was built to the chapel, and a fine six room parsonage adjoining the church was erected.

In 1884 the Rev. Dr. W. F. Butler was appointed, but owing to disease of the brain was unable to finish his year out. Father Joshua Brinkly, a superannuate, completed the year.

Rev. D. A. Ridout became in 1885 pastor and proved himself a successful organizer and driller of the people. The benevolent collections were increased, being taken the first part of the Conference year. Business-like methods introduced in the boards that have greatly increased the usefulness of Haven Chapel.

After a successful pastorate of three years, Rev. Ridout was succeeded by the writer, who was appointed in 1888.

There are now 65 members and a Sunday-school numbering 100. The present board of trustees are James Whartonberry, president; Ellis Jefferson, secretary; Moses Nichols, L. H. Collins, J. H. Woodlen, James Lewis, Ezekiel Townsend, Philip Garrison and Wm. Price.

Haven is a frame building in need of repairs, which we are now planning to have speedily done. She is, however, spiritually alive. Having heard the order, "Go forward," from the Captain of our salvation, her soldiers are pressing onward, bearing aloft the gospel banner. Hearing the sound of the gospel bugle, they have buckled on the armor of God and are charging against intemperance, Sabbath desecration, worldliness, yea, immorality of every kind. Haven intends to march and fight with the militant church of God against the foes of the Lord's annointed till she shall be mustered into the triumphant army of heaven.

The History of Kingswood Methodist Episcopal Church.

By the Rev. R. Irving Watkins, Pastor.

The history of Kingswood Church is so closely connected with that of its Sunday-school, that to give the one is essentially to give the other. The church is the natural outgrowth of the school.

Prior to 1872 there was comparatively little to attract the attention of the church on the east side of Eleventh street bridge. True, Father Taylor preached to those who gathered at a point, now known as the S. W. corner of Thirteenth and Forrest streets ; and afterwards, under the "shady maples," not far distant, he, with simple earnestness, preached the Gospel to the masses.

A true itinerant was he, having the Methodistic standards as his guides ; and realizing that "the field is the world," he entered its wide domain to seek some soil into which Methodist seed might be planted.

What has been the harvest? An answer is attempted. About the first of May, 1672, there lived on Forrest street a godly couple, Wm. and Alice Rinker, members at that time, of Brandywine M. E. Church.

Sister Rinker, seeing the children running around the streets on Sunday, and feeling the necessity of their being instructed in Bible truth, conceived the idea of gathering them into her home on Sunday afternoons, and teaching them the lessons of scripture.

With true Methodist zeal, she collected eight scholars, and with the assistance of several good neighbors, began a Sunday-school. This was the nucleus from which the church has grown.

In a short time the room was too small to hold those who came to be taught, and two rooms became necessary. Meanwhile the interest was increasing, and Brother and Sister Rinker moving from that part of the town, it was necessary to change quarters. This was done, and the scholars entered the home of Wesley Beerbrower, next door, and continued to grow.

At Christmas, the records tell us, the children were given a jubilee under the direction of Esther Bangs. This proved to be a success, and now the school was formerly organized under the name of East Wilmington Methodist Episcopal Sunday-school, having the following officers and teachers: superintendent, Alice Rinker; secretary and treasurer, Eli Bangs; musical director, Esther Bangs; teachers, Wesley Beerbrower and wife, and Wm. Rinker.

The school prospered, and help was needed. More room became a necessity. A more permanent place of meeting was sought, and after much thought and prayer, application was made to St. Paul's Methodist Episcopal Church for assistance. After much solicitation the society at St. Paul's accepted the school, and about February, 1873, the name of the school was changed to St. Paul's Methodist Episcopal Mission of Wilmington, Delaware.

Geo. R. Greenman was appointed supterintendent and M. D. Lamborn, secretary and treasurer, with following teachers: Brothers Enos W. Clair and Peters, and Sisters Alice Rinker, Amanda Clair and E. B. Dorman. At this time the school was still held in the home of Wesley Beerbrower, where it was continued to be held until his removal from the city in the spring of 1873. Brother and Sister Bangs, then kindly offered the use of their home, on Claymont street, as a place of meeting. This offer was accepted, and there the school went in April of 1873.

About this time the teachers' association of St. Paul's appointed a committee to procure a suitable lot, and build a chapel. A lot was soon procured from Eli Mendinhall, at the corner of Fourth and Claymont streets, but the erection of a building was not begun until about the first of September, when the project was put into the hands of Bro. Jacob F. Sharp, who put new life and energy into the enterprise. A building was begun and completed about the first of November. The dedication occurred about the middle of the month, and the name was again changed to "Kingswood Chapel of St. Paul's Methodist Episcopal Church of Wilmington." About this time the school met with a severe loss by the removal of Brother and Sister Bangs to Baltimore. Sister Bangs taught the children the sweet songs of Zion. The record tells us that she would gather the children into her home during the week evenings and teach them to sing. This added testimony is given: "God's Holy Spirit came very close to us, making His presence felt." For the two Sundays prior to going into the chapel the school was held in the home of Wm. Powell. It was thought the school would flourish in its new chapel, but like many another, it met with its reverses. The loss of a leader for the singing, and several changes in the officers and teachers weakened the school for a time.

On March 8, 1874, M. D. Lamborn took charge as superintendent. On July 19, 1874, Jacob F. Sharp succeeded him, with Brother Zach. Pickels as musical director. At this time I find on the minutes the following record: "It is hoped that Kingswood Chapel may yet be known as a church in Wilmington." The school began to grow again, and on November 22, 1874, the first anniversary was held. Addresses were made by Rev. J. B. Merritt, pastor of St. Paul's, and Bro. Joseph Pyle, who took a deep interest in the work.

Brother Sharp's health failing, H. M. Rile was appointed superintendent on March 7, 1875. He served until February 13, 1876, when Bro. Alfred W. Guest, a member of Kingswood Chapel succeeded him. Brother Guest served until October 7, 1877, when he severed his connection, as he was about to remove to Cambridge, Md.

He was succeeded by Wm. Powick, who served until February 8, 1878, when he was followed by Jabez Hodson.

Under his superintendency it was suggested that some improvements be made to the chapel, viz: painting the outside, and kalsomining it within. This was begun and completed under the supervision of George W. Todd, who was appointed to succeed Brother Hodson as superintendent, April 13, 1879.

From then till now Brother Todd has given Kingswood his entire services, and not only so, but he has during all these years, Sunday after Sunday, gathered and brought with him help in the shape of volunteer teachers from St. Paul's Church.

Some six or seven years ago, the interest of the school having steadily increased under Brother Todd's guidance, the members of Kingswood Sunday-school Association appointed a committee to prepare plans for an addition to the chapel for the use of the 'infant department.

After much delay, and the appointment of several committees, Brother Todd thinking that the time had come when the improvement must be made, again brought the matter to the attention of the trustees of St. Paul's Church. Their approval and assistance was asked and a committee was appointed to put the matter on a working basis.

With Brother Todd as leader in this enterprise the work was faithfully performed, and the infant department was separated, so that it could the more successfully prosecute its work. In this improvement much help was given by the friends at St. Paul's; added to this was the energy and business tact of Bro. Geo. W. Todd, which made it a financial success.

Little can be gathered of the infant department, save that for many years it was most faithfully ministered unto by Sister Amanda Clair.

Thus the work has grown, until at present there is a flourishing school. On Sunday, October 6, 1889, the school was formally organized under the provisions of the discipline, as an "independent" school, with Bro. Geo. W. Todd, as superintendent, Alex. Z. Clair, as secretary. The last named has for several years been punctually at at his post, and deserves great credit for the manner in which he has done his work.

In connection with the school special mention should be made of the services of Aubrey Vandever, who served as secretary for a number of years; Mrs. S. E. Hoffecker, who aided as assistant superintendent, and Mrs. Fannie Forbes, superintendent infant school, who has lately removed to her home in Maine.

To-day the school is in a condition which foretokens advancement in all lines of Sunday-school work.

During all the years from 1873 until 1884, the pulpit was supplied, for the most part, by the local preachers of St. Paul's Church. Among them were Bros. Isaac L. Cronch, Jabez Hodson, Jacob F. Sharp, and Albert Thatcher; the last two being familiarly known as David and Jonathan. Sunday after Sunday these faithful brethren came to preach the word of life to the Kingswood people. During a part of this time the Rev. A. T. Scott, a supernumerary of the Wilmington Conference, supplied this work.

With him were associated Bro. Alfred W. Guest and wife, and Sisters Amanda Clair and Elizabeth B. Dorman, who, in the dark hours of Kingswood Church life, were always on hand to do good, and aid in keeping the church doors open.

The first revival occurred during Bro. Scott's pastorate. There was a quickening in spiritual life, and as a result the church grew for a time.

Nothing of a permanent character, however, was accomplished until the Rev. R. H. Adams was sent to St. Paul's Church. Kingswood lay very near his heart, and it was during his pastorate that a gracious revival broke out in the chapel, and many were soundly converted.

Brother Adams was aided in this revival by some of the members of St. Paul's, who night after night wended their way to the little chapel, and helped on the good work.

Among those who so nobly stood by Kingswood, may be mentioned Brothers Joseph Pyle, Jabez Hodson, Jacob F. Sharp, Albert Thatcher, and Geo. W. Todd, and Sisters S. E. Hoffecker, and Sue Simpson. The result of this meeting was that at the ensuing session of the Conference, in 1884, the Rev. W. A. Wise was associated with Rev. R. H. Adams as assistant pastor of St. Paul's Church, and assigned to Kingswood.

Here begins the church-work regularly; the people felt as if they were at last getting to be a regular church. During Brother Wise's first year there was a wide-spread revival. The meetings were held in St. Paul's tent, which had been erected on the vacent lot adjoining the church. Here for many weeks services were held with good results.

It was during this pastorate that the church was improved by putting in gas, and papering the walls, and putting blinds to the windows. In 1886, at the end of Brother Wise's second year, Kingswood was left to be supplied. Bro. Chas. Hill was presiding elder. A committee, consisting of Brothers Daniel A. Forrest, William Leathem, Alfred Wilson, and Jno. W. McCauley, waited on Brother Hill and asked for the appointment of the Rev. Wm. L. White, a local preacher of Epworth Methodist Episcopal Church, as their pastor. The request was granted, and Brother White began his work.

For three years he rendered efficient service as pastor of Kingswood, having had during the last year quite an extensive revival. When it is remembered that this brother did the work in addition to following his daily avocation, it may be seen how heavily the burden fell upon him. The congregations increased greatly during the terms of Brothers Wise and White, so much so that it began to be whispered that a new and larger church was needed. But where could the necessary funds be found? The people at Kingswood were not able to do this work alone, and they must appeal to the large sympathies of Wilmington Methodism.

At the last Conference the present pastor was sent to Kingswood, which was still a mission of St. Paul's. Frequently the independence of Kingswood has been a mooted question, but no definite action was taken until the people of Kingswood, with their pastor, asked St. Paul's Quarterly Conference to set them apart in their official relations. St. Paul's still retaining the church property. Kingswood Chapel was thus formerly set apart on June 10, 1889.

On June 12, 1889, the Presiding Elder, Dr. W. L. S. Murray, organized and held the first Quarterly Conference of Kingswood Methodist Episcopal Church.

The following were the officers of the church: pastor, Rev. R. Irving Watkins; local preacher, Rev. Wm. L. White; class leaders, the pastor, Powell F. Clayton and Asel Stiles; stewards, Daniel A. Forrest, John W. McCauley, William Leathem, Alfred Wilson, Benjamin Price, Thomas Proven, Annie V. Guthrie, Ellen Dixon, and Reba B. Smith, the last named being the recording steward, and Geo. W. Todd Sunday-school superintendent.

Just prior to the meeting of the second Quarterly Conference, the official board of Kingswood sent a communication to the board of trustees of St. Paul's, asking for a transfer of the church property.

At St. Paul's second Quarterly Conference, held September 9, 1889, a resolution was passed by which the church property was to be transferred to a legal board of trustees, to be elected by Kingswood Methodist Episcopal Church, in accordance with the laws of the State.

On September 11, 1889, the second Quarterly Conference of Kingswood accepted the proposition made by St. Paul's in reference to the property, and joined in asking the Presiding Elder, Dr. Murray, to nominate the trustees to be elected by Kingswood. Thus, after many years, the wishes of the early workers of Kingswood have been fulfilled, and to-day Kingswood is no longer a mission, but is an independent church, and looks forward to the time when a new edifice will take the place of the present building.

Our people have already subscribed about $1,000 toward a new church. We have a Ladies' Mite Society in successful operation, and we hope, ere long, to have a church which will meet the demands of this part of the city. May I add, that, owing to the efforts on the part of the church and Sunday-school, in connection with the Swedish Mission and our local Women's Christian Temperance Union, we have rid our section of the city of the curse of many saloons; and to-day, with a population of more than three thousand, there is at present but one saloon in our midst.

Great credit is due Rev. Wm. L. White, a former pastor, and Geo. W. Todd, our Sunday-school superintendent, for the existing state of affairs. Methodism is alive on this great question, and in no church in the city more so than in Kingswood.

As a child of Methodism we hope to grow and keep pace with the onward progress of the coming century, and leave such memories as will be pleasant in the years to come to those who have so nobly stood by us in the day of small things.

History of the Whittington Methodist Episcopal Chapel.

By the Rev. J. A. Richardson, Pastor.

The task of preparing an historical paper of Whittington M. E. Chapel has been a difficult one, and indeed, this one is very imperfect, because there have been no records kept of the church, and I have been compelled to rely upon the treacherous memory of a few who were connected with its founding.

We do not claim to hold position in the ranks among the noted and more wealthy churches of our city, but as the proverb "He is truly great that is little in himself, and that maketh no account of any height of honor."

Whittington, the granddaughter of the illustrious Asbury, and the third or youngest daughter of Ezion, is situated on Buttonwood street, south of the Christiana creek, in the section commonly known as South Wilmington.

It was in this place that many persons from the lower part of this State and from the Eastern Shore of Maryland, who were not the aristocrats of society nor even the rich milk, much less the cream of the race, began to settle.

Of this place it could be truly said, as was said of Nazareth, "It was noted for its wickedness," and it has been a question, not of Nathaniel, but of many who are familiar with its history, "Can any good thing come out of South Wilmington?" Corruption had been allowed to prevail until it had wrought itself into men's characters so as to have affected their minds and become, as it were a part of themselves. Gambling, drunkenness, rioting and low class women, were the vices which pervaded the place. Virtue and morality kept their distance and dare not show themselves, but it was almost useless to expect an era of peace and prosperity among these people until they had been touched by the facilities instituted for their enlightenment. An ignorant people can be governed by despotic force, but none but an intelligent and moral people can govern themselves.

The negro, if educated, refined and christianized, will be a most faithful ally in the perpetuity of good government; but if left in ignorance, will remain a tool of evil and designing demagogues, a constant menace of the peace of society. This place was everything but attractive, only for those who wished to engage in these vices, or to do service in the Master's vineyard. No field was ever so inviting to the laborer for God than here. There was one feature connected with the early history of the place that made it especially attractive to a Methodist preacher, and I have no proof that this was not the chief inducement which attracted the preacher. To many of the primitive inhabitants this place is better known as "Turkeytown," and a good fat turkey for a Thanksgiving dinner was then quite a treat to a poor Methodist preacher; however, whether this be the cause or not, there were a few persons in whose hearts dwelt a love for God's church. Among them were Francis Byrd and wife, who had tasted the rich blessings of God's grace, and feeling a deep interest in these semi-heathens, began to agitate the organization of a Sunday-school. Their knowledge of procedure was somewhat limited and they therefore applied to Abraham Murray, one of the leading men of the Ezion M. E. Church, for advice.

Brother Murray, a man of great influence and whose name is dear to many hearts in this city, gave the command to "Go forward." Accordingly in the early part of the year 1873, a Sunday-school consisting of five children was started in a private house on Buttonwood street, then occupied by Francis Byrd and family.

The founders of this school were Francis Byrd, Solomon T. Bantum and Charles H. Smith. Francis Byrd and Charles Smith were then exhorters and Solomon T. Bantum a local preacher in Ezion M. E. Church. Wm. Blake was appointed the first superintendent. In this organization a resolution was passed to have preaching at ten o'clock each Sunday morning, and Rev. Charles H. Smith preached the first sermon and God poured out His spirit upon them. The superintendent, William Blake, who was indeed zealous for the cause, and grasping every opportunity to make the school a success, labored faithfully, going into the highways and hedges and persuading the children to come to Sunday-school. In the face of hundreds of excuses he did not despair, and on several occasions met the excuses at his own expense.

furnishing some of the children with sufficient clothing to attend the school, and even paying some of them to attend. Through his earnest and faithful efforts the school prospered, and soon they needed larger quarters. Their condition was made known to Rev. Hooper Jolley, who was then pastor of Ezion, and an effort was immediately put forth for a church. They first attempted to purchase a lot on A street, where the St. Paul's A. U. M. P. Church now stands, but failed.

Afterwards they succeeded in purchasing a lot on Buttonwood street in a low, marshy place, and built a small chapel thereon, which was dedicated to the service of God in the month of August, 1873, by Rev. Hooper Jolley, and a mission was organized consisting of twenty in the Sunday-school and about thirteen church members. John E. Johnson, Francis Byrd and William Blake were selected by the trustees of Ezion and appointed as the first trustees, and Francis Byrd was made the first class leader.

The chapel was named in honor of one of the old veterans of the cross of Christ, Rev. Joseph Whittington, a former pastor of Ezion, under whose preaching many souls were awakened to a knowledge of sin and sought the blessing of God's grace. He was a good Christian and a powerful gospel preacher, and many both white and colored have had their souls fed while listening to his simple yet forcible manner of preaching the story of the cross; he was a blessing to the church. We cherish his memory, and as he has crossed the line of battle below and is standing on Zion's hill, may we follow his precepts and examples, until we cross the dead lines and stand with him around the throne of God. The mission now seemed to gain new vigor, and a life of prosperity seemed inevitable; but alas! in February, 1875, it became a prey to the devouring flames and was entirely burned.

The hearts of the people were sad, their hopes seemed for a while blasted, their only beloved Zion was gone, and they were compelled to return to their primitive mission house, where they stayed only one week and then rented a house on the corner of A and Buttonwood streets, where they remained about six months during which time the Rev. Solomon Cooper, then pastor of Ezion, came to their relief and rebuilt the chapel, and they were once more made happy in a new chapel, which was dedicated to the service of Almighty God in the summer of 1875 by Revs. Lewis Y. Cox and Perry G. Walker.

In the autumn of this year the public school, through the untiring efforts of Girard Rollins, one of the members of Whittington, had its origin in the church where it was held for nearly one year. From this little chapel emanated our public school which now numbers on roll one hundred and three pupils, with an average attendance of eighty-seven and one-half per cent., ranging from the first to the tenth grade, under the principalship of the efficient teacher, Miss Emilie N. Dorster, who has served as principal nine successive years.

This work remained a mission under the supervision of Ezion until the Conference of 1876, when it was organized into a circuit with Browntown M. E. Chapel, and Rev. William Holland, a local preacher from Zoar M. E. Church, Philadelphia, was appointed as pastor. He remained one year. During his administration the church was in a prosperous condition; the present choir was organized and everything bid fair, but another calamity befell it. In September of that year, during a terrific storm which swept over this city, the banks of the Christiana yielded to the rolling waters, and this section of Wilmington was overflowed, the church became, as it were, a pool, but quite unlike the noted Bethesda, for instead of desiring to be put in, the people were anxious to get out, and the pastor, who was by no means a Baptist, was carried out by one more used to the water. God's word, the bread of life, was cast upon the water, but the sign was soon seen and gathered after a few hours, as the Bible was washed from the pulpit and floated upon the water in the church. This was indeed bad enough, but the worst was not yet, after the waters subsided the serpent made his appearance in the church. We do not pretend to say that this was his first time there, but his first visible appearance. Snakes, frogs, lizards, etc., found refuge in God's sanctuary, and for three weeks the people were compelled to abandon the church.

Where they worshiped I have not been able to ascertain. The inhabitants were forced to their upper stories, and some of them beyond that. Many left their homes and made room for the reptiles which were constantly coming in. Times looked desperate, but God was all sufficient, and the faithful of God seemed to hear that soul-cheering promise so full of consolation to the Christian, "Lo, I am with you always."

In 1877 Rev. I. H. White, now Presiding Elder of the Salisbury District of the Delaware Conference, was the first regularly appointed pastor, he was appointed by Bishop Levi Scott, who presided over the Conference then in session at Chestertown. Rev. White continued pastor for two years, during which time the organization was greatly strengthened financially.

In 1879 he was succeeded by Rev. Thomas M. Hubbard, who rearranged and reseated the church during his pastorate. An organ was purchased by the choir. The church prospered financially. Having served two years, Rev. Hubbard was removed and Rev. Harrison D. Webb was appointed his successor.

Brother Webb was much beloved by the people; he was a good financier, and did a good work in building up the church in every respect. On July 17, 1882, the chapel was turned over to the board of trustees, which had already been appointed by the trustees of Ezion, in consideration of the sum of $200. Brother Webb served two years, and in 1883 was succeeded by Rev. J. J. Campbell, who remained one year; during which time an effort was put forth to purchase a new and better site on which to build, and a lot 30 x 100 feet, on the east side of Townsend street, between A and B streets, and adjoining the public school ground, was purchased at a cost of $250, and the first payment made.

In 1884 Rev. William F. Butler, D. D., was appointed pastor, but owing to mental derangement he was not able to complete his year. Whittington was at this time taken from the circuit and made a station, and Rev. Hezekiah Grinnage, a local preacher, and a son of Rev. Asbury Grinnage, one of the fathers of the Delaware Conference, was appointed by Presiding Elder I. H. White to finish the year out. In 1885 Rev. Andrew J. Wallace became pastor and proved himself efficient for the work during his administration. The building lot was paid for, the Sunday-school was greatly increased, and a new board of stewards was appointed, and the trustees were newly elected and duly incorporated February 10, 1886. A seal of the incorporation was purchased by the church, and new life began to spring up. Brother Wallace spent two years of sucessful but hard labor. In 1887 Rev C. A. Tindley, who had been for two years pastor of Cape May Circuit, was appointed pastor and made his first visit, preached on Sunday, May 7, morning and evening, and completely captivated the people. At this junction a new work was established in Cape May City and Rev. Tindley, being quite a favorite among the people of both classes in Cape May, was asked for as pastor, he was therefore removed from his work in South Wilmington, and it was supplied with Rev. Wm. Hilton, a local preacher from Zoar M. E. Church, Philadelphia. Rev. Hilton made one visit and stayed one day, but because of some dissatisfaction returned home the following morning and never came back.

For a while they were without a pastor, and the sheep began to stray; darkness seemed to overshadow them, the members became discouraged and the people dissatisfied. At length Rev. William J. Hudson, a local preacher from Salisbury, Md., was appointed as a supply, making the third pastor within the period of three months. By his efforts and the constant appeals of the leading officials and a few faithful members, the fort was held until 1888, when it was connected with New Castle Circuit, and your humble servant, (J. A. Richardson,) was appointed pastor by Bishop Cyrus D. Foss, at the session of the Delaware Conference, held in Whatcoat M. E. Church, Dover, Delaware. Being nothing but a babe in the ministry, and having learned of the character of the place, I shuddered at the thought of being pastor here, and to make it worse, one of my predecessors on leaving the Conference said to me: "Richardson, rise, go to South Wilmington, that great city, and cry against it, for their wickedness has gone up before Him." And I, like Jonah, desired to flee, but hearing the voice of God in His many promises to sustain me, and being encouraged by my Presiding Elder, Rev. William H. Coffey, who had been my faithful friend, I came trusting in God and with faithful prayers. Here I pause and sigh. Could I have said that in these fifteen years of trial and conflict through which Whittington Chapel had passed, she had captured the monstrous foe, I would have been happy; but no, although vigorously assaulted by these heroic captains of the Lord's hosts, he was still raging, and I thought that if ever there was a place in God's vast domain, where the naked, plain, simple word of God's truth was needed without a satin dress on, it was here.

The devil and his infernal army having combined with the whisky men, seemed to destroy our God-given Sabbath, our blessed sanctuaries and our Christian homes, and make that section of Wilmington a wilderness, and men and women brutes. They had hoisted high the black flag and were defying the righteousness of our church, but we smote them with our sermons, our prayers and our influence, and thank God that He is coming to our rescue. Some of the liquor dens have been closed, and we pray God they shall all be closed and buried beyond the hope of a resurrection, and our God-blessed sanctuaries preserved from this cursed evil. In this place I found much missionary work to do and with the burden of souls upon me and the upbuilding of my race and humanity. I took the opportunity of going not so much where I was wanted but where I was needed. I visited some of the most degraded houses in the place, and found many who had not attended any church for several years. The sound of prayer had been silenced by the blaspheming of God's name, and His holy word knew no place in the family. Yet among them were some who had been nursed at a Methodist breast, rocked in a Methodist cradle, reared in a Methodist church and converted under Methodist preaching. They had come here strangers and poor, were neglected by pastors and church people, and feeling themselves forsaken fell into this state of degradation. By our earnest entreaties and best advice, good results were accomplished. Last year our membership increased considerably and we had a good revival.

The lot 30 x 100 feet on the east side of Townsend street was exchanged for one 40 x 100 feet on the west side, nearly opposite, costing $600, which was paid for, and a brick parsonage adjoining costing $700, was purchased. At the Conference of 1889, held in St. Daniel's M. E. Church, Chester, Pa., Whittington was taken from New Castle Circuit, and again made a station, and the writer reappointed as pastor. Efforts were immediately put forth for the erection of a new brick church, 34 x 55 feet, costing nearly $6,000; and on April 29, Leal Collins broke the ground for the cellar. The foundation was completed June 12, and the corner-stone was laid with appropriate ceremonies, on Sunday, June 23, by Rev. Harvey W. Ewing, assisted by Rev. J. R. Waters and the pastor, at which time $325 in cash were raised.

Many, like Simeon, had waited long for the consolation of Israel. It was the joy of every heart in Whittington Chapel, and on account of the joy which filled the hearts of the people arising from the possession of a fit temple for the worship of God, the name was changed to Mt. Joy M. E. Church. The benevolences and ministerial support have been increased each year of my pastorate, the membership is now 85. Earnest attention is given to the child army which is being marshaled for the future conquest of the world. The Sunday school has increased from five to one hundred and forty-eight, and under the superintendency of L. H. Bantum, is in a prosperous condition.

Whittington is spiritually alive and financially is not dead. I have learned in my experience here, that the sweet that man chooses turns bitter, but the bitter that God chooses turns sweet. A more heroic band than the members and congregation of Whittington cannot be found. God helping us we are coming up higher, and though poor, we ask for a recognition of kinship among her wealthy relatives of aunts and cousins, and as relatives in distress we shall certainly call on our relatives for help who are in better condition. The secret of our success lies in the one word, union; pastor and people have worked in perfect harmony, and in looking over the past we may exclaim together, "Hitherto the Lord hath helped us."

The day now dawns upon Whittington, the true character of Christianity is being better understood, and the evils of the past are fading. Order and peace now predominate. Our wants are the prayers from every Methodist pulpit and family altar for the success of our work, and as children of the same family, born of the same father, filled with the same Methodist blood, we shall look for sympathy and help from every Methodist hand. I beseech you who boast in your wealth and greatness to heed the cry which comes to you from this once degraded place, and now a struggling people for God, "Come over to Macedonia and help us." It may cost you sacrifice, but I hazard nothing when I say that God has placed the work of redeeming from ignorance, vice and superstition the race whom centuries of oppression have placed at so terrible a disadvantage, not in the hands of political adventurers, but very largely upon the hands and hearts of the Christian people of the great Methodist church. We need just now prayers whose amens shall be cash, and a little while from now the saints on earth, the saints in heaven, and all the angelic host of heaven and the army of the dark region shall hear these soldiers of the cross with General Jesus at their head, making this known city of Wilmington ring with the triumphant shout.

> "All hail! the age of crime and suffering ends,
> The reign of righteousness from heaven descends;
> Ring out the darkness of the land,
> Ring in the Christ that is to be."

History of the Swedish Mission.

By the Rev. W. L. S. Murray, Ph. D., Presiding Elder of
the Wilmington District.

If from a few fossil bones, comparative anatomists can construct a skeleton of the entire animal whose species is now extinct, why may not the future historian bring together in chronological order and in historical form, fragmentary statements from various boards, Quarterly Conference records and pastoral reports? To aid the historian in his work, and to give some account of the Swedish Mission is the object of this paper.

A thought conceived by a brain always thinking about the poor; spoken by lips now sealed in death, which have plead eloquently for the needy; written by a hand that wielded the sword against slavery; backed by liberal laymen; fashioned into a church building by skilled mechanics, some of whom toiled at night, making overtime that they might see the desire of their heart, has become a house of worship for foreigners and strangers, brought nigh by the blood of Christ. The thought originated with Rev. Lucius C. Matlack, D. D., Presiding Elder at the time of Wilmington District.

We take the following from report, of the Rev. Charles Hill, Presiding Elder to the Wilmington Annual Conference, March, 1884:

"The Swedish Mission organized by Dr. Matlack last October, one year ago, and recognized by this Conference at its last session, and recommended to the General Missionary Committee, now numbers thirty members and five probationers, with a Sunday-school of forty-one officers, teachers and scholars. In April, a lot at the corner Eleventh and Claymont streets, in East Wilmington, was purchased. A deed was executed in due form of law and in accord with the discipline to a corporate board of trustees. On this lot a brick chapel 30 x 50 has been erected. The liberality of the friends of the mission has provided for this amount, $1,000, all except about $800. I am inclined to the opinion that the whole amount would have been provided for had it not been for the continued sickness of the president of the board of trustees. For the success of this enterprise we are largely indebted to the large-hearted liberality and the untiring Christian zeal and energy of Capt. Alexander Kelly." The first pastor was Rev. Carl O. Carlson, who served the church nearly two years; when it was left to be supplied. Rev. Charles Hill to the Annual Conference, March, 1885, says: "The Swedish Mission of Wilmington was without a pastor from March, 1884, until August. After making several ineffectual attempts to supply it from the Swedish work, I obtained, through the influence of Rev. B. T. Carlston, the delegate from Sweden to the late General Conference (1884), Rev. Alexl. Z. Fryxell, direct from Sweden, who is extending his labor among the Swedes in Chester and Philadelphia, and has formed a class in each place. This is an important work.

There are many Swedish families in these cities, and yet there is not an ordained Methodist minister among them in all the region of country extending from Wilmington to New York.

Rev. Alexl. Z. Fryxell served the church in 1885-7, when he was succeeded by Rev. Konrad Hartwig, direct from Sweden, who continued pastor from 1887 to 1889, when he was transferred to Philadelphia Conference, by Bishop R. S. Foster; but in the absence of a supply for the Swedish Mission of Wilmington, he has been appointed to give half of his Sabbaths to its service.

The alternate Sabbaths have been filled by a Wilmington member, an exhorter who has been very faithful and earnest in his labor of love. It is but due Sister Hartwig, the wife of Rev. Konrad R. Hartwig, to say that she rendered most efficient and acceptable service in the mission, aiding her husband in every possible way, serving as organist for the church and as superintendent of the Sunday-school. Her good English education prepared her also to act as interpreter and as secretary of the Quarterly Conference. The salary of the mission was made at first $500, $300 of which were paid by the General Missionary Society.

At a meeting held at Capt. Alexander Kelly's residence, December 15, 1886, it was advanced to $600.

The first board of trustees elected October 22, and organized October 25, 1883:

Alexander Kelly, president; John W. Deifendorf, secretary; Geo. W. Todd, chairman finance committee; Joseph Pyle, O. M. Fandin, Andrew Nilson, Gustaf L. Gustafson, Adolph Erickson, Andrew Wall.

The present board: Alexander Kelly, J. W. Deifendorf, Robert W. Wheeler; terms expired February, 1889. John Hedlund, Chas. Fosberg, Chas. Osholm; terms expire February, 1890. Joseph Pyle, Andrew Neilson, C. Berg; terms expire February, 1891.

On acount of the indisposition of the president of the board no election was ordered in February, 1889.

The benevolent citizens of Wilmington were encouraged to aid the Swedes for two reasons; first, their great need of divine services in their own tongue on the holy Sabbath, and also their need of an ordained minister to administer the sacraments of Baptism, and the Lord's Supper, and to do pastoral work for the sick, despondent and dying among this people. In the second place, because that portion of Delaware where Wilmington now stands was largely settled at first by Swedes, and the Christiana, on which so many of our large industries are located, bears the name of a beautiful Queen of Sweden. A few of the most liberal towards this much needed enterprise have been Alexander Kelly, Joseph Pyle, J. Taylor Gause, G. W. Todd, R. W. Wheeler, Wm. M. Fields, C. Wesley Weldin, Job H. Jackson, H. C. Robinson and John G. Baker, Hillis & Jones, Seidel & Hastings Co., St. Paul's and Grace Churches.

The debt which was referred to in Brother Hill's report as having provided for, except $800, increased to $1,350, for which Capt. Alexander Kelly holds a mortgage.

The probable value of the property is $3,600. The society is earnest and systematic in all its business. Removals to different parts of the country and occasions which make it necessary for others to return to Sweden, forbid a rapid growth, and the society may be considered a success if it but fills the vacancies caused by removals and death. It will also be well to remember that but one Methodist has come to the society from Sweden, pastors excepted, since its organization.

The friends of the mission have often been called on to aid, and Rev. Jacob Todd, D. D., pastor of Grace Church, delivered a lecture in St. Paul's Church, April 25th, 1888, on "Jaunting Through Ireland," from which the board of trustees realized $268. I close this paper by expressing my appreciation and the gratitude of the mission to the General Missionary Committee and also to the generous friends who have so liberally assisted this worthy society of toiling Methodists.

History of Silverbrook Methodist Episcopal Church.

By the Rev. Chas. K. Morris, Pastor.

There being no date from which to write, we appear before you with a very incomplete sketch of the history of Mother Asbury's seventh daughter, Silverbrook, some four years older than her baby sister, Wesley. Silverbrook having no records to refer to, the items that make up this paper have been picked up wherever we could find them. We are indebted to Rev. G. Howard Smedley for the most of them; and if we don't get excited we'll try and read them to you as we have collected them.

Silverbrook, a missionary enterprise of Mother Asbury, was started in the summer of 1880. On a bright Sabbath afternoon in the month of June, Andrew J. Dalbow, a licensed exhorter of Asbury M. E. Church, with a friend, took a walk to the little hamlet of Silverbrook, situated just outside the city limits, on the Lancaster Pike. In their walk they came to a beech tree, very large and beautiful. Under this tree were several gentlemen seated in conversation, in which Brother Dalbow and his friend joined. After conversing for a while about the place and its surroundings, Brother Dalbow, ever on the lookout for opportunities of doing good and building up the waste places in Zion, remarked that this would be a delightful place to hold meetings on the Sabbath. The gentlemen replied they would be glad if some one would do so, as there was no place of worship near for them to attend. So it was agreed they would begin the next Sabbath afternoon. When Brother Dalbow arrived the following Sabbath, he found quite a congregation assembled for divine worship. He then commenced evangelistic services in the open air, beneath the shade of that beautiful

Rev. CHAS. K. MORRIS,

Pastor of Silverbrook Methodist Episcopal Church

beech tree, after the fashion of Jesse Lee, in his pioneer work in New England. The people came from all directions, and of all denominations, from city and country, to these open air services. Many times several hundred people were assembled under and around that tree, in their carriages and wagons, in regular old camp-meeting style to engage in these open-air meetings. In the summer of 1881 a Sunday-school was formed, with Chas. A. Foster as superintendent. These meetings were continued through two summers and part of another; much good was done, and many souls were saved. In the meantime Brother Dalbow resolved to establish an M. E. Church there. He collected money sufficient to buy a lot, and to build the foundations of a church, when along came the new B. & O. railroad and took both tree and lot. Financially they made something by this operation, as the railroad company paid them liberally for their loss. They then made application to be a mission of Asbury Church, which application was accepted. The money received from the railroad company was then turned over to the trustees of Asbury Church, who then purchased another lot some five squares farther north; but being beyond the new railroad, it was deemed too far out of the way.

The local workers of Silverbrook then went to work independently and purchased a lot 36x84 feet from Mrs. M. E. Riley, at Second and Rodman streets, upon which the foundations and corner-stone for a new Methodist Episcopal church were laid on Thursday afternoon, January 8th, 1885, by Rev. W. L. S. Murray, pastor of Asbury M. E. Church, assisted by Rev. E. L. Hubbard, of Brandywine M. E. Church. The attendance was large and respectable, and much interest was manifested, as laying the corner-stone of the first church building in the place was an occasion of no small importance. A copy each of the city papers, a Methodist discipline, and other mementoes of interest were placed within the stone. Between $70 and $80 was taken up in a collection to aid in the erection of the building. The Asbury authorities recognizing this movement of the local workers, Rev. W. L. S. Murray organized the society, comprising twenty members and some fifteen probationers. We are sorry we have not been able to get the names of those members, so they could have the credit which is due them, but having never seen the class-book or any other record of the church, we are compelled to pass them by. The second lot purchased and paid for is still held by the Asbury trustees, but in such a way as to be of no use whatever, unless they could sell it to some denomination to build a church on. When the beech tree was cut down to make way for the new railroad, the meetings were suspended for a while. For about three months in 1883 two rooms in the house of a

Mr. Robert West were placed at the service of the society, with Brother Chas. A. Foster as leader, Brother Dolbow having taken up new territory elsewhere. Subsequently, the stable of a colored man was rented at $2 per month; the horses and mules were turned out and the stable fitted up with seats, platform pulpit, and provided with an organ. Here Dr. J. H. Simms and Rev. Chas. Moore, with a good portion of Asbury fire in them, preached some of their soul-stiring gospel sermons, under which many were awakened and converted. The memory of the grand glorious meetings held in that stable will not soon be forgotten by those who took part in them, and by those who were there born again and made new creature in Christ Jesus. From that time forward the enterprise was carried on mainly by Brothers Chas. A. Foster, Harry C. Webb and Edward Spencer.

Although the enterprise originated among members of Mother Asbury, it was helped very liberally by members of other M. E. Churches, notably by Joseph Pyle and Mrs. Riley, and others living in the immediate neighborhood. Other denominations also contributed very liberally. The whole cost of the church and lot, Rev. Chas. Hill, in his report to Conference says, was $2,242. The building, which cost $1,800, is of frame and built in gothic style. It is 28x42 feet, with an extreme height, beneath the crown of the roof, of forty feet. It is surmounted by a tower and bell, and has a vestibule 6x10 feet where the library is kept, and the pulpit platform occupies a recess in the rear of the church. The seating capacity is about four hundred. The pulpit furniture was donated by Dr. J. H. Simms of Asbury. May 31st, 1885, was fixed upon as the day of dedication. Brother Chas. A. Foster conducted a prayer meeting at 6 A. M. and Rev. W. L. S. Murray a love-feast at 9 A. M. The Rev. E. L. Hubbard preached a sermon at 10.30 A. M. from II Cor. iii: 2, "Known and read of all men." At its close it was announced that $825 of the $1,800 must yet be provided for before the church could be dedicated, and $351 was subscribed. Rev. R. C. Jones preached at 3 P. M. from Songs of Solomon iv: 4, "The Church of Christ is a tower of strength." The collection amounted to $160, which, with an old subscription list of $153 handed in, left still $161. Consequently, the dedication was postponed. In the evening Rev. C. W. Prettyman preached from 51st Psalm, 7th verse, "Wash me and I shall be whiter than snow."

A further sum of $61 was raised, when all present felt they had contributed all that they could afford. Then a number present pledged themselves to raise the remaining $100 in sums of $5 to $10 each, so that the church could be dedicated free of debt. Dr. J. H. Simms, president of the board of trustees, then presented the building for dedication, and the dedicatory services were performed by Rev. W. L. S. Murray, assisted by Rev. C. W. Prettyman. Until the Conference of '87, the pastor of Asbury supplied the pulpit with local preachers, with occasional preaching by the pastors of the city churches. Of the local preachers, Rev. Chas. Moore, Father Taylor, of precious memory, Dr. J. H. Simms, who also preached under the beech tree, Brother Thatcher, and Brother Rodgers, were the most punctual, never disappointing a congregation. Revs. Henry Sanderson and A. T. Scott, of the itinerant rank, also, were very efficient laborers in that part of the vineyard, and whenever the Macedonian cry was heard, Come over and help us, were always ready and willing, and we find them so to this day. In 1887 Rev. W. E. Tomkinson was appointed by the presiding elder as the first pastor of Silverbrook, and served them faithfully a part of the year, when he was appointed to Hockessin to supply the vacancy caused by the death of its pastor, Rev. Joseph Dare. After which the local brethren supplied it with preaching under the direction of the pastor of Mother Asbury, Rev. J. E. Bryan. In April, 1888, the writer having removed from the eastern shore of Maryland, and just here permit me to say with Dr. Roche, that I consider it an honor that I was born in Kent county, Maryland, near the village of Sassafras, at the head of Sassafras River. My grandfather was a local preacher, his house was a preaching place for the early Methodists; so you see if I am not a very good preacher, I come from good old Methodist stock. For twenty years I was engaged in mission work in what was called the big forest, lying between Sassafras and Smyrna, and all the way from Chestertown to Smyrna I was known by the familiar title of the swamp preacher. Many of the inhabitants of that region were considered little better than heathen; and in going through that forest visiting the sick, and burying the dead, I have gone into some as mean, low, dirty, and filthy hovels, as Father Abbott ever entered. Coming from that rough field to your beautiful city, and being well acquainted with Rev. J. E. Bryan, pastor of Asbury Church, I was requested by him to serve as a supply for Silverbrook, saying they will pay you probably $200 or $250. To their credit, be it said, they paid me $400. A stranger, among strange people, it was with much fear and trembling we entered upon our work. Not for fear of being stoned, however, or otherwise roughly used; but, lest we should not be acceptable as a preacher of the gospel in the midst of such a refined and cultured people. But owing to their indulgence and ready willingness to pass our many imperfections by, and their earnest prayers to the God of Heaven for our success, we were soon led to say with the Psalmist, "Truly, the lines have fallen to us in pleasant places; yea, we have a goodly heritage." We had a very pleasant, happy and prosperous year. The church raised last year for all purposes $875. At the fourth quarterly conference last year, the trustees of Silverbrook asked Mother Asbury to set them off as a separate charge, which request was granted; they also asked the presiding elder to return their pastor for another year, which he did at the ensuing Conference. The first Thursday evening in April, the annual election to fill vacancies in the board of trustees was held, and there were four vacancies. J. W. Coley, J. W. Hyrons, J. L. Vandyke, and A. W. Brilely were elected. The present board of trustees for Silverbrook are, J. W. Coley, of St. Paul's, president; Dr. J. H. Simms and C. A. Foster, of Asbury; J. L. Vandyke, J. W. Hyrons, A. W. Brilely, J. C. Jones, F. R. Wilde and J. F. Leach, of Silverbrook. May 2d Dr. Murray held our first quarterly conference, and organized Silverbrook as a separate charge. The following were elected a board of stewards: J. L. Vankyke, J. W. Hyrons, J. C. Jones, Chas. Simmonds, A. W. Brilely, Sallie Vandyke, and Retta Jones. We have a Ladies' Aid Society which is doing good work. We could not get along at all without the good Christian ladies who have been such efficient workers from the beginning of this enterprise unto the present, both in church and Sunday-school. The Sunday-school which numbers one hundred and twenty-five scholars and twenty officers and teachers is in a flourishing condition, with bright prospects for the future. The Misses Laura and Bertie Harris have been teachers in this school from its first organization under the beech tree until the present, and none more faithful than they have been can be found. Sister Annie Vandergrift has also been a very faithful and efficient teacher for a long time, but whether she taught under the beech tree or not we have not been informed. Sister Parr also comes in as a faithful co-worker in the good cause. The present board of officers and teachers are as follows: A. W. Brilely, superintendent, G. H. Smedley, first assistant superintendent; Sister Retta Jones, second assistant superintendent; secretary, G. T. Vandyke; treasurer, Katie Morris; librarian, Miles Barrett; first assistant librarian, Clarence Hyrons; second assistant, Albert Wilde; chorister, J. W. Coley; organist, Mrs. Etta Briley; assistant, Albert Wilde. Female teachers, Mrs. Margaret Hyrons, Miss Bertie Harris, Miss Laura Harris, Mrs. Annie Vandergrift, Mrs. Retta Jones, Miss Katie Morris, Mrs. Sallie Vandyke, Mrs. Etta Brilely, Mrs. Emma Barratt, Mrs. Hiller. Male teachers, Chas. Simmons, J. L. Vandyke and J. W. Hyrons.

To the indomitable energy and perseverance of Brother Foster, the Sunday-school owes much of its success. It was never too cold or too hot, too stormy or too muddy for Brother Foster to be at his post of duty. He was superintendent from its organization in '81 until the 3d of August, '88, when he resigned, and removed his membership to Mother Asbury. Brother A. W. Brilely was elected his successor, and still occupies the position; he is a very devoted and efficient officer.

We deeply deplore the removal of Sister W. E. Tomkinson from our midst, who for nearly two years had been a faithful worker in this Sunday-school. Besides having a class of young ladies to whom she was very attentive, she has illustrated the lesson for the day upon the blackboard, and given interesting talks to the school in explanation of the same. She is greatly missed by the many friends who have become so much attached to her in church work and fellowship. Our church now has fifty-three members; some of whom were converted under the beech tree, and others in the stable, the birth place of the Saviour. In the autumn of 85 Mrs. Martha J. Inskip and Miss Carrie Foster spent some two weeks here in revival meetings, and quite a number of conversions were the result, a few of whom remain unto this present. We have two local preachers, Revs. Chas. Simmons and G. Howard Smedley, who are always ready when called upon to preach a good sermon. There is but one class, which is led by the pastor. The trustees concluding that the church needed some repairs and improvements, set about the work in August last, and by the 22d of September had the church ready for reopening. The walls and ceiling have been painted, the seats and wainscoting beautifully grained, new window-shades put up, the old stoves taken out, a cellar dug and a new heater put in. The church now presents quite an attractive appearance, and will be much more comfortable in cold weather. The whole cost of these improvements was about $350; and in addition to this, the trustees desire to purchase the adjoining lot, which will be about $350 more, making a total of $700. Much credit is due Brother J. W. Coley, the president of the board of trustees, and the noble few who aided him in pressing this enterprise to such a successful completion. Dr. Murray, Presiding Elder, was present at the reopening, and preached at 10.30, from Gen. xv: 1. $350 were subscribed in the morning. The Rev. L. E. Barrett preached at 3 P. M., from Acts xxvi: 19. The collection amounted to $100.

At 7.30 P. M. the Rev. J. D. C. Hanna preached from St. John vi: 16, 20. Brother Coley then made a statement of the repairs made, and what had been raised during the day. Brother Hanna took the finances in hand and asked for the remaining $250. Bro. Joseph Pyle being present, and having a deep interest in Silverbrook's success, and anxious that the whole amount should be secured, made a proposition that if the congregation would raise $200, he would pay the last $50 when a deed was given for the lot. Brother Coley then very agreeably surprised us by reading a list of the names of those who had previously contributed, amounting to $105, leaving $95 to be provided for, which was soon done; and the grand total of $700 raised in one day. The people here are loyal to Methodism, and all seemed pleased with the work done, but were impressed with the fact, that we now need a Sunday-school room in addition, which the trustees purpose to build during the coming year. Silverbrook stands in the southwestern suburbs of the city, as one of the light-houses of Methodism.

> "Immovably founded in Grace,
> She stands as she ever hath stood;
> And brightly her Builder displays,
> And flames with the glory of God."

In conclusion we will add one thing more: as Brother Watkins, of Kingswood, stated in his paper that no saloons or bar-rooms surrounded the light-house in the northeastern part of the city; so we are happy to say that none of these dens of vice surround the light-house in the southwestern part. We have had them, but they are among the things of the past. Some years ago a brewery was started by the side of the beautiful stream from which this part of the city takes its name; but it was of short duration, the proprietor, in a drunken riot, took the life of his fellow man, and fled the country to save himself; so that ended the brewery. In a few months another party concluded that he would try the sale of intoxicants, fitted up a room in his house for a bar, and hung out his sign; but like the brewery, it was short-lived, he proving to be the best customer; and one evening on retiring for the night, after having imbibed rather too freely of the ardent, and being unable to steady himself on reaching the top of the stairs, lost his equilibrium, fell down the steps and broke his neck: so that closed the bar.

In March or April of '88, the brewery again started up, and just as it got in full blast, one bright, beautiful sunshiny day, about two o'clock, it was discovered to be on fire, and despite all efforts to save it, in a few hours it was in ashes. There has never been anything of the kind in Silverbrook since, and our earnest prayer is that there never will be again. Our heart's desire and prayer to God is that this beautiful little church may be the birthplace of scores and hundreds.

"And in the great decisive day.
When God the nations shall survey;
May it before the world appear
That crowds were born to glory here."

When Mother Asbury, with her daughters, granddaughters, and great-granddaughters, with the many thousands saved through their instrumentality, shall come in triumph from North and South, East and West, into the kingdom of glory, lookout for Silverbrook, for she expects to come with rejoicing, bringing her sheaves with her.

History of Wesley Methodist Episcopal Church.

By the Rev. W. G. Koons, Pastor.

Asbury has so many children that only a short time can be allotted each to tell its story in this Centennial home-gathering.

Wesley is next to the youngest child; comparatively a baby. The history of a baby is soon told. However, this baby has been blessed with good health and has grown very fast, and is to-day considerably larger than some of her sisters six times as old.

There was a time in our history when none of the churches claimed our paternity; but when success came we were surprised to hear members of Asbury, Union, St. Paul's and Grace, each laying claim to us. While with all the other Methodist Episcopal churches of this city, we trace our origin back to Asbury, as the Eve of Wilmington Methodism, we profess to belong to no one except the great Head of the church. As a spiritual power we trace our origin to a series of prayer meetings held in houses near where the church now stands. As our organization we ascribe our origin to the preachers' meeting of this city.

There had been a growing impression in the minds of both ministers and laymen, that Wilmington Methodism had not kept step with the march of improvement in our rapidly-growing city. This was and is to-day emphatically true of West Wilmington. Our church usually at the front, had allowed two of our sister denominations to plant their batteries on the frontier heights of our city ahead of us. All honor to our brethren of the Presbyterian and Baptist churches for their greater zeal. We have come not to fight them, but to help them to fight.

REV. W. G. KOONS,

Pastor of Wesley Methodist Episcopal Church.

The Wilmington Preachers' Meeting at its session June 9, 1884, in Asbury Church, on motion of Rev. B. F. Price, adopted the following resolution:

"*Resolved*, That as pastors of the Methodist Episcopal churches of this city, it is our judgment that those parts of our city unoccupied by churches, furnishing opportunity for introducing and organizing religious service, ought to be entered by us at once; and that a committee be appointed to inquire into the case, and report as soon as possible."

The committee consisted of Rev. J. E. Smith, Rev. S. T. Gardner, and Rev. C. W. Prettyman. At the next meeting of preachers, June 16, 1884, the committee reported that they had carefully surveyed the ground, and found necessity for two Methodist Episcopal churches in the western part of the city.

The first meeting on the ground was held December 23, 1884, at the house of Jas. Shakespeare, 306 South Jackson street. Both ministers and laymen were present. Rev. W. B. Gregg was made chairman and Rev. S. T. Gardner secretary. The need of a church in the community was urged by all. Other meetings for the same purpose were held at Asbury and St. Paul's. At the meeting in the latter church, Rev. Chas. Hill, Presiding Elder, was requested to appoint a pastor for a church and a superintendent for a Sunday-school, to be located near Maryland avenue and Jackson street. Rev. Jabez Hodson, a local preacher of St. Paul's, was made superintendent, and Rev. S. T. Gardner pastor.

A small room was obtained as a place of meeting at the corner of Maryland avenue and Linden street. On the following Sabbath twelve persons came to the preaching service, and twenty-four children gathered in the Sunday-school. The school was formally organized June 11, 1885, with Rev. Jabez Hodson superintendent. The room was very uncomfortable, so on March 25th, church and school moved into a store-room on the corner Maryland avenue and Bird street, now Newell's liquor saloon. The counter was removed and the partition between the store and sitting room taken down, making the place moderately comfortable, yet there was no place for the infant school, so the back kitchen was rented for the use of the infant school. Devices are numerous when we are in dead earnest. A smoky back kitchen is good enough for a young Methodist Sunday-school when God is at its back. In the early part of September, 1885, a large tent was purchased for $60, and pitched on the lots of Carlisle and Mitchel, near where the church now stands. Rev. Andrew Manship was engaged to assist the pastor in revival work, which was done with considerable success. The community was rough. While songs of praise and the voice of prayer were rising within, a mob was raging without the tent. Sometimes the brethren were compelled to arise from prayer without saying "amen," to collar the roughs who were trying to break up the meeting with eggs and stones.

Winter drove the church back again to its rented room, corner Maryland avenue and Bird street, where they worshiped till early in spring of 1889, when the owner of the property sold it to E. J. Newell, to be used as a liquor saloon. The church did not give up its rented right to use the property without a legal contest. The lawyer who argued the case against us said, "These people are so noisy that they are a disgrace to any community." The disgraceful church was thrust out to make place for a graceful saloon. The lawyer who argued the case against the church, though young in years, died a few months after that speech. Our interpretation will be according to our faith, but I am persuaded that others, beside Uzzah, have died because they laid irreverent hands on the ark of God.

We will now return to the formal organization of the church, which took place June 4, 1885. After a legal call of the members by Rev. Chas. Hill, Presiding Elder, seventeen names were enrolled as members of the new church. In the selection of a name there was considerable debate between those advocating Cookman and Wesley, but the founder of Methodism as was his wont won. The following were elected trustees: Wm. E. Gray, president; Wm. H. Mullin, secretary; John S. Stone, treasurer; E. S. Meeteer, Wm. T. Morris and John R. Wright. Wm. T. Morris was appointed class leader.

When compelled to vacate, as above related, the church moved to the private house of John A. Stone, 205 Maryland avenue. This was a time of great discouragement. I don't know that it is very pious to feel resentment, but some of the brethren told me that they gritted their teeth very frequently as they walked past the place where they ought to have been worshiping God and saw a lager beer sign decking its front, while they walked on to a private house to worship God. In the month of May the tent was again pitched, and services were continued in it till late in the fall when it was found again necessary to seek shelter indoors. This time the old Weccacoe Engine House, on Jackson street, near Second, was rented of Jos. L. Carpenter, Jr., whose liberality made the rent easy on the struggling church. Services were held in the second-story. The long flight of stairs, the small dingy room, the carpetless floor, the rude furniture, gave the worship of the little band an element of heroism.

In the spring of 1886 three sixteen-foot lots were purchased of Swithin Chandler, and one sixteen-foot lot of J. C. Johnson, at the corner of Jackson and Linden streets, where the church now stands. Plans were secured from E. A. Thorn for a church 50x70 feet and two stories high. The foundation was dug, the cellar walls and piers were built, the first set of joists put into place, when a lack of funds and the cold weather stopped the building.

The corner-stone was laid October 23, 1886. A heavy blowing rain drenched the congregation and but very little money was subscribed, and but very little of that subscribed was ever paid, so it was found after all possible collections had been made that there was a debt of $1,375 on the lots and $375 on the foundation.

In March, 1887, the writer was appointed pastor. He came to Wilmington all puffed up with pride at the idea of being a city preacher, but was rather shocked when he inquired for his church and found none, but was invited to peep through a crevice in a high fence, and saw a hole in the ground, walling in three feet of water and covered with $1,750 debt. His heart almost failed him as he was ushered into the dingy little Weccacoe hall, where the services were then held. The choir did something unusually appropriate on Sabbath morning when they sang as a voluntary before the new pastor's first sermon, "Cast thy burden on the Lord."

Services were continued in the Weccacoe through the summer with congregations frequently equal to the capacity of the hall. During this time money was collected to pay off the debt on the foundation. With the special assistance of Rev. W. L. S. Murray and Rev. Eli Mendinhall and Bro. C. W. Howland, the pastor set about to get subscriptions to complete the church. After carefully surveying the field, a meeting was called at the Presiding Elder's, 307 West Seventh street, in June; a number of the prominent Methodists met with the officials of the church to consider plans. It was agreed that the original plan should be cut down to a single story 50 x 70; this was afterward reduced to a single story 35 x 50.

The board of church extension having granted us $400, and the subscriptions having reached $1,200, it was thought safe to begin the building. Lewis T. Grubb, the contractor, started work September 1, 1887, and the building in its present form was dedicated December 4, 1887. A Ladies' Aid Society had been organized and had provided carpet and chairs for the new church. St. Paul's had donated a lot of cast-off pews which the members of the church scraped, repainted and had them in place by dedication. Chas. Crossgrove and Wesley Meeteer, two young men of the church, made with their own hands and presented a beautiful pulpit stand. Geo. W. Childs gave the Bible and J. Miller Thomas the hymn book. S. H. Baynard presented us a large clock to give us what all free-hearted Methodists so greatly enjoy—a good time. Rev. W. L. S. Murray preached in the morning, Rev. E. L. Hubbard in the afternoon, and Dr. Jacob Todd at night. Subscriptions and cash were secured, more than covering the cost of the building. The building was then formally dedicated and the doxology was sung with a good will. Thus far had we come after three years of bloody conflict for mere existence. Six months before the doxology was sung on the night of dedication, the most stout-hearted thought Wesley a forlorn hope.

June 1, 1888, a revival began which lasted till March 10th, the time of Conference. I took the names of one hundred and sixty who professed conversion, and received one hundred and three on probation. After the revival had continued about three weeks, and thirty-five had been converted, the pastor called to his assistance Andrew J. Dolbow, an exhorter in Asbury Church, who rendered very efficient service. It was an old-fashioned meeting. Christians shouted, leaping from the floor, and clapping their hands to express their joy. Sinners cried out loud for mercy, not only at the altar but also in the pews.

Another gracious revival came in the fall of 1888, beginning the 7th of October, and lasting six weeks; one hundred professed conversion and seventy-five joined church.

May 13, 1888, a Young Christians' Association was founded to help the young converts. It is still alive and doing excellent work.

The present officials of the church are: Rev. W. G. Koons, pastor; Rev. J. W. Harris, local preacher; H. L. George, Sunday-school superintendent; R. C. Jones, assistant; Mary S. Gray, superintendent of infant school.

Class leaders.—J. J. Wilhelm, Jas. E. Adams, Jas. E. Wirt and H. L. George.

Trustees.—Jacob Lamplugh, Chas. Ayers, Robert Carlisle, Jas. Wirt, Wm. E. Gray, Joseph Hildreth, H. L. George, John Gordon and Samuel Coyle.

Stewards.—Wm. E. Gray, H. L. George, R. C. Jones, J. W. Harris, L. L. Saunders, Baldwin Hygate, Geo. Murray, Thos. White and Z. T. Gross.

The rapid growth of Wesley is shown by the following figures taken from the Conference minutes and the church record: Organized

June 4, 1885, with seventeen members; number of members reported March, 1888, 22; reported March, 1887, 41; reported March, 1888, 70; reported March, 1880, 170; now on record, October, 1889, 225 full members and 15 probationers, making a total of 240.

These are the outlines of our history. They show the goodness of God. Paul has planted and Apollos has watered, and God has given the increase. There was a time when Wesley was considered a reproach to Methodism, but no reproaches could drive us to the wall, because God was in the midst of us; no persecution could sink us, because underneath were the everlasting arms. Wesley was started for the salvation of souls. She is on that line. Her type of religion is as warm-hearted and fiery as that of Asbury.

We do not exhort the people to shout, but if any one can't help it, we're not too badly scared to say Amen. We have laid the foundations, the oncoming years will see the present building giving way to a larger one, and the roll of membership enlarging, until by the next centennial, Baby Wesley will be as big as Mother Asbury.

History of Cookman Methodist Episcopal Church.

BY THE REV. ALFRED T. SCOTT, PASTOR.

Eleven squares west of Grace Church, three quarters of a mile east of Mt. Salem, there was a portion of the city bounded on the north by Gilpin avenue and extending southward ten squares, unoccupied by a Methodist church. With commendable zeal, our Presbyterian and Baptist brethren have planted their churches in that locality, and are getting the children of the Methodist families into their schools. On this as well as other accounts, the need of a Methodist church has for years been felt and talked of.

During the presiding eldership of Rev. Charles Hill, this feeling found expression in the call for a meeting at the home of Mr. William I. Buck, on Van Buren street, beyond Delaware avenue. By request the writer was present at that meeting. Although after a full discussion of the matter, it became evident that those there present were generally convinced that something ought to be done, yet the Rev. R. C. Jones, then pastor of Mt. Salem, because of an earnest effort being in progress to rid that church of an old debt, seemed to use his influence against the movement, fearing a division of interest might frustrate their desires. So all efforts to supply the recognized want were soon abandoned.

On the Fourth of July, 1888, an honored local preacher, then connected with this (Asbury) church, Rev. W. W. Taylor, who had formerly resided in the neighborhood, and who was well acquainted with the condition of affairs, determined that something must be done. Accompanied by Mr. Benjamin McVey, of Mt. Salem, he proceeded to examine the region already named to see if any building could be secured in which to preach the gospel and hold a Sunday-school. They succeeded in renting of Mr. Geo. Gregg, the lower story of the building No. 1307 Scott street. The upper room was already rented by a fife and drum corps.

Brother Taylor at once began to prepare the room for religious services. With the assistance of Rev. J. H. Simms and other friends, he succeeded in having some plain benches made; the aisles and platform carpeted, and a pulpit built. Thus the room, capable of seating about one hundred and fifty persons, was ready for occupancy.

The first service was held on the afternoon of July 29, 1888. Rev. Jas. E. Bryan, pastor of Asbury Church preached the first sermon.

Among those present were: Father Taylor, Mrs. Mary L. Crozier, the widow of one of the members of our Conference; Mrs. Mary Ingram and Brothers J. H. Simms, Lewis Maxwell, Charles A. Foster and Andrew J. Dalbow. On the following Sabbath about twenty children were gathered in Bro. Solomon Hersey, of Union Church acted as superintendent. Preaching services were held under the direction of Father Taylor every Sabbath afternoon after the Sabbath-school had closed its session.

At a meeting of the school on August 26th, a Sabbath-school board was elected according to the provisions of the dicipline. Wm. L. Buck, to whom reference has already been made was elected superintendent, Solomon Hersey, assistant; W. T. Morris, also of Union Church, was elected secretary, Mrs. W. L. Buck, treasurer, and Millard T. Toft, librarian. A constitution and by-laws were adopted, but it was not until the 30th of August, that, after some discussion, it was decided to adopt the name of "Cookman Methodist Episcopal Sabbath-school."

At a meeting held October 17th, to consider the interests of the enterprise, the presiding elder, Rev. W. L. S. Murray, Ph. D., appointed Rev. W. W. Taylor, Wm. L. Buck, Millard T. Toft and Mrs. Mary L. Crozier as a committe of ways and means to supervise the affairs of the church. On the 25th of the same month Solomon Hersey, W. T. Morris, W. J. H. Lingo, Charles Beadenkopf, George Gregg, Mrs. W. L. Buck and Mrs. W. J. H. Lingo were added to the committee.

At the quarterly conference held in Asbury Church, September 1, 1888, a request was received from the Cookman school asking to be received as one of the Asbury Sabbath-schools. This was agreed to on condition that "no pecuniary liability should be incurred." Thus was this work brought into connection with Asbury Church. Whether

Cookman is to regard itself as a child or grandchild of Asbury, under such a connection, is a puzzle our brains have not been able to solve. Had not Father Taylor been a local preacher connected with Asbury quarterly conference it would seem as if Cookman were a stray waif born out of wedlock and coming to Asbury for adoption.

Thus the work in both departments was well under way. The people were attending the church service, and the Sabbath-school was increasing in number. Father Taylor's heart rejoiced to see the work of the Lord prospering. But a shadow was about to darken the prospect. Father Taylor was taken sick, and on December 1st was called from labor to reward. Death found him prepared and fully ready to go to be "forever with the Lord." The funeral services were held in Asbury Church, Rev. J. E. Bryan, assisted by Rev. H. S. Sanderson and the writer, gave expression to their love. Brother Solomon Hersey read some verses he had composed for the occasion and presented the resolutions of respect and regard which were passed by the ways and means committee of Cookman. A large and deeply interested audience gave evidence of the hold this simple-minded, entirely devoted man of God had gained over them.

Thus again is illustrated the usefulness of the local branch of our ministry. So far as the work at Cookman is concerned, there is little ground to believe that this effort so long talked of would yet have been commenced, had not Father Taylor set himself to do it. Out of this conviction grew the desire on the part of those interested to keep this fact in remembrance, and to do honor to this worthy man; and so they have erected a neat monument over his grave in Mt. Salem Cemetery, on which is the inscription, "The founder of Cookman M. E. Church." As the Methodist Episcopal church looks back with grateful remembrance to a local preacher, Philip Embury, as the man under God, to take the first steps toward calling her into being, so may Cookman when she shall have become a large and useful organization, thank God for the work of Rev. Wm. W. Taylor.

It soon became apparent that the arduous duties devolving upon Brother Bryan would not permit him to give that attention to this work that was needed, and being satisfied it was better to have some one to take special charge of its spiritual interests, at a meeting of the ways and means committee, held December 9, 1888, it was resolved to ask the writer to attend to this matter in connection with Rev. Jas. E. Bryan, until the ensuing session of the annual Conference. Accordingly he was appointed by the Presiding Elder.

Brother Bryan had commenced an extra meeting, and had formed a class of eight persons, consisting of Mrs. Rebecca Thompson,

Millard T. Toft and wife, Elijah A. Toft, Miss Mamie Flynn, Miss Lena Weible, Mrs. Martha J. West and her daughter Mary Lizzie, and Miss Indiana Thompson. Several of these had been converted during the meeting then in progress. As a further result of this meeting five other converts were added.

Feeling his need of Divine help, the new pastor commenced his work by preaching on Sabbath morning, December 13th, from "Finally, brethren, pray for us that the word of the Lord may have free course and be glorified."

Visiting in the neighborhood it was soon found that there were Methodists who did not go to church, having almost lost their church relation, and that there were others who, because of early training and associations, if ever saved must be reached through Methodist influences; and so he informed the community that we had not come there to hinder our Baptist or Presbyterian friends in their work, but to bid them God-speed, and to do a work for God and for souls, which they could not do.

When the time came to hold watch-night services as the pastor approached the church he found the fife and drum corps in full blast in the upper room. Rev. W. E. Thompkinson was preacher for the evening, and while those who cared not for the things of God amused themselves above, the children of God listened to His word, and worshiped Him with praise and prayer in the room below. For a time it was matter of doubt as to whether both parties would see the Old Year out, and greet the incoming of the New. But a little before twelve the drum ceased to beat, the fife was laid aside, and our friends quietly left us alone with the Lord.

Another short extra meeting was held, during which other souls were converted. Thus we labored on until the approach of Conference, when the writer was asked if he would consent to act as pastor for the ensuing year. To this he agreed and at the Conference at Easton, the name of Cookman Chapel was for the first time announced with Alfred T. Scott as pastor.

It is with regret that our duty as historian requires us to state that some of our friends deemed it needful, in order to secure the money to purchase another organ to be used in the lower room while the one then in use should be taken to the upper room which had been secured for an infant department, to hold an "apron bazaar." Satisfied from long and careful investigation that it is better for the church to lay aside all such methods for raising supplies, the pastor and some of the members had hoped Cookman's record would be found free from such affairs. On his return from Conference, before he reached his home, the pastor was greeted with the news of the financial success of the bazaar and that it was also proposed to follow it with "a strawberry festival," so as to help "pay the preacher." Up to Conference, in order to pay off all bills for furniture, etc., the pastoral service had been free of charge. At a meeting of the ways and means committee, held soon after Conference, the matter was brought up and the pastor declared his purpose not to receive any money toward his support raised by any such method; but, if need be, to relinquish part of the salary, the $260 agreed upon, and take only what was given directly for that purpose. After considerable discussion a motion prevailed directing the treasurer to pay the pastor five dollars each week. He is thankful to say that with the exception of one week this has been done; and as yet the "strawberry festival" has not been held, nor have we resorted to anything of the kind. All other expenses have been met. We have tried to lead everyone to feel it a privilege to give to the support of the Lord's cause and to give regularly. A number of friends, not connected with Cookman, but feeling an interest in it have regularly given their assistance.

As our membership increased it soon became apparent that it would be better for us—specially as Asbury had been true to the contract (not to incur any financial responsibility) to take our place as one—although a small and weak one—yet as one of the Methodist Episcopal churches of the city. Accordingly Asbury Quarterly Conference granted the request made by Cookman to be severed from connection with her at the Quarterly Conference held August 31, 1889. And on the following Thursday evening, September 5, 1889, the Presiding Elder preached an installation and a charge sermon from the first Psalm, and afterwards organized us into a church. The following are the names of the persons thus formed into Cookman Methodist Episcopal Church: Mrs. M. L. Crozier, Mrs. Mary Ingram, Miss Emma J. Ingram, Miss Mary J. Ingram, Samuel F. Bannar, Mrs. Martha Bannar, D. T. Harman, Mrs. Maggie Harman, Mrs. Eleanor S. Clark, Joseph T. Cannon, Mrs. Minerva Salfner, Miss Maggie Salfner, Mrs. M. J. Cannon, Miss M. Elizabeth West, Miss Indiana Thompson, Miss Mary Dillon, Millard T. Toft, Mrs. Elizabeth A. Toft, Miss Lena Weible, Mrs. Rachel MacConnell, Arthur Clinton Davis, Clara V. Toft, Mrs. Rebecca Thompson—full members. On probation there remain Miss Mamie Flynn, Miss Lizzie MacConnell, Alderman B. Sentman, Mrs. Clara V. Sentman, Mrs. Isabella Sharp, Miss Ruth Toft, Cecil C. Lynch, Mrs. Mary E. Lynch and Miss Ida Salfner. Brother Millard T. Toft was appointed class-leader; Joseph T. Cannon,

Samuel F. Bannar, M. T. Toft, Mrs. M. L. Crozier and Mrs. Mary Ingram were appointed stewards.

M. T. Toft was appointed recording steward and Jos. T. Cannon a committee on church records.

As we recognized ourselves as a Christian Endeavor Society, all the members with exception of two residing at a distance, were put on the various committees.

Our Sabbath-school has an average attendance of sixty-seven. We are in need of devoted teachers.

It was judged expedient to secure from Bro. Jno. S. Miller, of Mt. Salem, into whose hands the property had fallen, a lease for the building until March 25, 1892, as there was no other room anywhere in that locality suitable for our purpose, and it might be some time before we secured a lot and a church home. We have been anxious to secure the kernel of the living church—a band of converted people—assured that sooner or later it would gather to itself a proper outer form.

We have on the wall of our church the portrait of the sainted man after whom we are named, and as he rejoiced to consider himself "dead indeed unto sin, and alive unto God," and as "holiness to the Lord" was his motto, so we are striving to gather a holy people zealous of good work.

History of Newport Methodist Episcopal Church.

By the Rev. Vincent G. Flinn, Local Preacher.*

In coming to take part in this Centennial anniversary, Newport does not come as one of the offspring of old Asbury, or as part of the result of her large success; but rather as a sister, a sister indeed, lacking only a few years of being as old as she is herself, our church being built only twenty years after. We come therefore to unite our rejoicings with yours, and to mingle our professions of gratitude to God with yours, feeling drawn by the bands of Christian *brotherhoood*, and glad to add our offering of thanksgiving to our common Father.

Methodism at Newport began in a very small way. The best sources of information on the subject furnish us with the fact that about the year 1786 or '87, there came to Newport a young Irish girl, who was employed in one of the families there. This young girl had been converted at a Methodist altar in her own country, and inquiring if there were any Methodist people about, she was told there were some in Wilmington. Thither she went and called upon one John Thelwell, the same who pitched the tunes for Capt. Webb, when he preached there in 1769. Thelwell told her of a Methodist preacher named Caldwell stopping with a family in town, and when she called upon him and stated her case to him, he at once consented to go to Newport and preach. The school house was secured for the service, and so great was the novelty of the proceeding, that the house was crowded, while many stood around and listened at the windows.

*The Rev. Vincent G. Flinn, who prepared this excellent paper, a good man full of faith and the Holy Ghost, was buried from the Newport Church on November 15, 1889, exactly one month from the day on which he read this history at Asbury.

REV. JAMES E. BRYAN,

Pastor of Newport Methodist Episcopal Church, and of Asbury in 1886–'89.

Here began Methodism at Newport, and there is every reason to believe that from that time, 1786 or 1787, to the present, there has always been a Methodist society here. There does not seem to be much information obtainable at this distant date as to just where they worshiped, or how they prospered; no doubt they had their share of persecution and opposition, in the years that followed; but we find that in the year 1796 at the annual Conference held in Philadelphia, Ezekial Cooper was appointed pastor of Asbury Church, Wilmington, and Newport. He preached at Asbury in the morning and evening, and at Newport in the afternoon. Under date of February 11, 1797, which would be the following spring after his appointment, he gives an account of our society at Newport, which is perhaps the first reliable account of this society in existence. He says: "Our society here is small, but I am very much pleased with it. Mrs. Lattimore, Mrs. Robertson, and Mrs. Miller, are three excellent souls. There is but one white man in society, that is Mr. Miller. After preaching and class I returned to Wilmington and preached again in the evening. Preaching three times a day, and class and general society meeting, is rather too much for me."

After a service of five months, at which time the Philadelphia Conference was again convened, Mr. Cooper reported an increase of members at Newport of eight whites and eleven blacks, a greater per centum of increase, probably, than we have ever reached since. Mr. Cooper was again appointed to Wilmington and Newport, and preached as before, until the yellow fever broke out in Wilmington that summer, when he came to Newport to live, and went in and preached at Asbury on Sunday. While living here he was entertained at the house of Major Robertson.

To "Lights on Early Methodism" by Dr. Phœbus, we are indebted for some incidents occurring about this time. On Sunday, July 8, 1798, about the close of his sermon, a violent storm of rain, wind, thunder and lightning arose, detaining the congregation while it lasted. So severe was it that the people became intensely alarmed, and the windows of the building not being glazed, the storm beat in and through the house, whilst they took refuge under the pulpit and in it, and huddled together wherever they could until the fury of the storm was over. On the 28th of the following October, 1798, Mr. Cooper preached his last sermon at Newport, having been appointed book agent by Bishop Asbury.

The question might be asked why Newport seemed to get a start in Methodism earlier than other points adjacent. The answer probably lies in the fact that we are on what was then the main line of travel between Philadelphia and Baltimore. This was the old stage route, as well as the mail route carried by stage. The oldest citizens tell of crisp rumbling of the mail coach as it came driving through the crumbling snow up to the hotel where the horses were changed. Here also at that time two lines of vessels sailed to Philadelphia, carrying the grain and produce of the farms for miles around, and bringing back merchandise for the needs of the community in return. It was, therefore, most natural for the pioneers of Methodism to drop into this channel and thoroughfare of business, and plant her banners and set up her altars.

It will be remembered that white and colored people sometimes worshiped together in the Methodist churches in those days; it was so at Newport, and there seems to have been some colored persons living and worshiping here that enjoyed the confidence and esteem of the entire community. One of these, Grace Bailey, was much interested for the success of the cause here and opened her house and entertained the preachers when on their visits to preach the gospel.

Another item of interest is found in the fact that Anderson Brinkley, a colored man, and Joseph Springer Lynam, well remembered by many present, were converted the same night in the old church.

Thus they went on meeting in school house, in private house or shop, or wherever they could, until finally, in 1809, the first church was built. The lot on which the church stands was sold by Thomas Latimer for one dollar, and the original deed, bearing the names of Joseph Lynam, Benjamin Hersey, John Miller, Dennis Dougherty and Samuel Wood, is still in the keeping of Bro. Abram Chandler, our oldest active member. It would be very interesting to have a picture of the congregation as it then assembled; our fathers and mothers in the simple and plain attire of eighty years ago, most of them coming afoot, some walking for miles, few had means of riding. I am told there were *three* families who came in vehicles. Father Lynam and wife, in one of the first of carriages, Mother Miller and family in about the same style, and Shadrach Morris (colored,) with his ox team.

Newport was connected with other churches from 1809 to 1825, forming Cecil circuit. In 1825 New Castle and Newport were placed together; but New Castle may not have liked her company or vice-versa; at any rate the arrangement continued but one year, and we were again placed on Cecil circuit, where we remained until about 1851, at which time the circuit was divided, and Newport, Christiana and Salem were placed together. In 1859 this was changed and Newport and Brandywine Springs were our appointments.

In 1863 Chandlerville and Ebenezer were connected with Newport and this was the plan of appointment until 1868 when we became a station. In 1876 and 77 Stanton Church was built during the pastorate of Rev. H. S. Thompson, and continued with Newport until last Conference, 1889, when we became a station again.

The names of the preachers who were in charge of Newport from 1810 are as follows:

1810, Thos. Smith and Geo. Sheets ; 1811, James Aikins and Wm Torbert ; 1812, James Aikins and Thos. Miller ; 1813, James Moore and Thos. Miller ; 1814, Thos. Walker and John Poice ; 1815, John Goforth and Samuel P. Levis ; 1816, John Sharpley and Edward Stout ; 1817, John Sharpley and David Ireland ; 1818-19, Wm. Torbert and John Woolson ; 1820, Samuel J. Griffith and Thomas Miller ; 1821, Samuel J. Griffith and Daniel Fidler ; 1822, John Smith and William Lummis ; 1823, William Rider and Jesse Thompson ; 1824, William Rider and James Long ; 1825, Edward Page and John Goforth ; 1826, Edward Page and John Goforth ; 1827, Solomon Sharp and James B. Ayars ; 1828, Solomon Sharp and William Cooper ; 1829, Thomas Miller, and William Rider ; 1830, William Rider and Samuel D. Jones ; 1831, William Torbert and James Nicols ; 1832, William Torbert and William Spry ; 1833, E. Reed and George M. Yard ; 1834, E. Reed and J. Woolley ; 1835, E. Kennard and J. D. Onins ; 1836, E. Kennard and J. S. Inskip; 1837, William Rider and John Dutot; 1838, William Rider and William W. McMichael ; 1839, S. Grace and H. S Atmore ; 1840, Edward Kennard and John Ruth ; 1841, Edward Kennard and J. Aspril ; 1842, William C. Thomas and D. L. Patterson ; 1843, William C. Thomas and George Quigley ; 1844, Gassaway Oram and William Campbell ; 1845, Gassaway Oram and Abram Freed ; 1846 James Cunningham and Stearns Patterson ; 1847, James B. Ayars and William Robb ; 1848, James B. Ayars and J. Bayne ; 1849, Christopher J. Crouch and W. L. Boswell ; 1850, Christopher J. Crouch ; 1851, Levi Storks ; 1852, S. R. Gillingham ; 1853, S. R. Gillingham and William M. Dalrymple; 1854, Henry Sanderson ; 1855, Thomas W. Simpers and J. Dison ; 1856, Thomas W. Simpers ; 1857-58, James Hand ; 1859, Thomas Sumption ; 1860, Thomas Sumption and David Makee ; 1861, J. Carlisle and David MaKee ; 1862, J. Carlysle ; 1863, Joseph N. Magee ; 1864, Samuel Powers. during this year the building of the present church was commenced and completed the following year and dedicated by Rev. Thomas T. Tasker ; 1865-66, William H. Fries ; 1867-68, H. H. Bodine ; 1869-70, Joshua Humphriss ; 1871-72, John Allen; 1873-74-75, John D. Rigg; 1876-77-78, Henry S. Thompson; 1879-80, John D. Rigg; 1881-82-83, James E. Bryan; 1884-85-86, Edwin H. Nelson; 1887-88, John D. C. Hanna; 1889, James E. Bryan.

I wish also to call up the names of some of the early laymen and women of the church here. Those who were the class-leaders, the stewards, the trustees and the pastors' assistants in those days. What could he do without their co-operation and aid? What would all his efforts amount to, especially in these first attempts to found a society without the faithful few on whom he could depend and in whom he could trust? What faithful men those Methodist fathers were; full of faith, zealous, true, devoted to God and Methodism. We had such at Newport, and while I find it the greatest pleasure to trace out and reproduce the names of the faithful itinerants who in the past have been stationed here and proclaimed the unsearchable riches of God's word, and who have many times been successful under God in leading souls to him, yet, to me there comes a desire to place side by side with these the names of those old veterans of the cross, who, in the primitive days of our beloved Methodism, gave support to the preacher, encouraged him, prayed for him, and bore the burdens of the church in the heat of the day. Oh! that our churches were filled with the same kind to-day. May there always be life and vitality enough in our congregations to say amen to what the preacher says, "and be able always to give a reason for the hope that is within us to him that asketh."

Absolam Thomas was one of the early pioneers of Methodism here, and it was at his house preaching was often held previous to the building of the church.

Benjamin Hersey was another, and mentioned as one of the first trustees. He lived near Marshallton and with him Bishop Asbury stopped on his way up and down the Peninsula.

John Miller another, being owner of horse and vehicle, was often called on to take the preacher from one point to another.

Mrs. Lattimore, mentioned by Mr. Cooper, was the mother of John R. and Henry Lattimore, then living at Newport. She seemed to take a deep interest in religious services, and with Mrs. Robinson and Mrs. Miller were ever ready to do what they could to help on the good cause.

Joseph Lynam, J. Springer Lynam and Jacob Lynam, a father and two sons, deserve to be remembered while time shall last, for their efforts to bless and benefit the neighborhood, and for their zeal for God's house. The first named of these, known for many years as father Lynam, lived to be nearly 102 years of age, and died February 4th, 1872, and was buried at Newport, Rev. Jacob Todd preaching his funeral.

This old man delighted to the last of life to converse with the preachers, and had one question which he always propounded to them, namely, "what is the best word in the Bible?" and while some would answer God, or love, etc., his own answer was the word Truth. His wife, Joanna, is said to have been one of those sweet spirited, meek and kind women, whose appeals to sinners were hard to withstand. It is said of her that she sometimes visited from house to house and talked with the people about religion, and besought them to be saved. I was told of one instance where she called on a hardened old sinner living alone on the banks of the Christiana, who on seeing her coming, left the house, got into his boat and rowed over to the other side. When taken to task about it, he said "if Josey, (meaning her husband,) had come, he would not have left but he could not stand Joanna." Springer Lynam, a son of these two, inherited their zeal and love for God's house and for many years was an exhorter and class-leader in the church. Nivin C. Miller, Thomas Lamplugh, Joseph Grubb, Peter Torbert, Joseph Killgore, fifty years a class-leader, and later on, John R. Lynam, Albert J. Lynam, and Lewis Weldon, with others that might be mentioned, who have been the active men of the church, and guarded her interests with jealous care during the past eighty years of her life, have now all passed from labor to reward. The church owes all these a debt of gratitude for what they did, and generations to come will bless them for their interest in the church and community, in their day and generation.

Now what has been accomplished in the past eighty years? Who can tell? By what rule can it be measured? Where will the influences of saintly life and christian example end? Eternity alone will reveal. The church in our community is as a light house giving light to all around. What would the community be without it?

In these years agone some have been marked by sweeping revivals of religion. I have heard of one which occurred during the pastorate of Rev. Thomas Miller, which was remarkable for its attractive and saving power. Another was in 1842, during the pastorate of Rev. Wm. C. Thomas and Daniel L. Patterson, spoken of as extensive and wide-spread. But the greatest revival perhaps ever known on Cecil Circuit occurred in 1848, under Jas. Brooks Ayers and William C. Robb. The whole circuit seems to have been in a blaze of revival power and glory. At the Union appointment there were one hundred and sixty-eight conversions; at Cherry Hill, one hundred and forty-seven conversions; at Newark, seventy-three conversions; at Wesley Chapel fifty conversions; at Christiana, one hundred conversions, and at Newport, one hundred and seventy-three conversions. The meeting at Newport commenced February 14, with both the preachers away at other points on the circuit; but after an exhortation by that man of God, Springer Lynam, the power of the Holy One seemed to come upon the assembly, and then and there a most wonderful revival commenced. A record kept by Rev Jas. L. Killgore, then a youth of sixteen years, shows the number of penitents, and the number converted each night until the 25th day of March following, giving the whole number saved to be one hundred and seventy three, probably the greatest revival Newport has ever known. In 1855 and '56, Rev. Thos. W. Simpers, a man who being without horse and carriage, walked his way to the homes and hearts of his people, was blessed with another large ingathering of souls; and of later years a revival that should be mentioned on account of the blessed results and large number that were added to the church, occurred in 1874 and '75. At this time over one hundred and fifty were converted, and many who were in official place in our church to-day are of the fruits of that revival.

This then is intented as a brief epitome of Methodism in Newport from its infancy. I wish it were fuller. I wish it were more complete. It has been indeed very meagre. I have only touched the subject here and there along the line of years. Another pen might have done better than my own, but no man could properly portray the grand results attained, nor the wonders that God hath here wrought. Suffice it that here He choose to meet with his people, and here He poured out his spirit. Our fathers named the church Peniel, signifying face to face with God, and verily upon her His face has shined in the past May her future be as blessed as her foregoing years.

REV. E. L. HUBBARD, PH. D.,
Pastor of New Castle Methodist Episcopal Church.

History of the New Castle Methodist Episcopal Church.

By the Rev. E. L. Hubbard, Ph. D., Pastor.

As early as 1772 Bishop Asbury preached in New Castle. He stopped at a tavern kept by a Methodist, and preached to a handful of people, meeting with great opposition. The Court House which was open for dancing and all frolicking was closed against a Methodist service. So hot was the blood of antagonism that all the guests of the hotel left, when the Bishop was registered as a lodger for the night. Asbury characterized the people of New Castle as "full of pride, vanity and folly." Three years later after preaching twice in New Castle on one day, the Bishop writes, "I hope my skirts are clean of the blood of the people of this little town, whether they reject or accept an offered salvation."

This statement allows the conclusion that no visible effects followed the preaching that day. However the word preached was seed sown. The barrenness of soil was more apparent than zeal. Conversions followed, and in 1820, a society was organized. The membership was twenty, and were led in class by Thomas Challenger.

By this reckoning it was forty-eight years after Bishop Asbury's first sermon in New Castle, before an organization of twenty, guaranteeing permanence could be effected. This slow movement in religious matters is conspiciously characteristic of all ages, but not ordinarily of any movement in America. I doubt if Methodism has so long knocked at the door of any other town. Immediately after organizing, the society began active preparations for building a meeting house; and one was dedicated to Almighty God in the year 1821. The progress of Methodism was slow. New Castle was in the keeping of other churches. The names of the Methodists were not well suited to the religious taste of people delighted with the ball room and race-course. The itinerant preacher was too little in sympathy with the devil, or any of his works, to gloss iniquity, embellish trifles, or make an unholy life palatable. The theology of the horsebacker was too near the fountain, too freshly drawn from the Bible to distinguish between hades and hell, or allow the preacher to ramble for an hour about the prairie lying between literal and material fire. These men knew the gospel of the Son of God to be the power of God.

This glorious fact was burned into their souls by a *literal* flame. This they *could* preach and this they *did* preach. In the Bible they read about heaven, hell, the resurrection and the judgment. By the wayside they halted to read a chapter, and lighting on Daniel in the den, Noah in the ark, John on the island, Paul in prison, or Jesus on the cross, they mounted their fleet-footed friend, and bounded away to the nearest village to tell the story, and shout over personal deliverance by simple faith in Jesus. The strong points of their sermons were wedged apart by righteously indignant denunciations of all worldliness. Particularly declaring against the great common vices of that day, as this, to which the people were given, and of which professing christians were guilty. New Castle has never loved to have the Bible looking-glass held too near to their eyes. The unsavoury reputation of the little city to-day is not a libel. In the wicked sons can be seen the sires. The same difficulty encountered by the early Methodists would have met any reforming effort.

Does the rose emit no fragrance when blooming in the forest? Or will there be no luscious grape on the uninhabited mountain side? So acceptance of the gospel by those to whom it is presented is not all there is of it.

Though the people would not hear and receive generally, there were a few who arose from bowing before Baal.

To these the word was precious, and they neither left the town nor left off shouting because their neighbors pelted them with mockery. God sets tables in the wilderness for His people and loads them with the edibles that make angels' mouths water. In the life of the few Methodists of New Castle there was peace and power, and God added to the Church one after another until the membership in New Castle and elsewhere, and in heaven, are a great company.

The building of 1821 gave way to a larger one, but before it gave way it was all over written with the hieroglyphics of Him who writes invisibly, and can now only be interpreted by a few holy persons, yet lingering about the shining way awaiting their turn to step into the chariot. Of these I will relate but one. Brother John D. Cannon was the companion of a few godly young men, who were accustomed to meet after dark, week days and in the afternoon Sabbath days, for seasons of prayer and praise, adding to their number such godly disposed young men as they could influence. The little church boasted no sexton nor fire and no light to spare, so this little band would enter the building by a window and hold their service in the dark. After one of the afternoon meetings where Brother Cannon had been a mourner, on his way home he stopped at a pump to get a drink; as he lifted the pump handle and saw the clear stream flowing from the spout his thirsty soul said, "O Lord, give me drink," and instantly looking up there came into his heart such a refreshing that he dropped the pump handle and tin cup, shouting "glory" with all his might. In this way he went through the streets. Jehovah had turned the flood of salvation on him and has never turned it off. Brother Cannon is now an old man, but a veritable saint of God.

In 1860 the main building of the present edifice was erected. It was a great triumph. Perhaps its necessity and possibility were due to the iron works being in the hands of that staunch Methodist, Thos. Tasker, who took great interest in the church. It is a single story building, seats five hundred persons, with tower front and magnificent acoustic properties. It has a carpeted floor, hard wood pews, stained glass windows of a most exquisitely beautiful pattern, and a handsome pipe organ.

It has a membership of over two hundred, weekly meets all expenses and moves with increasing excellence and influence in the community. The officials are in number, twenty-one, who work without a jar, who vote on all questions, submitting to the majority and fellowship in all undertakings. In 1876 a building for class and Sunday-school purposes was erected across the rear of the main building, two stories high. This building is also handsomely frescoed and carpeted.

Besides this double building there is across the street a three story brick building, elegant in all directions, where the Bishop could now find a resting place without disturbing and distressing either the hotel or its guests. In this home the Methodists of New Castle comfortably shelter their pastor.

Was it because the mother of Wilmington Methodism named her children in the city Scott, Union, Brandywine, St. Paul's, Grace, Silverbrook, Madeley, Epworth, Kingswood, Mt. Salem, Cookman and Wesley, that her child left five miles down stream should be named Nazareth? Was this an attempt to read the character of New

Castle into the title of the Methodist Church? As the men of other times ignorantly mocked the city in which was born our Saviour, so may this have been. Nazareth and Methodism! What two names were ever mentioned more contemptuously? Think of it; the text for the dedicatory sermon of the church first erected in New Castle was this, "Can there any good thing come out of Nazareth? Come and see." How hopeless a case when the Methodists of New Castle named their church Nazareth. These were men of faith and experience, men believing that great good would come.

When Lawrence Laurenson and John Henry were joint pastors of Asbury, New Castle was one of their regular appointments.

In 1837 New Castle was made a station with Pennel Combs pastor. A great revival blessed the year's work, making the church strong enough to attempt to go alone.

For a long while the congregation struggled. Never were men more heroic in the effort to be self-supporting. Only those quite familiar with the real situation understood the genuine liberality of the people.

It has not been the lack of disposition to give. This is one of there most commendable characteristics; their lack is in the ability to give. The church is composed to-day, entirely of people earning their living. But they are salt, fire and light. To-day the Nazareth Methodist Episcopal Church of New Castle is one great, glorious, established fact; a living fact in the city and factor in her moral life.

Remove this church and the darkness resulting would amaze an infidel. Asbury need not be ashamed of her child Nazareth. She may not be so deep toned and big around, but she is in tune and wears no corsets. She may not have so wide a reputation as the mother, but she successfully enters every opportunity. She may not have so many attentive auditors each Sunday, but she has no untaken seats. She may not have so wide a brow as her mother, but it is as high and encircled by pearls made in the same shop. She may not have so eloquent and zealous a domine, but she is fired by the same steam, lighted by the same fluid, and led by the same hand. Her singers may not say so many hallelujahs, but they can pronounce as many musical shibboleths. And as you have no need to be ashamed of us because we track you so closely, so we beg that you will not be jealous of us because of our extreme beauty and pardonable pride; for we beg to assure our mother that no bedeckment will cause us to lag in the war, and, mother, when we look at your bronzed, but unwrinkled brow; your deep set, but undimmed eye; your powerfully developed, but ungouty physique; when we note your age and see no decay, we are reminded of the eternal fireside, and the blessed elixir of life.

Since the organization of the church the following have served as pastors: 1821, Joseph Rustling, Ezekiel Cooper and James Smith; 1822, Lawrence Laurenson and John Henry; 1823, Henry G. King; 1824, Joseph Holdridge; 1825, John Goforth and Edward Page; 1825-37, Solomon Sharp, George M. Yard, John Inskip and James B. Ayers; 1837-38, Pennel Coombs; 1839-40, James McFarland; 1841-42, John D. Long; 1843, J. T. Taft; 1844, Nicholas Ridgely; 1845, Samuel G. Hare; 1846, Authur W. Milby; 1847, Thomas Miller; 1848, Peter Hallowell and John D. Long; 1849, Andrew Manship; 1850, J. H. Wythes; 1852, William B. Walton; 1854, J. N. King; 1855, J. S. Lane; 1856, William J. Paxson; 1858, Joseph O'Niell; 1859-60, John W. Pierson; 1861-62, Thomas Montgomery; 1863-64, M. H. Sisty; 1865-66, S. N. Chew; 1867, Daniel George; 1868-69, Leonides Dobson ; 1870-71, William B. Walton ; 1872-73, Henry Colclazer; 1874-76, J. B. Mann ; 1877-78, George R. Bristor; 1879, David C. Ridgeway; 1880, Madison A. Richardson; 1881, George R. Bristor; 1882-84, N. M. Browne; 1885-86, Thomas E. Terry; 1887 until, I don't know when, E. L. Hubbard.

History of the Edgemoor Methodist Episcopal Church.

BY THE REV. J. T. VAN BURKALOW, PASTOR.

The Edgemoor Methodist Episcopal Church is the granddaughter of the Asbury Church in Wilmington.

Like many other churches erected in the nineteenth century, it had its origin in a Sunday-school.

Edgemoor is a little proprietary village on the land of, and belonging to the Edgemoor Iron Company, built for, and rented solely to their workmen.

On the 29th of January 1871, there being about eighty inhabitants, a number of them belonging to several different religious denominations, organized a Sunday-school in the gate-house, and elected Mr. George Morrison, superintendent.

Revs. Marks, Smith, Shaw and Moore, and Mr. James Morrow, took an interest in it, and encouraged and aided the workers.

But in consequence of removals, it was closed after being in operation about a year. It was re-opened about two years and eight months afterward, in September, 1874, in Mr. Morrison's residence, and was kept in operation till October 1875, thirteen months, when it was closed again.

In March, 1876, the Edgemoor Iron Company consented for the school house to be used for religious purposes, and the Sunday-school was re-organized in it, with Mr. John T. Bradbury as superintendent, and it has been kept up ever since.

Prayer meetings were, also, held in the school house from time to time, and Rev. Wm. B. Gregg, of Mt. Pleasant charge, and Rev. John Simmons, a local preacher, frequently preached there, and R. M. Biddle and others, occasionally exhorted.

At a little prayer meeting, to the glad surprise of the brethren, several persons presented themselves to the altar as penitents, and were converted. Then a regular revival meeting was held for sometime, and a considerable number made profession of faith.

Among the chief workers in the revival, were Bros. John Simmons, John T. Bradbury, James B. Coleman, Robert M. Biddle, and Sisters Abbie Biddle, and Lydia J. Rambo.

They all being Methodists, a class was formed, and Bro. James B. Coleman, was elected class-leader.

Rev. E. L. Hubbard, pastor of Brandywine M. E. Church, took hold of the work soon after the revival arose, and was so successful, and he so endeared himself to the people, that they requested him to take the society under his pastoral care.

Accordingly, after due legal notice being given, a meeting was held on the 28th of January, 1885, at which it was decided to ask for the society to be united with Brandywine M. E. Church, and a board of six trustees was elected.

At a meeting of the trustees eight days after, it was resolved to build a church, and soon subscription books were opened. On the 8th of March, 1886, after a thirteen months canvass for contributions, the society was incorporated as The Edge Moor Methodist Episcopal Church, the Edge Moor Iron Company having given a lot, 60x100 feet, on the corner of Second avenue and B street, for the church, for which the trustees received a deed, to be good and valid as long as the property is used for religious purposes, the size and style of the edifice to be erected thereon to meet with their approval.

After a further delay of over six months, on the 17th of August, 1886, ground was broken for the church, and the corner-stone was laid on the 18th of the following September, by Rev. J. E. Bryan. Nearly all the other Methodist pastors of Wilmington, and four local preachers being present and taking part, and the choir of Brandywine Church furnishing the music, both instrumental and vocal.

The superstructure was begun on the 16th of October and it was closed in by New Year's day, 1887, but the plastering, on account of the cold weather, was deferred till next spring. The plastering was commenced about the 1st of April and in less than two months the church was ready for dedication.

In the meantime, at the Nineteenth Session of the Wilmington Annual Conference at Crisfield, Md., the Edge Moor Society was separated from the Brandywine Church and united to Mt. Pleasant, forming Mt. Pleasant and Edge Moor Charge, with Rev. Julius Dodd, as pastor. This union of the two churches was agreed to and requested by a committee of three from each, at a meeting at Edge Moor, on the 8th of March, 1887.

On the 29th of May, 1887, before the pulpit was made, the heater and carpet purchased, or the painting finished, the edifice was dedicated to the worship of Almighty God by Rev. W. L. S. Murray. Rev. Jacob Todd, D. D., preached in the morning, Rev. W. L. S. Murray, Presiding Elder, in the afternoon, and Rev. E. L. Hubbard in the evening. Subscriptions to the amount of $500.00 were secured during the day, which together with those made before, left a debt of only $400.00 on the church when fully finished and furnished. Early in that year, Bro. J. B. Coleman resigned as class-leader, and Bro. R. M. Biddle was appointed in his stead.

During that autumn a number were converted and received on probation, and the class was divided. Brother James A. Smith, a recent accession from Maryland, being made leader of the second class. Class number one, being thus depleted and not being sustained, Brother Biddle resigned the leadership in the spring and Brother A. W. Young was given the place, but he soon removed to Wilmington, and the class not having improved in attendance, it was disbanded and its members put into Brother Smith's, number two becoming number one. This was done by Rev. J. T. Van Burkalow, who was appointed preacher in charge, in March, 1888. During that year alienations arose among the members which paralyzed the work, and the society has been greatly reduced both in number and in moral and monetary power by removals.

The operatives of the Edge Moor Iron Works are mainly a floating population. But few remain long in the village and many are non church-going and apathetic and indifferent to the cause of God, and others, who claim to be, at least, nominal Christians, evince no sympathy with the Methodist church; hence, the status and strength of our little society there are very variable and uncertain, and at present, from these and other causes, the membership and attendance is very small.

There are now but four male members in the place and but seven anywhere. There are but sixteen members and two probationers *in toto*, some of whom live in Wilmington and Philadelphia, and but few of whom are earnest workers in the cause of God.

In view of these facts, it may well be asked with the ancient Hebrew prophet, applying the interrogatory to Edgemoor Methodists, "How shall Jacob arise, for he is small?" But, "Who hath despised the day of small things?" Not the Lord. "God hath chosen the weak things of the world to confound the things which are mighty." He can cause "One to chase a thousand and two to put ten thousand to flight." The few Methodists of Edgemoor are getting nearer together, and are looking up in prayer for a revival, and it is hoped "The Lord will send showers of blessings."—"Amen and Amen."

www.ingramcontent.com/pod-product-compliance
Lightning Source LLC
Chambersburg PA
CBHW031849220426
43663CB00006B/553